PATENTS, PROFITS& POWER

How intellectual property rules the global economy

Curtis Cook

KOGAN
PAGE

To my beautiful wife, Michelle.

*You are my soulmate, my best friend and my hero. I would not have pursued
this project without your encouragement and unwavering support.
I am amazed by your intuitive gifts and your powerful intellect.
But it is your courage, strength and love that inspire me most.*

First published in 2002

Kogan Page Limited
120 Pentonville Road
London N1 9JN
UK

Kogan Page US
22 Broad Street
Milford CT 06460
USA

British Library Cataloguing in Publication Data

A CIP record for this book is available from the British Library.

ISBN 0 7494 3641 7

Typeset by Saxon Graphics Ltd, Derby
Printed and bound in Great Britain by Biddles Ltd, Guildford and King's Lynn
www.biddles.co.uk

CONTENTS

Acknowledgements   *vi*

Introduction   1

1   The ghost of IP past   10
      The path to intellectual property protection   13
      The world without intellectual property   16
      Creativity without interference   21

2   Intellectual assets: the new wealth   22
      How it works   25
      Linking industrialization and intellectual property   26
      A modern scenario   27
      The IBM example   28
      Knowledge management   30
      Intellectual capital   33

3   That's brilliant – what is it?   38
      Patents   39
      Trademarks   45
      Copyright   50
      Geographical indications   53
      Industrial designs   57
      Trade secrets   58

Layout designs (topographies) of integrated circuits 58
Breeders' rights 59

4   The enforcers   **61**
WIPO 63
Intellectual property protection treaties 64
Global protection treaties 74
Classification treaties 78
Administrative agreements 82
WTO 84
The European Patent Office 90
National intellectual property agencies 90

5   The new currency   **93**
Information and power 95
Microsoft: intellectual property warrior 97
Prosecuting intellectual property crimes 98
Protecting trade secrets and other intellectual assets 102
Intellectual property protection strategies 106
Due diligence 109

6   Rogue nations and false creations   **112**
A Canadian example 114
Why nations condone intellectual property theft 116
The economics of intellectual property theft 118
International enforcement mechanisms: power or
   pushover? 119
Corporate offenders 121
Teachers, students and copyright abuses 123
Intellectual property theft quiz 127

7   Thoughts on the future of thought   **128**
The future of the international institutions 129
Future disputes and controversies 131
Intellectual property alternatives 137
Festo: challenging the power of patents 140
Questioning the right to intellectual property rights 143
Future innovation, high stakes and market instability 144
Choosing our destiny 147

8   Internet rules: intellectual property at cyberspeed   149
Internet piracy   152
The Digital Millennium Copyright Act   154
Felten, copyrights and freedom of speech   158
Protecting property on the Net   162
Intellectual property resources on the Web   165

9   Developing intellectual property in developing nations   170
Honouring international obligations   174
The problem with piracy   175
Where there's a will…   177
India   178
China   180
The technology solution   182
Hope and help from developed nations   183

10   Losing your mind   187
Nothing is really new   191
Intellectual property and the wrong kind of growth   194
The power of ideas   197

References   *199*
Index   *200*

ACKNOWLEDGEMENTS

To all the people who have contributed to the creation of this book, I thank you. In particular, I would like to thank Michelle Cook, my wife and business partner, for taking on considerably more responsibility than was fair so that I could undertake this project. Thank you for your support and generosity throughout the process. To William Fisher, Mauri Gronroos and Mark Cuban, your contributions and time are greatly appreciated. Thank you for sharing both with me. To R Mark Halligan, your expertise has been invaluable for both of my books. I am also grateful to Brent Sheffler for his excellent research contributions that helped 'kick start' my writing. Thank you Emily Steel, for your support of this title and for making the publication process as smooth as possible. And, to all of the dedicated people at Kogan Page, thank you for taking all of the words I gave you and creating a book.

INTRODUCTION

Property has its duties as well as its rights.

Thomas Drummond

What had gone wrong? I stood in my office reading the letter from the Intellectual Property Office repeatedly. As my partner walked in, I muttered, 'Trademark abandoned.' She stared at me for a moment before responding with a disbelieving 'Pardon me?' I handed her the letter and said, 'Our trademark has been abandoned.' According to this official government correspondence, the deadline to finalize our trademark registration had passed, our application process had not been completed, and we were being informed that, as far as the people responsible for approving trademarks were concerned, we had abandoned the pursuit of our trademark. And, if this was not enough bad news for one day, I held an unopened identical-looking letter in my other hand. It was quite evident that this was the correspondence from the same office indicating that our other trademark application had also been abandoned.

We spent approximately 30 seconds trying to figure out how two years of planning, patience, revisions and clarifications had gone wrong before contacting the Intellectual Property Office in an attempt to salvage all of our time and effort. Our trademarks – the name of our company and a slogan relating to our services – were critical elements of our branding and our identity. We had already had various types of infringements and minor conflicts with other entities using similar or identical slogans in related business activities. Would we now lose the advantage of having applied for these marks before anyone else? Would the competition know what had transpired? Would some opportunistic rival or another business apply for our company name? As our initial paranoia gave way to reason, we received our instructions from the public servants responsible for trademarks. We simply had to write to their boss, explain why we missed the specific deadline and beg for forgiveness. If we were adequately convincing, and caught the boss on a good day, we would pay a late penalty in addition to the outstanding application fees and wait until the process was completed. I did not even ask what would happen if we caught the boss on a bad day. It was time for positive thinking. About a month after sending the payment and the letter of atonement, my partner and I celebrated the completion of our trademark process, with both registered trademarks in hand. Shortly thereafter, our office received not one, but two invoices from different sources in Eastern Europe for amounts far in excess of the actual cost of our trademark procedure. Considering our company had not applied for a trademark in that part of the world, we were somewhat surprised and very curious. The invoices were quite official in appearance, but a scam nevertheless. We provided as much information as we could to our national Intellectual Property Office regarding the origin of these notices. We also contacted the local business newspaper to run a story on these intellectual property scam artists. Apparently, they are quite common and use public documents like trademark journals to discover potential targets. By invoicing the company listed in the journal, the scam artist hopes payment will be made by an unwitting administrator or manager unfamiliar with the company's intellectual property strategy. As long as the employee does not verify the legitimacy of the bogus trademark invoice, the scam artist will continue to make money. It seems to happen with sufficient frequency to keep these criminals in business.

These experiences triggered a great deal of reflection on the significance of intellectual property. I had impressed upon clients the importance of protecting their corporate identities, innovations, strategies, trade secrets and other valuable elements of their business. I had written extensively on the subject. Yet, it was not until my partner and I came very close to losing part of our firm's 'hidden value' that I began giving careful consideration to what intellectual property really means to a business. Or, more accurately, what it can mean to a business. Why, for example, is a name, a style, a sound or a thought captured on paper or audiotape so important that an ever-expanding area of law could develop around it? Why are these items so valuable that nations become more upset about foreign abuses of intellectual property than foreign abuses of human rights? Why would a normally calm man like myself experience such distress at the thought of not possessing two combinations of words? Surely, our business would not go under simply because we had lost a couple of trademarks. Clients would not deem us less capable and seek other firms to provide our specialized services. Or would they? It seems foolish looking back on the situation but those feelings were very real. Our intellectual property wielded considerable power, even if it was only to insiders in the company. We truly felt it was an integral part of the reliable, credible and profitable business we had established.

I then began to ponder the significance of intellectual property on a global level. In many commercially driven societies around the world, billions of dollars are lost and gained on the basis of protecting these great ideas, catchy names, innovative designs and inspiring words. For example, the main industries concerned with copyright, which include the entertainment (movies, music, and other media) and advertising realms account for an estimated 7 per cent of the global economy, according to John Howkins, author of *The Creative Economy*. The financial value of all of these ideas, names and designs is staggering and often difficult to comprehend. Did we really choose for this to happen? And, if this is the way we choose to operate – attaching such importance and financial worth to these concepts – how can we make sure we are well equipped to hold our own, to compete? These initial thoughts have expanded into this book.

You might be getting the idea that this is not your average book on intellectual property. Let's face it: intellectual property is not usually considered the most stimulating of topics, even if you work in the legal profession or government offices dedicated to the rules and regulations governing the subject. But that does not have to be the case. Intellectual property is a complex and fascinating element of our recent recorded history. The protection of intellectual property also serves a valuable and essential role in the socio-economic environment that we have created in much of this world; namely a consumer-oriented, market-driven, complex environment. Additionally, intellectual property has become a disturbing, dangerous and insidious force in many areas of our daily routine. It is pervasive in our lives yet we often do not even consider its existence. Yes, it is all these things and more. The objective of *Patents, Profits and Power* is to share these concepts with you. In addition, I want to give you some practical things to think about. For instance, it helps to know what institutions are out there to protect your ideas and projects. It helps to know how you can effectively deal with them. Equally important, however, is an understanding of the ways in which they may complicate your life, or even fail you. If you have aspirations of taking your great ideas across the globe, it is a good idea to understand what you are getting into. There is no shortage of sad tales recounting how entrepreneurs with great software programs, innovative tools, appliances, or other works or concepts have lost control of their projects when they leave the safety of their home turf. Unscrupulous foreign business partners, distributors, or complete strangers operating in places where intellectual property laws are non-existent or poorly enforced may simply take your great idea and run with it. That is not to say that you and your innovations are always safe within your own borders. It is just that much more difficult to take action outside your own jurisdiction. We will explore why this is the case.

Fear not, however. The globalization of trade and commerce has hardly been dented by the prospects of patent or trademark abuses, copyright infringements or other alleged misuses of intellectual property. But a slight dent still amounts to billions of dollars. A small e-business in the United Kingdom will be upset if it discovers a German company duplicated its Web site and directed traffic, including consumers, to the fake site. The fake site may contain all of the elements that comprise the UK firm's intellectual property: a trademarked logo, name and slogan as well as a line of copyright protected software programs. If the firm lost £10,000 or £100,000 worth of business, the immediate damage is visibly apparent. If the German thief actually took the online orders by credit card, the orders would obviously not be filled and the credit card information of numerous customers and prospective customers would now be in the hands of an unknown entity. In this scenario, the UK firm also must deal with a flood of consumer complaints, as well as the fallout when word spreads about the firm's unreliability. The damaged reputation is quite likely worse than the original loss. And that is a small local firm. Consider a corporate giant like Nike or Coca-Cola. How much money does Nike lose each year because unauthorized reproductions of its clothing are sold at prices that most people can afford? What would happen if Coca-Cola could no longer protect its secret formula and it was made available for commercial use by others? Businesses, both small and large, have a vested interested in protecting their intellectual assets.

Your journey in *Patents, Profits and Power* begins in the past, with an exploration of the genesis of intellectual property. We will look at some possible sources of its development, as well as its application at various times throughout recorded history. While we will focus on culture types that have fully embraced the rationale for protecting creations of all kinds, the book will also contrast this development with cultures that did not adopt the concept of intellectual property. Too often, modern Westernized societies forget about the considerable number of cultures that have neither the knowledge of, nor the use for intellectual property. And, bridging the gap between these cultures and the obsession for intellectual property in many industrialized nations are those tribes, communities and nations that are suffering from the exploitation of traditional resources by others seeking to monopolize and commercialize their heritage. This may be a book about a thoroughly Western creation, but I would be remiss to give it an entirely Western perspective. We can learn a great deal from adopting a global view to either challenge or reinforce our current belief systems. Throughout the book, you will encounter views, opinions and commentary that stray from the straight and narrow of standard intellectual property discussion. Consider it food for thought because there really is no straight and narrow with respect to intellectual property. You may begin to realize this even prior to finishing the first chapter.

The whirlwind history lesson in Chapter 1 will lead us to more contemporary times, examining both why and when 'brain power' surpassed 'brawn power' as the measure of worth, on an individual, corporate and national level. The second chapter will explore the shift from tangible assets that gave birth to and fuelled the early industrial economies to the intangible assets of today's knowledge economy. We will also examine topics that are undeniably linked to the proliferation of intellectual property in our modern business world. Business concepts such as intellectual capital and knowledge management are much more recent developments than intellectual property; however, they have brought the significance of valuing, organizing, using and profiting from the collective genius in an organization to the top of the business management checklist. If the tacit knowledge residing in the heads of employees is not directly used in the creation of intellectual assets, it is likely used in the marketing, sale, and protection of these assets. Though aspects of knowledge management and intellectual capital fall outside the realm of intellectual property and it is unlikely that the World Intellectual Property Organization (WIPO) will establish a treaty for the protection of individual brains, these issues are directly linked to our examination of intellectual property.

No book on intellectual property would be complete without looking at the various types of property that the 'powers that be' deem worthy of protection. These include patents, trademarks, copyrights, industrial designs, trade secrets and others. While we may not explore all of the types of intellectual property in Chapter 3, the main types will be presented in detail and will include a few stories to keep things light – or as light as an explanation of 'breeders' rights' can be, for example. You may be surprised to find out the many ways 'things' can be protected. In contrast, some readers may be dismayed by the extent of protection or by the types of items that are included or excluded from the intellectual property portfolio. However you choose to look at it, intellectual property statistics are staggering. For example, the European Patent Office estimates that there are over 4 million patents in force in the world today. Another 700,000 applications for inventions – just patent-related creations – are filed annually. Patent protection is sought, on average, in four countries per invention and the licensing revenues from patented products has increased tenfold since 1990, reaching an estimated US $100 billion worldwide in 2000.

As you continue to read, you will understand that intellectual property is a highly contentious and volatile element of the artistic, scientific and business world. Consequently, there are a number of regulatory and coordinating bodies around the world that have been established to deal with the complexity of intellectual property issues. Chapter 4 will examine these international, regional and national organizations and the rules they make. Specifically, it will look at the WIPO, the World Trade Organization (WTO) and their respective roles. These international institutions are powerful entities, driven primarily by the powerful member states within their constituencies. They strive for equality in decision-making based on the egalitarian membership system that affords one vote to each nation. Yet, we will discover how such a system fails certain members and continues to provide advantages to others. Additionally, we will explore how outside influences exert pressure on these organizations to come up with policies and laws that further specific agendas.

There is no shortage of business leaders and scientists who will tell you that ideas, innovation and intelligence are the most valuable commodities in today's world. Protecting the 'three I's' becomes paramount and Chapter 5 explores the effectiveness of the current protection system for individuals in the creative, scientific and business spheres. First we will look at the value of information by shedding new light on two old adages – 'information is power' and 'power corrupts'. Later in the chapter, we will learn why authorities find it challenging to prosecute intellectual property crimes. Once you understand the difficulties the legal people have in this regard, you will probably recognize the need to take some responsibility for securing your intellectual property. This will lead us to solutions and strategies that businesses can implement to protect their intellectual assets. Two trade secret experts will share their views on how to effectively secure these valuable assets against both internal and external threats.

In Chapter 5 it will become apparent that intellectual property is a global currency. In many ways, it is less susceptible to recessions and devaluations than our dollars, pounds and yens. Certain brands and inventions have close to universal appeal on this planet, creating lucrative global markets for legitimate products and literary or artistic works, as well as unscrupulous fakes. As a result, intellectual property is the target of criminal activity at the individual level, as well as the corporate and national level. Because the protection of intellectual property is not a global objective, theft, piracy and other infringements occur with disturbing regularity. Chapter 6 examines this situation, and looks at some of the less desirable players on the world stage and why they choose to defy the law, good sense or both.

Now that we have an idea about where intellectual property came from and where it is right now, we can have some fun exploring the future of intellectual property and the value of thought in the years to come. The rate of change we experience in our society is over-whelming. New developments occur in the field of law, the realm of international trade, the spheres of science, technology and the arts and the political, social and natural environments in which we live. Changes in any or all of these areas can have an impact on the devel-opment and definition of intellectual property. We will consider a few of these in Chapter 7 by examining upcoming events and seeking out trends that may influence the future.

Crystal-ball gazing would not be complete without taking into consid-eration the impact of the Internet. Its effect on intellectual property protection has already been enormous, and we will look at the implica-tions of stopping (or encouraging) this runaway train in Chapter 8. You will understand why a billionaire Internet entrepreneur/professional basketball team owner despises the Digital Millennium Copyright Act and why online arbitration of domain name use and abuse is growing in popularity. You will be exposed to the epidemic known as software piracy and learn about some of the solutions that are being offered to combat the apparent lawlessness of cyberspace.

By the end of the Chapter 8 this book will have focused to a large extent on the success and failures of the intellectual property system from a fairly Western perspective. Yet there is another facet of intel-lectual property that often goes unexplored by the trademark lawyer in London, the drug company executive in Switzerland and the optical

networking entrepreneur in Silicon Valley. The economic and technological burden felt by developing economies around the world is
enormous. These nations are losing the battle to gain intellectual
capital and the prosperity that it brings. Chapter 9 will explore the
barriers facing developing nations, the strategies employed by governments to adhere to, or ignore, intellectual property laws in an effort to
sustain their economies, and how industrialized nations both help and
hinder the development process. Despite the best intentions of the
'have' nations of this world to create a just and equitable system, they
simply do not seem prepared to make sufficient concessions to change
the fate of the 'have not' countries with which they share this planet.

In conclusion, we will try to put it all together – the good, the bad
and the ugly. By the time you hit the last chapter, you will probably
have a good sense about your feelings on the subject. If that is the case,
and you know where you stand, I will try to turn it all upside down
again. You may think you are, indeed, losing your mind, or that I am.
Either way, it is never a good idea to get too comfortable with our
beliefs about right and wrong. We may prefer black and white;
however, there is a huge patch of grey when it comes to intellectual
property. As William Shakespeare so aptly wrote in the first Act of
Hamlet, 'There are more things in heaven and earth, Horatio, than are
dreamt of in your philosophy.' Do you think he created that line?

When you have turned the last page and taken another look at the
cover, I hope that you have a better idea of what comprises your intellectual assets, or those of your company. I hope that you understand
the ways in which you can transform these assets into your intellectual
property. I hope that you recognize all the means at your disposal to
protect your intellectual property and use them to your advantage. As
much as I wanted to write *The 12-Step Programme to Understanding and
Protecting Intellectual Property* I could not do it. It simply is not a 12-step
programme. Each reader will find titbits of information that apply to
his or her respective situation. One example will intrigue the
programmer with the software company, while a contribution from an
attorney in the United States will shed some light on a confusing situation for the marketing executive at the tool manufacturing firm.

In addition, I hope that when you finish the last page of *Patents,
Profits and Power*, you will ponder the ways in which you use your
intellectual assets or those of your company. I encourage you to put
them to work in ways that not only contribute to your profits and
wealth but in ways that enrich every aspect of your life and the lives of
others. There can be little satisfaction in knowing that your company's
patent-protected drug brought in 20 million in revenues in its first year,

but was the contributing factor in the deaths of a dozen pregnant women. What is the reward in copying the words of a journalist from an article on the Internet and pasting them directly into your term paper as your own thoughts? What are the long-term consequences of genetically modifying foods? Should nature be altered so that someone can claim it as personal property?

For all that intellectual property is and all that it does, it presents few easy answers. The complexity of the topic and its related issues makes it tempting to proclaim 'we can live without it, as we have for centuries' or 'the world could not function without this rules-based system to protect the livelihood of so many people'. We seek out extremes in order to divorce ourselves from the possibility that we could make things better. I prefer to believe that the evolution of the intellectual property system will lead to improvements and a more equitable system for the global community. However, this is a long-term vision. Until then, I still shudder when I read about the exploitation, excess and environmental damage we accept to further commercialize our world. We always have the opportunity to change our minds, our actions and our future. There is no compelling reason to suggest that the intellectual property system be eliminated from that future. Likewise, there is no need for it to necessarily resemble the system we have in place. Armed with the information, stories, knowledge, discoveries and examples you find in *Patents, Profits and Power*, I urge you to seek out and create alternatives. Innovate to improve. Invent the future of intellectual property. Enjoy.

ONE

THE GHOST OF IP PAST

Inventions reached their limit long ago, and I see no hope for further development.

Julius Frontinus, 1st century AD

Human creativity is as old as civilization. In fact, it is probably safe to say that creativity predates what we commonly refer to as civilization. Prehistoric art, cutting and stabbing implements, scraps of clothing or coverings are not necessarily symbolic of organized groupings of humanity with shared goals and objectives but they are evidence of ingenuity. Neanderthals, for example, lived throughout Europe and parts of Asia by 70,000 BC. They used stones for cutting and scraping and they used bones and sinew to join skins together. Cro-Magnons are believed to have appeared in Europe from regions to the east 35,000 years later. They created artwork among other things, painting fascinating images of animals deep inside caves. By this time, people had already been living in Australia for 20,000 years or so (more by some accounts, and who can really question these estimates?), as well as other remote geographic territories around the globe.

We can look back at the little scraps of bone and stone, 'primitive' drawings and shelters, smile at their primitiveness and marvel at how far we have progressed as a species. Yet, these artifacts are clearly signs of intelligent minds at work, attempting to improve upon a current situation or labouring to solve a dilemma. As a species, we have operated in this manner every day since. For example, you may be impressed by your neighbour's design for a natural water filtration system for her house so that she does not have to rely on questionable and expensive municipal water sources. And you congratulate your friend who designed a self-filling bird feeder so that the birds do not starve during the winter and he does not freeze every time it needs to be re-filled. Humans, by nature, create. Whether these creations are stories, tools or art, they form the foundation of our common body of knowledge as a species. Combined, all of these creations form human culture and shed light on the human saga.

Our recorded history has captured numerous stories, myths and tales as evidence of the great thinkers of the past. It has also left material evidence in the form of documents, structures, implements and equipment to reveal the extraordinary creativity that humanity has always possessed. Consider the following:

- Archimedes, a Greek mathematician discovered a number of physical and geometrical principles almost 2,300 years ago that many of us still struggle to understand today. He also invented catapults, a cylindrical screw used to move water for irrigation and demonstrated the principle of the lever by moving large objects by himself. Who knows how far he would have gone had a Roman soldier not murdered him.
- Even earlier than Archimedes, Democritus proposed the theory that matter is composed of a seemingly infinite supply of tiny particles. The use of the term atom, meaning 'uncuttable', is first attributed to the Greek philosopher, who is quoted as stating, 'Nothing exists except atoms and empty space; everything else is opinion'. Even more remarkable is that similar beliefs based on an atomic theory developed in India at virtually the same period in history.
- Galileo Galilei did not invent the telescope but his improvements to the design allowed him to observe a far larger and more complex universe than powerful 17th-century belief systems were prepared to accept. Among other things, his theory of relativity asserted that the earth moved around the sun. For his efforts, he was labelled a heretic by the Roman Catholic Church and condemned by the Inquisition to life in prison. While he was forced to retract his beliefs regarding the movement of the sun and the earth, he never surrendered his convictions.
- Leonardo da Vinci is well known as one of Italy's premiere painters and sculptors spanning the 15th and 16th centuries. In addition to his artistic talent, he conceptualized numerous devices and

machinery that did not become commonplace until the 20th century, and he drew reasonably accurate depictions of how these contraptions looked and operated.

■ Over a span of 25 years in the 12th century, a visionary named Hildegard von Bingen produced an extraordinary collection of works devoted to the role of humankind in the divine plan of God and the mysteries of creation. A sickly child who was given to a nun as a tithe from God, Hildegard von Bingen became the abbess of St Disibrod and toiled tirelessly for her Christian beliefs. In addition, she produced two scientific studies in the fields of nature and medicine and close to 80 liturgical songs for her nuns. At a time when women (including women in the Christian Church) were considered little more than property or the direct cause of sin on Earth, Hildegard von Bingen obtained considerable influence in her spiritual community. Her music, in particular, has been resurrected in recent years and is inspirational regardless of religious or spiritual belief.

These are five well-known examples of incredible minds contributing knowledge to the global repository. They have a number of things in common. They were obviously brilliant and very much in touch with their personal genius. They made their beliefs, discoveries and inventions public, at great personal cost in some cases. Even today, we still draw upon these characters for inspiration and motivation. For example, a recent book instructs modern-age readers to think like Leonardo da Vinci. How many others lived before these great minds yet were lost in history? How many followed but fell into obscurity as a result of a military campaign or religious crusades? And how many brilliant minds have no outlet for their creativity today because of stifling regimes or starvation?

This minor detour is designed to support the following argument: there was no intellectual property protection for Democritus, da Vinci, or Hildegard von Bingen, yet they forged forward to enrich the future with their creations, ideas and wisdom. They may have been lucky to have their creations attributed to them to this day. I remember English professors speculating on the possibility that William Shakespeare was not the author of many of the plays and sonnets graced by his name. History is maddening in that respect. Yet it seems fairly clear that intellectual property protection as we know it did not exist in ancient Greece or 12th-century Germany. We must also speculate on the various reasons why these individuals pursued their paths of innovation and creativity. We can guess that Archimedes and Democritus were immersed in a culture that cherished learning and fostered intellectual advancement. We can propose that Galileo was caught up in the scientific revolution of the time, questioning the Ptolemaic (as Copernicus did before him) and Aristotelian views of physics and astronomy that were gospel at the time. We can conclude that Hildegard von Bingen was inspired by her spiritual beliefs and her devotion to what she experienced as the Divine. Not one of these hypotheses would seem a stretch based on our current understanding of history. But that very same history does not support the notion that these great figures had monetary incentives to innovate. There does not appear to be much evidence to suggest that they prospered financially from their creations. Why did they do it? They may have created for the types of rewards that we now diminish: knowledge for the sake of knowledge; honouring, serving and celebrating a deity to secure a place in the afterlife; or intellectual and spiritual enlightenment. These can be powerful motivators as well as sources of power. History is full of such examples.

If we close the history books and take a look at our current environment, it is fairly apparent that the bulk of creativity is intended for commercialization. Creators in many of our societies expect some form of remuneration for their efforts and financial remuneration seems to be at the top of the list. Fame, notoriety or celebrity may be a close second. In our modern world, these 'rewards' are aspects of power. We are conditioned to believe that more money or more fame equates to more power. Yet is it a natural human phenomenon to create or invent something and use it as a means to gain power over others? When did such behaviour start, and why? Has it always been this way?

THE PATH TO INTELLECTUAL PROPERTY PROTECTION

This book is not intended to be a philosophical study of human nature as it pertains to intellectual property but these are curious questions. William Fisher, Professor of Law at Harvard University, acknowledges that invention has been a characteristic of human history for the past 15,000 years. He points out that, well before recorded history, there was the manifestation of art, such as the cave paintings mentioned above. As far as we can determine, all of that time prior to the last 500 years, humanity continued to create and innovate without any formal mechanism in place to assign ownership and rights. Nor was there any organized methodology for ensuring that rights to ownership were protected against others. On the contrary, ancestral legends and spear-hunting techniques were passed down from generation to generation. Clothing and implements were improved upon out of necessity. Agricultural techniques were discovered and weapons were enhanced.

It was and still is common for such discoveries and inventions to contribute to power shifts and radical upheavals in human development. If one tribe, society or culture was on to a 'good thing', another group would resort to any means to obtain it. Of course, this could include war and other barbaric acts. Many conquests resulted in the integration of knowledge and ideas. Specialized skills also spread, as did creations from diverse peoples and territories. Protection took the form of secrecy or threat of punishment by violence and force. Legal protection was an unknown concept for many millennia.

In contrast, the legal protection for ideas, as differentiated from the legal protection for objects, is quite a recent phenomenon. Fisher refers to the 15th century for early developments in patent law and the 17th century for copyright law. According to the European Patent Office, the first patent law was passed by the city of Venice in 1474. Not unlike the laws of today, it protected the interests of inventors by assuring them the right to their inventions and prohibiting the copying of their creations unless the inventor provided authorization. Consider some of the inventions that came before this time: compasses and clocks, windows, glass mirrors and magnifying glasses, chimneys on houses, gunpowder, air guns and muskets, and Gutenberg's moveable type printing press. By 1624, England had enacted the Statute of Monopolies, which provided for patents to be granted for a limited period to the 'true and first inventor'. Over the next two centuries, European nations developed additional patent laws, as well as laws to protect other forms of intellectual property. These national developments, coupled with the increase in international trade, led to the Paris Convention in the late 19th century and the modern intellectual property treaties that much of the world adheres to today. We will look at these treaties and their language in Chapter 4.

Technological progress and innovation has been a primary factor in the development of intellectual property. For example, ease of replication has contributed significantly to the concept of protecting one's creativity. As Fisher points out, the pressure for intellectual property protection increases as the facilities with which consumers of intellectual products can replicate the property increase. Consequently, the

invention of the printing press by Gutenberg as a means of mass replication of printed materials increased pressure for intellectual property
protection dramatically. Truthfully, we must admit to our 'euro-
centricity' and acknowledge that Gutenberg did not really invent the
printing press; rather, he invented it in Europe. The Chinese had
actually printed 400 years earlier using a moveable type method,
which they later discarded. In the 9th century, books were printed in
China using wooden blocks. Considering how insular China was at
this time, it seems obvious that Gutenberg had no prior knowledge of
the Chinese invention – not that it mattered, it was not patented!
Nevertheless, his invention revolutionized the way in which information was documented and distributed. Prior to Gutenberg's
printing press, the recording and printing of information was largely
the task of scribes and monks, who painstakingly copied works by
hand. Such methods obviously limited the quantity of books that could
be replicated. They also limited the types of information that could be
distributed, keeping books and other printed materials within the
domain of a select audience. The printing press brought books and
writing to a wider audience and it accomplished this feat at a rate that
scribes and monks could not match, had they wanted to. It has been
suggested that this invention was instrumental in the dissemination of
knowledge that led to the Protestant Reformation. One can imagine
that certain religious leaders would have gladly exercised copyright
protection, had it existed, to suppress the information flow that
Gutenberg's invention unleashed.

More recently, the development of copying technology such as Xerox
machines as well as the various digital technologies used to replicate
movies and music has resulted in active and vigorous lobbying for
increased intellectual property protection. Fisher (1999) suggests
another reason that contributes to the increased demand for protection
of intellectual property today: the upfront costs of specific types of
creativity are rising. 'To produce a novel requires a fair amount of time
and effort', says Fisher, 'not just time and effort to sit down at your
desk and write the novel, but also the time and effort necessary to train
yourself to be a good writer.' Fisher emphasizes that the magnitude of
the effort to produce a novel is dwarfed by the investment necessary to
generate a new drug, for instance. He adds that:

> One can expect that novels will be produced even in the absence
> of intellectual property protection and were indeed produced in
> the absence of thoroughgoing intellectual property protection in
> the eighteenth and early nineteenth centuries when copyright

15

*protection was much narrower than it is now. It is less plausible
to think that people would invest the money and time necessary
in new pharmaceuticals in the absence of any guarantee of
financial remuneration down the road.*

THE WORLD WITHOUT INTELLECTUAL PROPERTY

Intellectual property is such an ingrained element of our business
world that we assume it is, and has always been, a natural
phenomenon in society. However, there are many cultures and societies around the world that have little or no notion of intellectual
property. The Australian Aborigines, for example, survived for many
centuries without the concept of property. One of the oldest known
group of humans, the people of the Aboriginal tribes were highly
skilled creators of virtually everything they needed to survive;
however, they did not covet their creations or gain power positions as
a result of creating them. Rather, they viewed these creations as serving
a specific purpose at a specific time, after which they returned the
materials that they used back to nature. Individuals were not revered
for their particular skill, or rewarded for it in a way that most people in
Western society would understand. They were respected for their
contribution, their gift and their willingness to share it for the greater
good. Whether the person was gifted at healing, singing songs or
telling stories, or predicting weather patterns, they honoured their gift
and found methods to pass it down from generation to generation.

This type of relationship with innovation is demonstrated in numerous
cultures, yet most people would consider this representative of the
behaviour found in a less advanced society than the possessive cultures
in which many of us live. Two important and underlying factors
contribute significantly to the development of societies that place a
premium on knowledge and innovation. First, there have been periods
throughout recorded history where humans have explored and celebrated the importance of the self and individual creativity. It appears that
during these times, information becomes a valuable commodity and
something is expected in exchange for it. For example, books were traded
in Greece 2,500 years ago. Prior to that time, information was exchanged
through speech. In the earlier Greek oral culture, creative works and
information were more of a collective asset to be shared, imitated or
expanded upon. Information was shared for information's sake.

At other times in history, the concept of being a part of something greater, a valuable contributor to the 'oneness' that extends beyond individual actions, desires and functions has been prevalent. It appears that during these periods, there is very little focus on personal profit (particularly at the expense of others) or expectation of something in return. It is important to remember that both of these situations occur in different cultures, at different times, to various degrees and for different reasons. I consider virtually all of what the Western world commonly refers to as modern history – focusing on the Greek, Roman and Western European records and traditions – as corresponding with the former example. Granted, there have been long periods over the last 20 centuries where very little occurred in terms of advancing information and contributing to its evolution into a commodity. However, this has had very little to do with the existence of that latter state of 'oneness' described above. In many instances, oppressive forces such as religious or state tyranny had stifled or extinguished information exchange and possibilities for growth in any way, shape or form. For example, Medieval Europe combined authoritarian leadership with a culture accustomed to an oral tradition of communication. Neither of these elements promotes the advancement of intellectual property. The invention of the printing press, however, was a significant milestone that allowed for far greater dissemination of information. It has been suggested that the word 'information' correlates with Gutenberg's great creation of the 15th century. Coupled with increasing literacy rates, the seeds were being sown for a greater interest in protecting intellectual assets.

The second underlying factor may be more accurately described as an extension of the first. The development of trade and commerce opened the world to new ideas and exchanges: exchanges of products, services, stories, belief systems, virtues and vices, illnesses and cures. It would be a thankless task to evaluate whether international trade and the growth of commerce-based societies improved or worsened the planet, but it certainly contributed to the concepts of valuable ideas, desirable products and intellectual property. The expansion of trade and commerce was the driving force behind the growth of urban society. And urban society has been the driving force behind the development of businesses that deal in commodities of a physical and intellectual nature. Paul Kleinbert (1991) discusses the roots of our current economic culture and its preoccupation with intellectual property. He suggests that the decentralized Greek economic structures persisted through to Medieval times. In other words, trade and economic activity was fairly localized. Kleinbert examines how events like the Crusades spread economic activity over greater distances and across borders. Over time, economic practices and theories became widespread and accepted as part of the 'natural world order', according to Kleinbert. This contributed to greater attention to intellectual property issues by the 18th century, as well as that event we commonly refer to as the Industrial Revolution.

By the 18th century, the concept of skilled workers was taking root and the first examples of widespread technology transfer were taking place. Governments were taking notice of foreign recruitment efforts to lure skilled workers away from their native lands. As the leading industrial nation of the time, Britain was compelled to protect its workforce by banning the migration of skilled workers and introducing fines and imprisonment as deterrents to those who were tempted by continental rivals. Britain's restrictive policies and the responses of other nations is described wonderfully in *South Bulletin 19* (2001):

> *Emigrant workers who failed to return home within six months of warning could lose their land, property and citizenship. As technologies became embodied in machines, the focus shifted to controlling their export. In 1750 Britain banned the export of 'tools and utensils' in wool and silk industries, then in 1781 widened that to 'any machine, engine, tool, press, paper, utensil or implement whatsoever.' But in response, entrepreneurs and technicians in Belgium, Denmark, France, the Netherlands, Norway, Russia and Sweden devised new ways to get the technologies, often with explicit state consent or even active encouragement, including offers of bounty for specific technologies.*

Over the next century, the increasing complexity of technology coupled with the widespread introduction of patents rendered the practice of 'stealing' machines and workers ineffective. Licensing patented technology became more commonplace and much more important. Yet there were still many industrialized nations that avoided a complete commitment to respecting patents, copyright and trademarks until the 20th century. Unlike today, an international regime did not exist to push these nations. They created their own path and developed intellectual property strategies to meet their needs as they arose.

The United States provides an excellent illustration of the rapid growth of intellectual property protection over the last three centuries, primarily because the nation's economic growth has paralleled that of intellectual property. Arguably the most commercially diverse and technologically advanced country on the planet, the United States has been a hotbed of innovation for most of its existence. It has produced great minds in the fields of science and arts and it has attracted an equal number of brilliant people from beyond its borders. Not surprisingly, the US government upholds a constitution that protects its citizens, their property and their creations (but with a surprising twist that we will discover later in the book). The United States' Constitution states that Congress shall have power 'to promote the progress of science and useful arts, by securing for limited times to authors and inventors the exclusive right to their respective writings and discoveries'. With the financial stakes so high, the country protects its interests with a passion bordering on fanaticism.

Interestingly, the United States was not always so zealous when it came to protecting the right to ownership. Fisher (1999) alludes to this fact and suggests that the expansion of intellectual property rights in the United States can be linked to a couple of major transformations. First, agriculture was the primary industry in the British North American colonies and continued to be until the late-18th century. Fisher estimates that no more than 10 per cent of any colony's workforce was engaged in manufacturing. With the bulk of the population involved in farming, the need for copyrights, patents or other intellectual property was negligible. Throughout the 19th century, however, the United States became increasingly involved in diverse industries and over the last century, the nation evolved into a knowledge economy. Each of these shifts resulted in an increased perception that intellectual property rights were needed.

Fisher also points out that over that period of time, the nation also switched from a net consumer of intellectual property to a net producer. He states that, 'Until approximately the middle of the nineteenth century, more Americans had an interest in pirating copyrighted or patented materials produced by foreigners than had an interest in protecting copyrights or patents against piracy by foreigners.' He uses the example of Charles Dickens' requests to the US government to prevent US publishers from reprinting his works without his permission. According to Fisher, the United States was not particularly helpful with regard to its own authors as well. He writes that during this same period, 'a copyright owner enjoyed little more than protection against verbatim copying of his or her language. In other words, the work shielded by the statute was the literal text, nothing more'. For example, Fisher points to an 1853 decision by a federal Circuit Court to reject the claim of Harriet Beecher Stowe that an unauthorized German translation of *Uncle Tom's Cabin* was a copyright infringement. The court decision concluded that, 'A translation may, in loose phraseology, be called a transcript or copy of her thoughts or conceptions, but in no correct sense can it be called a copy of her book.' Pirated copies of her book were very popular in Britain as well. We have come a long way, Harriet.

Clearly, the development of intellectual property protection has not been without trials and tribulations. Dissenting opinions have existed and have been voiced throughout the process. As Dr Mauri Gronroos reminds us, protests against the intellectual property regime are not a contemporary fad. Gronroos is a doctor of economics and Associate Professor of Knowledge Management, with an emphasis on intellectual property rights, at Lappeenranta University of Technology in Finland. In addition to his books on the subject, he is also a corporate advisor and a popular speaker in seminars and conferences. Significant events protecting intellectual property rights took place before the two main conventions (the Paris Convention of 1883, which covered patents, trademarks and industrial designs and the Berne Convention of 1886, which covered copyright protection for literary and artistic works) came into force as a vital part of modern international law. There was an intensive public debate, and as Gronroos told me in an interview, 'The so-called anti-patent movement was especially loud and not far from being able to pull the rug out from under the Paris and Berne conventions.' According to Gronroos, the dissenting movement had its roots in the introduction of the Freedom of Trade in unified Germany in 1871. This liberalization had triggered an enormous increase in the country's gross domestic product and generated great optimism and enthusiasm. 'To grant new sole rights, as patents, trade marks or copyrights, sounded strange', says Gronroos. 'Actually that was considered by many as a return to the ancient privileges.'

Less than 40 years ago, the anti-patent movement re-surfaced. Gronroos refers to the protests of December 1963, relating to the United Nations General Assembly Resolution 1962 (XVIII). He recalls that the controversial principle of the 'common heritage of mankind' was mentioned for the first time, and that the developing countries in particular adapted this principle into a call for a New International Economic Order (NIEO). These countries claimed, among other things, that technology should be a part of this heritage and should therefore be available to the poor countries free of charge. Gronroos told me, 'The NIEO was intended to become legally binding by a "Charter of Economic Rights and Duties" in 1974. However, 15 OECD (Organisation for Economic Co-operation and Development) countries did not vote in favour of the resolution because they felt that it went too far. Thus, the charter remained without any consequences.' Presently, the anti-patent movement is again visible and a force to be reckoned with. Certain developing countries, following the example of Brazil, have ceased to respect international AIDS drug patents. We will explore this further in future chapters. One of the reasons for this blatant infringement against 'recognized' treaty law, as Gronroos also told me, is that the governments of these countries believe it is immoral to try to profit from the despair of the AIDS victims. Sadly, they also do not have the financial resources to approach their crises in any other way unless they begin to receive considerably more attention and effective assistance from the rest of the world.

CREATIVITY WITHOUT INTERFERENCE

Creativity over the ages has occurred for an infinite number of reasons. We can look back at the contributions of Mohammed, Jesus, Confucius and Buddha and express gratitude for their spiritual guidance and inspiration. We can also look at the ways people throughout history have distorted their teachings and abused their guidance for dishonourable ends. We can marvel at da Vinci's intuition. We applaud Galileo's curiosity while at the same time acknowledging the disturbing and shameful actions of the Roman Catholic Church. The trend that I have noticed is that interference from powerful institutions often has a negative impact on creativity. In the past, it has been religious or state-sponsored interference. In the 21st century, it would appear that powerful institutions are once again interfering with creativity by attempting to regulate it across the globe. It also appears that one of the primary purposes for this interference is to ensure that creativity is commercially profitable. We will explore these institutions and the influence they exert in Chapter 5; however, we must first discover why modern creativity and the minds responsible for it have become such powerful and profitable tools. In the next chapter we will examine intellectual assets and discover why they are referred to as the new wealth.

INTELLECTUAL ASSETS: THE NEW WEALTH

I not only use all the brains that I have, but all that I can borrow.

Woodrow Wilson (1856–1924)

Woodrow Wilson's comment is amusing but it was certainly not uttered in jest. The best leaders acknowledge both their strengths and their weaknesses and find the right people to eliminate the weaknesses. There are very few successful CEOs and presidents of companies (or countries for that matter) who can claim that they are unilaterally responsible for the achievements attributed to them. There is always an advisor or a team of strategists working diligently in the background ensuring that the boss appears brilliant. Those foolhardy souls who choose to go it alone will eventually stumble because no one is prepared to address every crisis that pops up. Certainly, no CEO can be expected to accomplish all the tasks necessary to run a profitable business. And in our modern business world, the profitable businesses are the innovators, creators and risk takers. They are using their intellectual assets for all they are worth.

Before we delve too deeply into the content of this chapter, let's look at some interesting statistics and data about modern business and the world we live in. Many readers will view these nuggets of information as a matter of fact. The newspapers are filled with these corporate 'accomplishments', theories and studies. We have become accustomed to the obscene profits that businesses make, the salaries they pay their executives and the pervasiveness with which their brands fill our magazines, commercials, movies and even schools. The wealth attached to these corporations is amazing and it is not all represented by the money in their bank accounts. Their worth is measured by innumerable assets and their success is dependent on how well they capitalize on these assets and protect them from outside interference. If you can read these facts and figures below without shaking your head or further pondering their significance, you may have become too comfortable with the way our business world operates:

- In 2000, IBM was granted an estimated 2,800 patents, the world leader for the eighth year in a row. The company now has over 19,000 US patents and 34,000 worldwide. Profits from the licensing of patents and technologies at IBM alone reached US $1.5 billion in 2000.
- Coca-Cola does not worry about spending a bit of money to protect its intellectual assets. It is the world's most valuable brand at an estimated US $72.5 billion.
- Can knowledge be quantified and valued in financial terms? According to many business gurus, it is a company's most valuable asset. According to Baruch Lev of New York University and developer of the Knowledge Capital Scoreboard, Microsoft has the most intellectual capital, estimated at US $211 billion.
- A KPMG Consulting study determined that, between 1998 and 2000, the business management theory known as 'knowledge management' moved from relative obscurity to high priority among business leaders in Europe and the United States. Knowledge management addresses the effectiveness with which businesses and organizations tap into and use the collective brain-power of their employees.
- The US pharmaceutical industry estimates that it loses US $500 million annually in India alone due to poor patent protection. Worldwide, however, it earns over US $36 billion in royalties from patent and other licences.
- A survey conducted by the Software and Information Industry Association (SIIA) and KPMG LLP concluded that nearly 30 per cent of business people who acquire software over the Internet could be classified as 'pirates' and half of the business users surveyed were

unaware of any corporate policies governing intellectual property protection.

■ The Canadian Alliance Against Software Theft (CAAST) and the Business Software Alliance (BSA) estimated that software piracy cost Canada C $457 million in lost retail sales of business software applications in 2000.

■ Applications for patents under the World Intellectual Property Organization's Patent Cooperation Treaty have grown from 2,600 in 1979 to almost 91,000 in 2000.

■ The US government maintains a 'priority watch list' of nations that are not pulling their weight when it comes to intellectual property protection. Not surprisingly, it includes countries like Argentina, Russia and the Dominican Republic. Surprisingly, it includes the European Union and South Korea. Down one notch, the 'watch list' includes such suspicious characters as Canada, Ireland and Spain. Intellectual property crimes are not restricted by any geographic or cultural constraints. They are only restricted by imagination and the occasional law enforcement action.

In the previous chapter, we took a whirlwind trip through the last two millennia to get an idea of how intellectual property protection evolved. In this chapter, we are going to consider why intellectual property rights have become such an integral element of modern business and why they appear so critical for corporate success. We are going to approach this task by looking at a broader sphere known as intellectual assets. These are the largely intangible assets found in the collective knowledge, ideas, innovation and wisdom of a company's employees. And, while some types of intellectual property can be measured to a certain degree, I consider them to be a subset of intellectual assets. Fabulous trademarks, profitable patents and award-winning industrial designs always originate from a human mind. Even if they were generated by a computer program, a human being created the program. Brain power (perhaps heart and soul power as well) is the root of all these types of intellectual assets. Put in these simple terms, it is difficult to argue against the significance of a team of great minds. Yet, this concept has been grossly undervalued for many years. That is no longer the case. Companies that recognize the value of intellectual assets have revolutionized the way businesses are operated. This approach has also revolutionized the way investors view the firms in which they invest. Let's try to shed some light on why this is the case.

How it works

Consider the Western world today. Its modern economy is based almost entirely on 'the next big thing' and 'new and improved'. Very few people on this material-based planet of ours want the same things their parents had. They want bigger and better, which is great if bigger and better are not destructive or harmful. There is nothing wrong with wanting a better relationship, a more comfortable home, more money and greater opportunities for learning. Contrary to popular belief, it is perfectly acceptable to be successful in all areas of your life. For most people, however, much of what is defined as 'better' or 'successful' consists of tangible acquisitions. This bodes well for our modern businesses because they are here to help us meet those bigger and better objectives. Not only do they find out what we want and give it to us in every colour of the rainbow, they have delved into even more profitable territory – they convince us that we need their products or services.

The company with the best team of 'convincers' is often the leader in its particular business realm. The team comprises marketing and business development executives, ad agencies, sales personnel, research and development scientists, engineers, public relations people, celebrity endorsers and maybe the CEO or president of the company. This team strives to create a competitive advantage for its employees. For example, it convinces prospective customers and clients that they need product X or service Y. Not only do they need it, they need it from this particular company, which is uniquely qualified to fill the order. The team may not be employed by the largest company in terms of number of employees, number of locations or number of products. These factors are increasingly irrelevant in the modern business world when one is considering competitive advantage.

Over the past decade, we have witnessed the success of companies like Dell, which has relied almost exclusively on advertising, mail orders, Internet orders, a 'customize your computer' strategy, reasonable prices and incomparable customer service guarantees. These are Dell's competitive advantages. They do not have the most employees, a store at every major intersection and hundreds of brand names to choose from. They do not even have hundreds of Dell products to choose from. But the team that conceptualized this business model was worth every penny they were paid and more. They were one of Dell's greatest assets. Other business models still flourish, such as 'big box retail outlets' and lucrative turnkey food franchises. But they are only as good as their 'brand power' or their trademark and its popularity. It has little to do with the building that the company can own or afford to lease. Real estate is, in many business models that thrive today, no longer a competitive advantage.

Intellectual property, on the other hand, is becoming an increasingly valuable asset for establishing competitive advantage in virtually all business models. It is the reward after years (or months for the truly gifted or lucky) of research, designing, crafting and experimenting. It is the happy, healthy corporate baby after a long and challenging pregnancy. It is the outward manifestation of a company's brilliant ideas put into action. On a macro-economic scale, it is the pay-off for those nations that were in advantageous positions at the time of the Industrial Revolution to recognize and embrace the shift from 'brawn power' to 'brain power.' This period of industrialization and its evolution up to the middle of the last century is critical in this discussion of intellectual assets.

LINKING INDUSTRIALIZATION AND INTELLECTUAL PROPERTY

In an effort to avoid the history lesson, I recommend Charles Dickens to anyone seeking a first hand perspective of the Industrial Revolution. For the purpose of our story, however, we will bypass the societal and environmental damage and focus on the relationship between the growth of industry and the growing interest in intellectual property rights. As industrialization increased, the number of inventions in the form of machines and industrial processes also increased. Industrialists sought out means to protect their 'property' and safeguard their businesses from rivals. As production increased, markets expanded beyond borders at a greater rate and protection for foreign competition became a more pressing issue. These larger markets contributed to larger profits and international trade grew in leaps and bounds. Intellectual property protection grew in step, as patents for machinery and industrial processes were joined by increased protection for literary and artistic works, as well as famous marks.

History texts of Europe's industrialization often focus on the machines and the money. Whenever people are considered, it is in the context of child labour, families uprooted from the farming lifestyle that they had known for generations, and the polluted and dangerous cities that teemed with poverty. Despite all the hardship and ugliness of the time, the concept of intellectual capital was born during this period. New and improved equipment, faster and more efficient means to accomplish difficult tasks, and effective ways to ship and distribute products around the world had to be developed by someone. They did not occur by chance. The companies with the most creative and skilled employees would lead the way. Brainpower was the underlying resource that provided the industrial brawn of these early industrializing nations. Strong workers were still required without a doubt. There was no shortage of backbreaking work to perform. The growth of the company and its profits, however, would be driven by the ingenuity and mental abilities within the company.

Once it was recognized that a clever mind could devise a machine to perform the tasks of 10 workers, the intangible asset of intellectual capital gained value. If the competition had a team that developed a machine that replaced 100 workers, it was critical to assemble a team to create a machine to perform the work of 500 workers – and patent it. And while it may have seemed like the machines were the answer to economic might, it was not really the case. Despite his inexcusable use of gender exclusive language, US writer Elbert Hubbard recognized what the future held in this regard when he said, 'One machine can do the work of fifty ordinary men. No machine can do the work of one extraordinary man.' The race for knowledge and innovation was under way. This time, however, the reward was financial profits.

A MODERN SCENARIO

Consider this example. Two top research scientists leave a leading optical networking company to start up their own firms. They both have international connections and are recognized in their area of expertise. They are first-rate inventors and have been largely responsible for their previous employer's success. Scientist Number One begins to enlist key people to his firm by relying on his reputation, his vision of a new line of optical networking products, and his strategy for developing the technology, obtaining the patents, and marketing like crazy to customers with whom he is already familiar. Prospective partners and potential investors believe that he can accomplish all that he claims. Except for one thing. Scientist Number Two is equally capable in all respects. She has her start-up name trademarked, the Internet domain name secured and her business plan has been professionally crafted. More importantly, she left her previous employer as the patent owner of some exciting new optical networking technologies, which form the basis of her new company's products. Where Scientist Number One has had to build in a research and development period – let's say 18–24 months – before hitting the market with products, Scientist Number Two will be using that time to manufacture and attract clients. By the time she has a salesforce in place taking orders, Scientist Number One is getting ready to manufacture. If you are the investor and you can only put your money in one company, who will you choose? If you have an equity stake in the company, as an employee, board member or legal advisor, which route looks shorter and smoother? While there is no such thing as a sure thing and anything can go wrong at any time in the volatile technology world, Scientist Number Two seems to have a distinct competitive advantage because of those patents. In addition to attracting the initial venture capital to her project, she may also capture better talent in all areas of her business: research scientists who view large investments of capital as an indication of a research budget for future 'patentable' products; executives who recognize that they can look better and prosper at a start-up that already appears to have a head start; and additional capital as long as things run according to plan.

THE IBM EXAMPLE

If you still do not believe that intellectual assets are as good (or better) than cold hard cash, consider two distinctly different businesses in the same general competitive environment. IBM is a powerhouse in the world of computer technology goods and services and a long-time survivor in this volatile realm. As we discovered earlier, IBM was granted an estimated 2,800 patents in 2000 – more than any other company in the world. That figure comprises more patents than some national intellectual property offices examine in a year. For eight consecutive years, IBM has registered more patents than any other company in the world, and since it was founded, it has accumulated more than 34,000 patents worldwide. Almost 20,000 of these patents are held in the United States alone. Considering that a patent in the United States can cost up to US $20,000 to obtain, this is a considerable investment in intellectual property.

Intellectual property is not simply the by-product of years of research and development by this innovative company. Nor is it simply a means to create new technology that is protected long enough for the company to profit from its commercial potential through direct sales. Granted, the company uses more of its patents than many other companies; however, this may be indicative not only of the talent of IBM's workforce but of the staggering amount of funds available to the company to commercialize its patented products. There is more to intellectual property at IBM than one may think. It generates an estimated US $1.5 billion in profits (not revenues) annually through licensing agreements with other companies that wish to use IBM's intellectual property and related intellectual assets. Many other companies become technology-sharing partners with IBM either willingly or unwillingly. The willing partners often enter into cross-licensing agreements that benefit both companies through the sharing of otherwise proprietary technologies and related innovations. The unwilling participants may have been confronted by IBM and asked to explain why they are infringing on an IBM patent. Coercion may be too strong a word to define the relationship that blossoms from Big Blue's aggressive intellectual property enforcement, so we can continue using agreement to describe the interaction from that point forward.

On the other end of the spectrum, a hot start-up is looking to become the next IBM. It wants to get its business plan in front of key investors so that it can secure sufficient funding to bring its products to market. Intellectual property and intellectual property rights will be among the many things that venture capitalists or other investors will examine to determine the potential of the start-up. In many instances, start-ups have flourished because investors have backed what they believe to be a sure thing: the brilliant individual who left another firm with a head full of ideas, also known as intellectual capital. When this intellectual capital is actually 'owned' by the individual and supported by laws regarding patents or copyrights, for example, investors will recognize the competitive advantages that could arise from this situation. Conversely, they must also gauge the likelihood of the brains behind the start-up staying with the company or departing with all that fabulous intellectual property in tow.

The general rule regarding intellectual property is that the inventor owns the invention. Therefore, the patent remains in the inventor's possession regardless of where the inventor works. A company would need a signed agreement with an inventor stating that all intellectual property arising from the inventor's efforts is owned by said company. In cases where the employee is hired specifically for the purpose of creating something that can become intellectual property, the company will own it. In the course of our work at Global Trade Solutions, we have used intellectual property ownership to successfully analyse and predict what area of the fibre optics field a new start-up would specialize in after key patent owners left an industry leading firm. Had the former employer owned the patents, it is conceivable to think that the firm would have been spared a new rival and may have developed the commercial potential of the patents itself.

To complicate things further, start-ups will also have to decide whether the risk of sharing their intellectual assets, property or trade secrets is required to attract the type of investment they are seeking. By hiding this information, investors may not have the complete picture they need to get involved. Yet revealing too much information may expose critical business planning to potential competitors. Critics suggest that in some industries, product turnaround is so quick that the promise of future intellectual assets holds considerably less weight in investment decisions. For example, a patent application can take years to approve and the industry may have undergone monumental changes in the interim. Such is the case with the semiconductor industry, where product cycles may be as short as six months. This would suggest that, while the promise of future patents is not necessarily going to attract immediate investment in your semiconductor firm, you should still analyse the benefits of securing your process or product as your own property. It may be useful in the future. In the short term, you can highlight the other intellectual assets in your company to impress the investors. All forms of intellectual assets carry considerable weight in the modern business world and their influence, though often imperceptible, is felt in most major corporate decisions.

KNOWLEDGE MANAGEMENT

There are different definitions for the area of theory called knowledge management. Some critics believe it is primarily a theoretical construct with limited practical application. Others view it as a valuable business tool that can clearly contribute to a company's value and competitiveness. Regardless of the number of definitions, it is clear that knowledge management is concerned with how we capitalize on those intangibles we refer to as intellectual assets. Knowledge management is Mauri Gronroos' field of research. He believes that knowledge management aims, among other things, to improve the organization's ability to produce new ideas and innovations. In an interview he told me, 'So far, it seems that ideas emerge by combining information, competence and creativity. To me the two formers are variables – one can have more or less information or one can be more or less competent. In this context, creativity is a constant. I believe that all human beings, with about the same IQ, possess about the same amount of creativity.' He is quick to add that we do not typically let people use their creativity. We either stifle it outright or at least do not encourage it.

Gronroos illustrates this defect in our society using a well-known example, when 500 pre-school children aged five and six were shown a picture of two towers situated about 200 feet apart. A small boy could be distinguished in one of the towers. The children were asked to innovate all possible and impossible ways the little boy could move from one tower to another. The children managed to average 16 different ways to move the boy in the tower. These same children were asked to undertake the same exercise after graduating from the high school at the age of 17. The average result among these teenagers was seven ways to get the boy to move from one tower to another. As Gronroos so aptly states, 'For me this reveals a frightening truth: there is a lot of inborn creativity but somehow the system manages to kill it under way!' This is one of the greatest downfalls of many education systems. Millions of little humans – each one unique – are being forced into a handful of roles perpetuated by uninspired teachers and administrators in uninspiring institutions. Schools churn out an astronomical number of followers and a negligible number of leaders. For this reason, we often see creative types cast as misfits or troublemakers. In reality, many of them are both bored by all aspects of school and oppressed by the education system. Very few schools can embrace and nurture creativity and, until recently, it was not considered a valuable trait for most forms of employment.

Fortunately, many businesses are starting to embrace creativity as a company asset. While creative skills were coveted in certain types of professions, such as writing, communications, marketing or promotion, one did not seek it out in engineers, scientists and middle managers. For the past few years, business magazines have been replete with articles about zany Internet start-ups and their wacky founders. Other technology companies caught the trend, as did more traditional types of businesses. Many failed yet others succeeded beyond anyone's wildest dreams. Quite frequently, the creative geniuses behind these companies took their magic to other ventures as well. In doing so, they spread the message that creativity in its myriad forms can be a valuable asset to any business. It is an intellectual asset to be nurtured and protected.

If we refer back to the KPMG Consulting study mentioned at the beginning of this chapter, the trend to understand, nurture and protect intellectual assets within a company appears to be growing. In the case of KPMG Consulting, it chose to examine the field of business theory loosely termed as knowledge management and published its first research report on the subject in 1998. At the time, knowledge management was a fairly new concept in the world of business. Two years later, KPMG's second study was released. Within those two years, knowledge management had jumped to the top of the list of known concepts, and businesses no longer underestimated how critical this element was to their overall success. The 2000 knowledge management findings were gathered over the summer of 1999 from 423 organizations in the United Kingdom, continental Europe and the United States. These organizations all had a turnover exceeding £200 million (US $347 million). Some of the key findings include:

- 81 per cent of organizations indicated that they had, or were considering a knowledge management programme.
- Companies believed that knowledge management could play an 'extremely significant' or 'significant' role in improving competitive advantage (79 per cent), in marketing (75 per cent), and in improving customer focus (72 per cent). Over half of the respondents indicated that the impact of knowledge management on product innovation (64 per cent), revenue growth and profit (63 per cent) and employee development (57 per cent) would also 'extremely significant' or 'significant'.
- 71 per cent of respondents with a knowledge management programme in place indicated that they had achieved better decision-making; while 68 per cent responded that the programme had contributed to a faster response to key business issues; and 64 per cent reported improved customer service as a result of knowledge management.

There was a downside as well. While companies predicted that they would see even greater benefits over time (increased profits, reduced costs, increase in the company's share price, for example) they were still struggling with the fundamental issues that make knowledge management a formidable challenge. Over half of the companies with knowledge management programmes pointed to internal problems, such as 'the lack of time to share knowledge' (62 per cent); 'failure to use knowledge effectively' (57 per cent); and 'difficulty in capturing tacit knowledge' (50 per cent). These three challenges all share at least one factor in common. In the business world, knowledge is power. This is why the concept of knowledge management is flourishing within corporations around the world. But knowledge is power on the individual level as well and many employees believe that they can leverage what they know, particularly if no one else knows it. This can reach levels close to paranoia in some organizations and is obviously crippling to any formal system that is intended to tap into the brains of each and every employee.

The KPMG Consulting study also found that employees were not adequately trained to understand how to manage the information and those who embraced 'knowledge working' were not rewarded. Two-thirds of the organizations complained of information overload, which can be the death of a knowledge management system. As in competitive intelligence, the collection of information for information's sake has a negative impact on effective and efficient decision making. Additionally, many of the respondents to the study appeared to view knowledge management as a technological issue. The use of the Internet, intranets, data mining and data warehouses, document management systems and other technology is valuable if the capabilities of the technology are fully realized. This requires commitment that extends beyond the willingness of the information technology group to spend the money and install the hardware and software. Employees must be trained to use the system and, equally important, educated in the significance of using it to benefit the company as a whole.

Technology aside, knowledge management is first and foremost concerned with effectively drawing on the tacit knowledge, wisdom and expertise within the company or organization. People, not technology, are the critical components for success. If they have no purpose or desire to share the wealth of information they possess, they simply will not. If the benefits of sharing their knowledge are clearly illustrated, they will likely become more willing to assist the company in this regard. If they are rewarded for doing so, experience personal satisfaction and witness the increased prosperity of their company (as a result of their contributions), they will make it a habit.

INTELLECTUAL CAPITAL

One of the more relevant points with regard to the topic of this book related to KPMG's finding that 'only 16 per cent of respondents whose organizations had or were considering a KM (knowledge management) programme measured intellectual capital – that part of an organization's value that is based on intangible assets such as knowledge, innovation and relationships. This mirrors organizations' failure to see KM in terms of creating shareholder value'. Intellectual capital – these intangible assets – are often the foundations upon which intellectual property is built. In fact, the companies that are the best at exploiting their intellectual capital in all ways (including the development of patents, trademarks or other forms of intellectual property) will reap the rewards and gain or sustain a competitive advantage in their respective markets. Such strategic approaches to business are clearly illustrated in many industry sectors: patents in biotechnology and copyright in software and media are two intellectual property-related examples.

There are no simple formulae that accurately assess the value of intellectual capital in an organization. According to Gronroos, two Swedes, Leif Edvinsson and Karl-Erik Sveiby, introduced the first model for assessing the intellectual capital of an organization. Skandia, a Swedish insurance giant, served as the guinea pig for their theories. Edvinsson and Sveiby became the founding fathers of the Scandinavian School of modern knowledge management. As Gronroos clarifies:

> Companies have of course always understood that 'capital' is not only money but also features or things that can be turned into cash – for example the brand of the company, customers, market share and so on. The novelty was, however, that they made the first attempts to develop the intellectual capital ('Skandia Navigator') and measure and report it ('Skandia Dolphin'). Naturally, the difficulty is that you cannot measure intangible variables as you measure tangibles. This is why Edvinsson and Sveiby developed a wide range of indicators for this purpose.

Their success may be measured by the fact that Skandia continues to publish an annual balance sheet of the company's intellectual capital.

These 'intangibles' of intellectual capital, as they are often called, include such elements as productivity, which has spawned a great deal of work in the area of growth accounting. Growth accounting is arguably more art than science and attempts to identify the contribution of diverse factors (skill, energy, knowledge of labour, for example) on the overall growth in productivity. Human capital is another of these 'intangibles' and may be loosely defined as 'the knowledge, skills and mobility of individuals' (Mortensen, 1999). Human capital issues for businesses include determining the return on investment for funding further education or training for employees.

There are also many 'intangibles' that fall under the umbrella of research and development and related innovation. Technology can also be lumped into this category. These elements are very difficult to measure in terms other than expenditures but it is these other terms that truly need to be measured in order to evaluate their worth.

We can look at this in a very simplistic way. Imagine that you are the president of a technology product company in a fiercely competitive market. You have a fixed amount to spend on training for your employees, who work in five main areas: administration, customer relations, research and development, manufacturing and executive management. If you train the administrative employees, your return on investment might include more efficient internal operations, a smoother running office. If you train the customer relations people, they may use their newfound skills to better serve your clients and customers. Improved customer relations may result in increased sales, repeat business and word of mouth promotion. Investing the training funds in the research and development team might cultivate innovation that results in product enhancements or new designs that can lead to a competitive advantage in the market. Productivity may increase if the manufacturing employees receive training that enables them to reorganize their equipment or assembly methods. And finally, the corporate executives might benefit from training that teaches them how to work effectively as a team, how to relate to their employees with respect, or how to make better strategic decisions. What do you do? The following questions would probably come to mind and I've given the answers that I suspect would follow:

- Do I have enough funds to train all of the groups? No.
- Do I know which group(s) should receive the training at this time? No.
- Do I know what training would benefit the company the most at this time? No.
- If I train any of these groups, will I be able to measure my return on investment? No.
- Will I be able to take these funds and complete an executive MBA without anyone else noticing? No.

If you knew that you could spend US $40,000 to train four of your engineers and that they would reward your company with a patentable product that generated millions of dollars in revenue through sales and licensing agreements, the decisions would be pretty easy. But such is the nature of intellectual assets and attempts to measure the 'intangibles'. Any investment in an employee is potentially risky for a number of reasons. And that risk increases when employees possess specialized skills or unusual talents that are in high demand. These are the issues that extend beyond the knowledge management that we have examined and the knowledge management as it is commonly perceived. Yet pure knowledge management is more complex than data mining, intranets and document management systems. Undoubtedly, the best knowledge manager would be psychic – someone who actually could get inside the heads of others and understand what they are thinking, what their motives may be, and the extent of their capabilities. Imagine the power of the company that could confidently state that all of its employees were committed to the firm without question, shared all of their expertise with their colleagues without reservation and protected the secrets of the company with their lives. Children would find such a fairy tale hard to swallow. It appears that companies are striving for this extreme loyalty in order to compete in a business world built on brainpower. Unfortunately, either the flawed human character gets in the way and attempts to exploit a situation in an unethical or illegal way or the indomitable human spirit recognizes that there is more to life (and business) than it is currently experiencing and sets out on a new adventure, taking its mind and all of the tacit knowledge that reside in it along for the ride. How does a company stop that from happening? In the former example, laws and dismissals can be reasonably effective deterrents. In the latter case, not even a beheading will help a company retain the knowledge of a key person who wants to leave. Granted, if you took that course of action, no one else would benefit from the knowledge, but that may be a small consolation as you sit in your prison cell.

To make a long story short, businesses are going to great lengths to secure brainpower and to increase their intellectual assets. It is no surprise that an intellectual property regime would flourish in such an environment. Every day, it appears that there are more things to protect, more rules to establish, and more threats that must be addressed with legal action. Yet, as Fisher suggests, intellectual property protection is only one of the ways in which businesses or inventors make money on their creations. 'Financial remuneration does not have to come in the form of patent protection or intellectual property protection. It can come in the form of government prizes or post hoc government rewards. It can come in the capacity to offer consumers ancillary services, such as a guarantee of originality or quality. But patent protection is one of the ways, the most common way in which the United States and most Western countries guarantee that financial remuneration is provided to the creators of highly expensive innovations.'

Fisher also believes that one must look at the context before deciding how effective a tool such as patent protection is for guaranteeing financial remuneration for creators. For example, he points out that patent protection is a very clumsy tool for basic scientific research for a couple of reasons. First, very little of basic scientific research produces commercially viable inventions that would enable the researcher to make money through the patent system by selling them to consumers. Also, says Fisher, 'There is no linkage between the subsets of scientific discovery that are suitable for commercialization and the subsets that are not, so it is a very crude source of incentive and creates a risk of distorting scientific research in the direction of commercial development.' A second defect, according to Fisher, is that patent protection applied to scientific work – biochemistry for example – creates a significant risk of impeding cumulative discoveries in the field. He uses the example of both businesses and universities having trouble securing the permissions necessary to continue doing cutting-edge research. Patent protection, in this regard, can cause substantial disadvantages.

It will be interesting to see how these different fields of study – knowledge management, intellectual capital and other similar areas of inquiry – will contribute to the belief that most of a company's worth may actually be immeasurable because it resides in the heads of employees and nowhere else. On that basis, is it really the company's worth at all? Exploring that question is definitely a subject for another book, although we will touch upon it in other chapters. Our present concern is how this apparent obsession with intellectual assets has contributed to the development of intellectual property – one of the few tangible means of looking at certain types of intellectual assets – and the development of laws to protect intellectual property.

THAT'S BRILLIANT – WHAT IS IT?

The best ideas are common property.

Seneca (4 BC–65 AD)

If Seneca were alive today, he would soon discover that humans in the 21st century are far more preoccupied with the commercially viable ideas than the best ideas. In some instances, the ideas are the same; however, we have still decided that the genius who comes up with the ideas must have the opportunity to be rewarded in some manner other than the respect of his or her peers and a place in history. Fair enough. Everyone, including geniuses, needs to make a living and virtually all brilliant ideas become common property over time. We know that humans created for millennia without needing their rights protected. Additionally, we have discovered some interesting historical evidence – the advancement of industrialization, technology and capitalist societies for example – that suggests that much of the creation over the last few centuries could not continue peacefully without some protection for the creator.

The question that I have is this: Was it 1) our innate sense of fairness; 2) our recognition of widespread human desire to exploit; or 3) some reason in between, that pushed us to formally protect the literary works, inventions and valuable marks of individuals? I am inclined to believe it was a combination of a number of factors loosely related to the fairness/exploitation dichotomy. Regardless, a group of men (I suspect few women, if any, were given the opportunity to participate) decided that protection was required and set about defining what was important enough to be protected and what was not. As we know from Chapters 2 and 3, the important stuff came to be known as intellectual property.

So what comprises intellectual property? According to the World Intellectual Property Organization (WIPO), intellectual property encompasses any creations of the mind. This is highly inaccurate. Hitler's mind created the Holocaust but he was not going to get a patent or trademark for it. The creations of the mind that WIPO more accurately wishes to encompass include inventions, artistic or literary works, and symbols, names and images used in commerce. Further, WIPO divides 'intellectual' into two categories: industrial property – this category includes inventions, industrial designs, integrated circuits, trademarks and geographic indications – and copyright – this category applies to books, poems, plays, films, musical works, drawings, paintings, sculptures, photographs and architectural designs.

The World Trade Organization (WTO) also includes the protection of undisclosed information and the control of anti-competitive practices in contractual licensing under its Agreement on Trade-Related Aspects of Intellectual Property (TRIPS). Regardless of the number of elements or the way they are categorized, the big three of the intellectual property world have been and continue to be, patents, trademarks and copyright. We will be finding out more about these assets in this chapter and throughout the book. Additionally, we will examine some of the less visible types of intellectual property covered by law.

PATENTS

A patent is a time-limited, exclusive right that is granted for an invention. This invention may be a new product or process and the patent protects the owner/inventor from others who may attempt to make, use, distribute or sell the invention without the patent owner's consent. Patent protection is generally limited to a period of 20 years. Patents provide the owners with the rights to decide who gets to use the patent by permission, licensing agreements, or other terms. Patent owners may also sell the rights to their invention to another party, which would also include the patent rights.

Once a patent expires, the invention enters the public domain, and may be used by anyone who may wish to exploit it commercially. One common example of this exploitation is generic or 'no-name' drugs that flood the market after a pharmaceutical company's patent for a particularly popular drug expires. Until that time, the patent owner is still obliged to share the information related to the patent publicly in order to contribute to the existing pool of expertise and innovation. This, presumably, fuels the fire for even greater inventions by inspiring creativity in other researchers and inventors. And, what kind of inventions can be protected? According to WIPO, there are some basic criteria that must be met in order to qualify for patent protection:

Practical use

How this is determined is beyond the scope of this book and quite possibly beyond definition. The practicality of something is entirely arbitrary and will undoubtedly be determined by the skill with which the applicant convinces the examiners of this point. A walk through the aisles of any department store or hardware outlet will reveal an unlimited supply of patented gadgets that one individual will find utterly useless. Yet, another individual will not be able to live without the product. Practicality is in the eye of the beholder. Considering that patents have been obtained for the method used to 'click' a button on an e-commerce Web site, we must question any guidelines that offer definitions of 'practical use'.

Novelty

If the inventor can reasonably prove that the invention in question incorporates some feature or characteristic that falls outside the pool of existing knowledge in the technical realm in which the invention fits, this criterion will likely be met. WIPO refers to this existing pool of knowledge as 'prior art'. For example, an inventor could create an exhaust system with a feature that filters out all of the harmful toxins that constitute the exhaust. The exhaust system itself may resemble that used on many other automobiles as long as no existing patents relating to exhaust systems and silencers are infringed upon. The inventor would not necessarily be looking for a patent for the exhaust system; rather, a patent would be sought for the filtering technology that, presumably, is a new characteristic in the field of automotive exhaust system technology.

In a recent article, Tim Campbell, Director of Business Development for IP.com, has suggested that prior art is incredibly powerful. According to Campbell (2000), 'Prior art has the ability to do something that powerful legal teams have often failed to accomplish: invalidate patents.' He writes that, in the past, there has always been a mad scramble by those opposed to a particular patent to find prior art that would invalidate the offensive patent. This reactive approach was often a costly gamble. A more proactive approach has been to adopt what Campbell refers to as 'defensive disclosures' or 'IP strategic publishing'. In short, this means that a company actively produces prior art and places it in the public domain. When such innovation comes to the awareness of patent examiners, for example, it provides effective evidence to prevent the issuing of similar or related patents. Campbell points out that the prevention of bad patents from being issued benefits virtually all the parties that could potentially be drawn into a dispute. There is no financial drain on companies fighting over an invalid patent and there is far less chance that a company will have to pay licensing fees for the use of obvious technology. Combined with effective patenting, defensive disclosures constitute an excellent strategy for businesses in intellectual property-intensive sectors. These include any businesses that have seen an increase in patents for business methods (the Amazon 'one click' fiasco is probably the most notorious example that we discuss in this book), software development or medical techniques as Campbell points out in his article.

'Patentability'

Additionally, the subject of the patent must be 'patentable' under law, which is not as easy as it may seem. Many countries refuse to issue patents for scientific theories and mathematical methods, for instance. Also, patents may not be obtainable for alterations to plant and animal varieties or discoveries of natural substances. Even some commercial methods or methods for medical treatment may not be 'patentable.'

Patents are applied for and granted in much the same way as other intellectual property, such as trademarks. They are typically issued at the national or regional level (such as the European Patent Office or the African Regional Industrial Property Office) following a lengthy process and much paperwork. WIPO also administers the Patent Cooperation Treaty (PCT), which enables an inventor to file for a single international patent in as many countries as he or she wishes, provided the countries are signatories to the Treaty. This Treaty will be discussed in greater detail in Chapter 4. The information pertaining to the invention or process is generally filed with the patent application. This also includes the title of the item for which the applicant is seeking a patent, as well as an indication of the technical field that is most relevant to the invention. The applicant must include background information, complete with a written and visual description of the invention as well as 'claims' relating to the invention. The skill with which the applicant prepares these claims can be a very significant determinant of the extent of protection granted by the patent. Once granted, the patent owner has a monopoly over how the invention is developed commercially. The invention can only be manufactured, distributed, sold or licensed with the consent of the patent owner. These patent rights are enforceable through the courts in most nations. Patents are not watertight, however, and the courts can also rule against a patent owner if a third party challenges the validity of the patent. Once a patent expires, it cannot be renewed, and the owner no longer retains exclusive rights regarding the use of the patent. The invention enters the public domain, where others may attempt to profit financially from it.

At the very beginning of the patent process, patent owners are required to share information relating to their inventions with the public. As mentioned above, specific information regarding the nature of every invention in the patent process is available to anyone who is interested in pursuing it. The intent of this requirement is to ensure that the 'total body of knowledge in the world', as WIPO refers to it, is enriched to further promote creativity and innovation. The patented invention remains protected for 20 years, but over the course of those 20 years, other inventors can use the knowledge they gained from studying the public information as well as the patented product to create something even more wonderful and financially lucrative. The really bright inventors seek out the loopholes and gaps in the patent applications, hoping to find areas where the slightest modification to an existing design could constitute an entirely new patent. If this strategy is used successfully, a new patent can be obtained and the inventor can reap the potential financial rewards much earlier.

Unfortunately, there is no book (including this one) that can adequately address the best possible way to file for a patent. Each case, each country, each invention and each examiner will be different. If you wish to file for a patent I recommend that you familiarize yourself with the patent office that you will be using and request all the documents relating to the patent process that the office makes available to potential applicants. Visit the Web site if there is one available (Chapter 4 lists some of the national offices around the world). And, if you can afford it, seek qualified legal counsel to help you. There is much to learn and it helps to have someone who has successfully completed the process a number of times on your side.

Patents and controversy

Patents are arguably the most controversial type of intellectual property from a moral, ethical and legal perspective. Historically, the patent reputation has not fared much better. In comments relating to the United Nations Development Programme's *Human Development Report 2001* (www.undp.org/hdr2001), Dean Baker, Co-Director of the Center for Economic and Policy Research in Washington, points to Medieval guilds as the origin of patents. He suggests that members of these guilds believed they had an exclusive right to practise their craft. Yet he is quick to acknowledge that no modern analyst would view these perceptions of guild restrictions as anything more than a form of protectionism. By extension, one might suggest that modern-day patents are protectionist as well. In the world of international trade, protectionism is synonymous with 'trade barrier', the more common term used by those who are trying to knock trade barriers down. Yet it appears that patents escape this scrutiny because they have been defined as 'rights' and afforded considerable influence in the international business sphere. By making the rights of patents available to everyone, one may argue, the charge of protectionism is unfounded. Yet, we will learn that while patent rights are theoretically available to anyone, especially anyone from a country that participates in the international intellectual property system, they are still primarily a tool implemented by businesses and individuals in wealthier nations for the protection of businesses and individuals in wealthier nations.

Clearly, the patent controversy in not a recent phenomenon. The issues multiply as time passes. For example, the issue of patenting life forms is highly contentious and has been so for many years. In 2001, a Federal Court of Appeal ruling in Canada stated that Harvard University could patent its 'oncomouse', a genetically altered mouse used in cancer research, in Canada. A lower court, as well as Canada's patent office, had earlier rejected the mouse patent because it did not fit the description of an invention. None of this is new, although it may still be disturbing to some people. The United States allowed the oncomouse patent over 12 years ago. European countries awarded the oncomouse patent 9 years ago. But where do you draw the line with patenting life forms? These issues will endless debate, not only in the realm of intellectual property, but in the hearts and minds of many people on this planet for many years to come. It will not be easily resolved.

There are other ways in which the patent regime as we experience it is not only ineffective, but actually interferes with potentially life-changing discoveries. Consider the example of cetyl myristoleate (CM), discovered by Dr Harry W Diehl in 1962. Dr Diehl was employed at the National Institute of Health, a US government research laboratory. As part of his research, Diehl injected rats with a bacteria-like organism called mycobacterium butyricum to create rats with severe arthritis. Diehl did the same thing with mice, injecting them with mycobacterium butyricum. Interestingly, the mice did not develop arthritis. Diehl isolated the only compound that he found different between the mice and the rats. This was CM. He conducted a further experiment by injecting the rats with CM prior to giving them the mycobacterium. Under these conditions, the rats did not develop arthritis. In other words, CM prevented rats from getting arthritis.

Further experiments in Diehl's home laboratory led to a patent for CM for rheumatoid arthritis in 1977. A second patent for osteoarthritis followed in 1996. Diehl found that he could eliminate arthritis in humans with CM. For many reasons, his government superiors did not deem this discovery worthy of further study. Arguably, it comes down to one very specific reason. According to Sherry A Rogers, MD (2001), 'As often has happened in the history of medicine with items that are not patentable or that could produce a cure thus driving the research organization into extinction (as it could no longer justify its existence), such research is ignored regardless of merit.' CM is available under a number of labels (in the United States, at least) and does not seem to require a prescription. More importantly, it does not have the life-threatening side effects of many pharmaceutical drugs. But it has not become mainstream – ask your doctor if he or she has heard of it – and has no big drugs company backing its advertising and promotion. What would such a drugs company do for a living if it cured arthritis and had no market for its drugs? And, as mentioned above, that is the bottom line when it comes to medical products. First, patent the products that are novel and that will appeal to a large population of suffering people. Second, market it like crazy to the medical community and the public and (excuse the phrase) make a killing from it. But, whatever you do, do not cure what ails them. Otherwise, you will not have a market for the stronger drug that you develop to mask the new symptoms plaguing the drug users. You want people to purchase the new product to treat the side effects they are experiencing from the original drug. Eventually, these side effects are more painful and life threatening than the original health problem. Without a market or a potential market, there is little use for a patent. And a real cure for a disease is not good business. The whole scenario seems analogous to the proliferation of intellectual property rights in some ways.

This may sound extreme but a good hard look at the ethics of many big businesses is a prerequisite for understanding intellectual property. Poor countries that are desperate for assistance to combat the diseases rampaging through their citizens are no longer waiting for the rich and influential nations of the world to help. They are demanding that drug companies relax patents on the costly drugs they develop for AIDS and other illnesses of epidemic proportion. Some patents are being relaxed but not to the extent that will make a difference in the life-prolonging category.

Clearly, there are many individuals who believe that patents infringe on basic human rights. Protesters waving 'Patents Kill' signs are likely protesting against the protection that patents afford pharmaceutical companies, thereby allowing them to keep drug prices inflated and beyond the reach of the vast majority of the world's population. Such practices have resulted in outright disregard of patents and international patent law in Brazil, for example. Brazil's decision to ignore international AIDS drug patents has been supported and imitated by other developing nations. For these countries, the moral and ethical issues of suffering and death have taken precedence over the legal concerns of the business world. Patents are often viewed as legalized monopolies for companies because of the lengthy patent protection periods. While these restrictions allow the patent holder an opportunity to seek reward for past efforts and investment, opponents may argue that the 20-year monopoly squelches competition, creates conditions of dependency and supports nothing more than a massive cash grab.

Currently, there are many questions and arguments but few answers or resolutions to the patent debate. Cautious progress in this area, combined with a critical analysis of past decisions, is critical if humankind is actually intended to benefit from patent rights.

TRADEMARKS

Trademarks have evolved from ancient times, when craftspeople would mark or sign the crafts, tools and other products they created to distinguish their particular works from those of other artisans or toolmakers.

Today, we recognize a trademark as a distinctive sign that indicates that specific goods or a service is produced or provided by a specific person, group or business. Trademarks may take many forms, including combinations of words, letters and numerals as well as drawings or symbols. More recently, trademarks have been applied to the shapes of packaging of various goods, as well as seemingly intangible phenomena such as music or vocal sounds, and fragrances used as distinguishing features. Even a colour or colours that are considered distinguishing features can be trademarked.

Trademarks identify ownership and rights of the commercial source of a product or service. They protect the owner by ensuring an exclusive right to use or by allowing the trademark owner to authorize use by another party for payment. Like patents, trademarks are protected for a set period of time that varies under different legal systems. Unlike patents, however, trademarks can be renewed indefinitely if the owner is willing to pay for the renewal. Perhaps the main value of a trademark is to offer an individual or a company an opportunity to develop a distinct and unique public signature that assists in building credibility and recognition. In turn, this promotes the individuals' or businesses' financial goals. Protection of trademarks is court enforced in most national intellectual property systems. As a result, trademark protection can hinder unfair competition from rivals offering imitation goods and services under a name or image that is identical or too similar to be coincidental.

Applications for trademarks follow processes similar to those for patents. In addition to providing a reproduction of the actual sign for which protection is sought (the words, letters, numerals, symbols, images, sounds, fragrances or colours, to name a few), the applicant must also include a list of goods and/or services to which the proposed trademark would apply. For example, a new accounting firm may apply for a trademark for its firm, Action Accountants. It may seek a trademark for that name, as well as the image of a stylized gender-neutral figure in business attire with a briefcase in one hand and a calculator in the other. The figure is also wearing a cape and is in a pose that suggests flying through the air like a superhero. Action Accountants obviously wants these signs as trademarks for its accounting services. But the company also wants them for promotional and marketing items, and publications relating to the field of accounting, such as newsletters, magazines and books. The company must list all these goods and services in its application if it wants protection in areas beyond the realm of accounting services. Article 15, paragraph 4 of the TRIPS Agreement states that 'The nature of the goods or services to which the trademark is to be applied shall in no case form an obstacle to registration of the trademark'. And if the relevant people at Action Accountants have done their homework, they will have checked in advance to determine if any of their words or images conflict with the rights previously granted to another trademark owner. Most countries register and protect trademarks and many have some type of database containing full information on all the registrations, renewals, oppositions and other relevant documentation relating to each application. Trademark seekers can conduct search and examinations on their own (this is now quite effective on the Internet) or they can hire a lawyer who specializes in trademarks to perform this work, as well as guide the applicant through the entire trademark process.

Related marks

Associations or other organizations that do not necessarily offer a commercial product or service may apply for and receive collective marks. These types of marks are used to identify members of such a group with a standard or level of quality or achievement relating to specific requirements for that group. Professional associations for accountants or engineers may have these types of collective marks. Certification marks are closely related; however, these do not 'belong' to any individual or particular group. They are not considered property in that regard. Rather, collective marks apply to such things as compliance to a defined and recognized standard. The ISO series of quality standards (ISO 9001, 9002, etc) is used by many businesses to identify that they have met a minimum level of quality standards – that prescribed by the ISO system – for various practices and processes within their operations. However, these businesses do not own any rights with regard to the certification mark. The mark is simply granted to them for use after they successfully fulfil the certification requirements.

Obtaining a trademark can be a challenging and costly experience. From the filing of the initial application with the regional or national office to the final approval, could take years. Even with the advent of electronic applications using the Internet, the process can be long and arduous. And what is your reward at the end? If you make it through the examiner's comments and concerns, potential opposition from third parties, and pay all the necessary fees when they are due, you have a trademark that is protected in the country or region in which you have registered it. At least, it is supposed to be protected. As for the rest of the world, you are out of luck unless you register with each national office in which you desire trademark protection. Alternatively, you can obtain an international registration through WIPO, which has effect in over 60 countries worldwide. Two treaties – the Madrid Agreement Concerning the International Registration of Marks and the Madrid Protocol – give some protection to trademark applicants from countries that are signatories to one or both of the treaties. Yet, how effective are these treaties at protecting valuable trademarks and other intellectual property? We will be exploring this issue throughout this book.

Next to the unauthorized use of copyright works, trademark abuses may be the most common form of intellectual property infringement. Clothing, fashion accessories and sporting goods are often easy targets. They are also lucrative because they are in high demand in many markets around the world. Mark Cuban, billionaire owner of the Dallas Mavericks basketball team, has a fairly easy-going approach to protecting his team's trademark and seemingly little concern for copyright issues relating to professional sports. Considerable revenue is obtained from the sale of sports memorabilia and clothing and flushing out culprits who sell unauthorized copies of the products is a full-time job. While the National Basketball Association takes a hard line with regard to intellectual property issues, Cuban is quite happy to leave it in the league's hands while he runs his team. 'From my perspective,' he says, 'if you dupe (copy) a Mavs game on tape, I would love it if you could give it to as many friends as possible. If you hear me give a speech and tape it, give it to as many people as possible.' Cuban does not even have a problem if you want to put his team's logo on an unofficial Web site; however, the National Basketball Association certainly does. Cuban draws the line with anyone who puts the Dallas Mavericks logo on merchandise for the purpose of selling it. 'I will come after you', he adds. 'I don't need any special laws. It is simple.'

Domain names

A domain name registration is not a trademark, nor is it the same as copyright. The first clue that these are distinct assets is that the intellectual property offices in nations around the world have nothing to do with the application, approval and registration of domain names. These are contracts between individuals and/or businesses and the organizations that provide domain registrations. The only legal aspects of this arrangement are with regard to your contract to use the domain name. There is little else protecting you or your business from infringements by others who choose a domain name that is virtually identical to the one you have registered. One of the best ways to protect your domain name is by registering it as a trademark. Securing both the trademark and the domain name at the same time is an excellent means to protect yourself and your new business. Find out if the trademark is available by doing a trademark search first. Then check to see if the domain name you want is available. If it is, register it with the domain name organization, and start your application for the trademark with the trademark office.

What happens if you are slow on the draw and the domain name that matches your trademark is already taken? A number of options are possible, including the use of online arbitration. Claire Barliant's article, entitled 'Rough Justice' (law.com, 5 September, 2000), follows the long and winding road taken by the Corinthians, a Brazilian professional soccer team. The owners of the team received an e-mail from the owner of the domain name 'corinthians.com' inquiring about the team's potential interest in purchasing the domain. Though they were interested, the Corinthians were not prepared to negotiate with a cyber-squatter, the term commonly used to describe individuals who register domain names (usually relating in some way to famous people, products or other potentially lucrative sources) with the intention of selling them for profit. These sales are frequently made to trademark owners who covet the domain name for obvious reasons. The Corinthians decided to use online dispute resolution in order to retrieve the domain. As Barliant points out in her article, this exercise was quite involved. From the Brazilian soccer club, to its lawyers in New York, to a WIPO-based arbitration service, to an Argentine lawyer serving as the arbitrator, the decision eventually settled in favour of the Corinthians. One of the decisive factors in the case was the offer for sale by the original domain name owner. Another factor, the author adds, was the fact that Corinthians held the trademark for the name, despite its use in the bible, as the name of the ancient city in Greece, and the Mississippi town where a Civil War battle was fought. Judgments in favour of trademark owners simply because they are trademark owners has been a common criticism of the dispute resolution system.

Similarly, Dow Jones and Company won two Internet addresses that were misspelt versions of *The Wall Street Journal*. An arbitrator ruled in favour of the owner of the prestigious newspaper after it claimed a Pennsylvania man had used 'wallstreetjounal.com' and 'wall-streetjournel' to create unauthorized links to the newspaper's online version. At the same time, users had to go through links to unrelated sites, wait until the pages opened, and then delete them prior to getting to the real page they wanted. These pages consisted of advertisements for products or services and literally trapped the user on other sites. The defendant's revenue source was the small amount of money (between 10 and 25 cents per 'click' on an advertisement) that the advertising companies paid him. As a result of people's misspellings, the man was making close to US $1 million annually.

The WIPO-based arbitrator ruled that the individual supplied no evidence of legitimate interest in the addresses and that he had acted in bad faith in both registering and using the two domain names. At the time of writing this book, the case could be found online at WIPO Arbitration and Mediation Center (Case No. D2000–0578) at www.arbiter.wipo.int.

Strong-arm tactics by trademark owners seeking domain names can backfire as well. Daniel Harris, an attorney with Brobeck, Phleger and Harrison in California, recounts one of these tales in 'Nabbing Trademark Trespassers' (Business 2.0, June 1999). Prema Toy Company, which created the Gumby and Pokey cartoon characters, decided to use the force of law to deal with what it perceived as a cybersquatter with the domain name 'pokey.org.' The law in question was the United States' Trademark Dilution Act, which came into force in 1995. The Act offers protection to famous marks (like Gumby and Pokey, for example) being used in a way that dilutes the trademark's distinctiveness. When the lawyers for Prema determined that the domain owner was not a cybersquatter looking to cash in on the famous mark, but a 12-year-old boy named Christopher 'Pokey' Van Allen, and that the domain name had been a birthday gift from his father, they did what they were paid to do. They threatened legal action and a costly battle over pokey.org, which was now a homepage on the Internet, complete with photographs of Christopher's puppy. Pokey decided he was up for the fight and within short order, it appeared that he had global popular opinion on his side. According to Harris' article, Australia's domain registrar created a top-level domain (.POKEY) which Van Allen now owns. The King of Tonga graciously offered the 'pokey.to' domain name to the boy. After a few months, the bad publicity brought Prema to its senses and they finally backed off. While Christopher retained the domain name, the Van Allen family also retained their legal bills. Battling the corporate giants does not come cheap.

COPYRIGHT

This book is protected by copyright. On the second page, there are a handful of sentences that tell the world that the rights to this work belong to the creator. There is a rights statement that identifies Curtis Cook as the author of the work as it has been asserted in accordance with the Copyright, Designs and Patents Act of 1988. Additionally, there are a few statements by the publishers regarding reproductions, storage or transmittal of the work in any form or by any means requiring permission by the publisher. And of course there is the very familiar and often disregarded copyrights symbol, ©, accompanied by the author's name and the year of publication. Will sections of this book be photocopied by teachers or business professionals wishing to share some of the ideas with students or colleagues? Quite possibly. Will paragraphs or chapters be reproduced on the Internet without permission? This is also possible. Are these offences against copyright? Absolutely.

Copyright is often regarded as the most rapidly evolving area of intellectual property over the past half century. In general, copyright is the right given to creators for their literary or artistic works. According to WIPO, copyright encompasses works such as:

■ books (both fiction and non-fiction);
■ poems;
■ plays;
■ reference works;
■ newspapers;
■ computer programs;
■ databases;
■ films;
■ musical compositions;
■ choreography;
■ paintings;
■ drawings;
■ photographs;
■ sculpture;
■ architecture;
■ advertisements;
■ maps;
■ technical drawings.

There is even a field of 'rights related to copyright' for performances by musicians and actors, producers of sound recordings, and broadcasting organizations delivering radio and television programmes. The TRIPS agreement includes Article 10, which is concerned specifically with computer programs and compilations of data, as well as Article 11, which addresses the rights of authors or their successors in title to authorize or prohibit the commercial rental of their copyright works. Copyright does not include ideas, processes or procedures, mathematical concepts or methods of operation. Rather, the protection offered by copyright is for the expression only. Fortunately, the parameters of expression have changed over time and legal interpretations have evolved so that authors have protection in more circumstances, such as translations of their written works.

The goal of copyright is to prevent the unauthorized use or piracy of any literary or artistic work by a third party. Since many of these types of works are intended for a mass audience and the investment in creating them is often significant, the potential for infringement of copyright is high. The actual creators often sell the rights to individuals or firms (such as a publishing house) who are equipped to deal with mass marketing, distribution, and (the creator hopes) protection of the works. In return the creator receives 'royalties' or payments based on a contract or agreement with the individual or firm.

Copyright is not infinite. Over the years it has expanded to cover the length of the creator's life and an additional 50 years for signatories of the WIPO treaties relating to copyright. In some cases, national laws may extend this right further. Historically, the Enlightenment Period was instrumental in the development of intellectual property rights, as writing became increasingly accepted as a profession, rather than an artistic pursuit. Famous writers of the day, such as William Wordsworth, were very much involved in the struggle to gain ownership and control of their works and to profit from them. As Sharman writes (1997): 'There was a sharp line drawn between the original genius or true artisan, disinterested in material fortune, and the crass commercialist looking to make a quick dollar'; and as Swartz (1992) writes:

> Even as they fought for economic control of their work, authors of the Enlightenment period still wanted to distance themselves from the image of the tradesperson or the mercantile. They wanted to be seen as artists, or cultural treasures, and above worldly concerns. Yet paradoxically, they also wanted to gain monetarily from their art. Justification for the 'disinterested genius' who still expects to profit from his or her writings was provided by a focus on the authors' need to provide for their families, whose estates should not be allowed to suffer.

Some things never change. Even today we struggle with the culture/commodity dichotomy.

Generally, there are no special procedures in place to register for copyright protection. In this regard, copyright is different from a patent or a trademark. Once a work is created, it is protected by copyright, particularly in countries that are parties to the Berne Convention for the Protection of Literary and Artistic Works. Some countries do have national copyright offices that serve to identify and distinguish titles of works and assist in providing evidence for potential copyright disputes. While such disputes can go to court (and we will examine some of these in later chapters), copyright may be the most difficult intellectual property protection to enforce. It may be relatively easy to determine if someone has pirated your creative works once you find them; however finding the culprit can be next to impossible. Technology – the Internet in particular – has facilitated the copying of material to such an extent that it is unreasonable to believe that any laws or enforcement efforts could possibly resolve the problem. It becomes an exercise in education and ethics more than anything else but that is a very challenging exercise to teach. WIPO has established and administers the 'Internet Treaties', comprising the Copyright Treaty and the Performances and Phonogram Treaty and, while these agreements are intended to create standards for the prevention of unauthorized access and use of copyrighted digital works, it is simply too easy for people to exploit this medium.

GEOGRAPHICAL INDICATIONS

According to WIPO, a geographical indication generally consists of the name of the place of origin of goods in order to emphasize certain positive qualities or reputation. A geographical indication often takes the form of a sign or label attached to or associated with the goods. Swiss watches and knives, maple syrup from Quebec or Vermont, or Cuban cigars may all constitute geographic indications because the quality and reputation of the product is directly related to where the product originates. And it is important that the link between the product and its place of origin be maintained.

Whether a particular sign serves as a geographical indication is a matter of both consumer perception and national law. The purpose of a geographical indication is fairly obvious. Consumers purchasing Columbian coffee want some kind of assurance that the coffee is indeed from Columbia. A Bordeaux wine is only a Bordeaux wine if it was produced in the Bordeaux region of France. The use of this name on any other wine is quite likely unauthorized and misrepresents the product. This type of geographical indication is called an 'appellation of origin'. The damage created by such misuse extends beyond misrepresentation. For example, the Swiss watchmaker loses business if unauthorized imitations claiming 'Swiss-crafted' precision are mass-manufactured in some other part of the world, sold at half the price and break down soon after they are purchased. Additionally, the watchmaker's reputation may be damaged as the unwitting consumer tells his or her friends of the poor quality of Swiss watches.

Geographical indications are protected primarily by national laws, and often fall under the umbrella of consumer protection or unfair competition regulations. Internationally, the ancient Paris Convention for the Protection of Industrial Property (1883) and the Lisbon Agreement for the Protection of Appellations of Origin and Their International Registration are invoked to protect geographical indications among signatories. In addition, the Agreement on Trade-Related Aspects of International Property Rights (TRIPS) includes three articles that address the international protection of geographical indications within policies and rules established by the WTO. These articles state the following:

Article 22: Protection of Geographical Indications

1. Geographical indications are, for the purposes of this Agreement, indications which identify a good as originating in the territory of a Member, or a region or locality in that territory, where a given quality, reputation or other characteristic of the good is essentially attributable to its geographical origin;
2. In respect of geographical indications, Members shall provide the legal means for interested parties to prevent:
   a. the use of any means in the designation or presentation of a good that indicates or suggests that the good in question originates in a geographical area other than the true place of origin in a manner which misleads the public as to the geographical origin of the good;
   b. any use which constitutes an act of unfair competition within the meaning of Article 10bis of the Paris Convention (1967).
3. A Member shall, ex officio if its legislation so permits or at the request of an interested party, refuse or invalidate the registration of a trademark which contains or consists of a geographical indication with respect to goods not originating in the territory indicated, if

use of the indication in the trademark for such goods in that Member is of such a nature as to mislead the public as to the true place of origin.

4. The protection under paragraphs 1, 2 and 3 shall be applicable against a geographical indication which, although literally true as to the territory, region or locality in which the goods originate, falsely represents to the public that the goods originate in another territory.

Article 23: Additional Protection for Geographical Indications for Wines and Spirits

1. Each Member shall provide the legal means for interested parties to prevent use of a geographical indication identifying wines for wines not originating in the place indicated by the geographical indication in question or identifying spirits for spirits not originating in the place indicated by the geographical indication in question, even where the true origin of the goods is indicated or the geographical indication is used in translation or accompanied by expressions such as 'kind', 'type', 'style', 'imitation' or the like.

2. The registration of a trademark for wines which contains or consists of a geographical indication identifying wines or for spirits which contains or consists of a geographical indication identifying spirits shall be refused or invalidated, ex officio if a Member's legislation so permits or at the request of an interested party, with respect to such wines or spirits not having this origin.

3. In the case of homonymous geographical indications for wines, protection shall be accorded to each indication, subject to the provisions of paragraph 4 of Article 22. Each Member shall determine the practical conditions under which the homonymous indications in question will be differentiated from each other, taking into account the need to ensure equitable treatment of the producers concerned and that consumers are not misled.

4. In order to facilitate the protection of geographical indications for wines, negotiations shall be undertaken in the Council for TRIPS concerning the establishment of a multilateral system of notification and registration of geographical indications for wines eligible for protection in those Members participating in the system.

Article 24: International Negotiations; Exceptions

1. Members agree to enter into negotiations aimed at increasing the protection of individual geographical indications under Article 23. The provisions of paragraphs 4 through 8 below shall not be used by a Member to refuse to conduct negotiations or to conclude bilateral or multilateral agreements. In the context of such negotiations, Members shall be willing to consider the continued applicability of

these provisions to individual geographical indications whose use was the subject of such negotiations.

2. The Council for TRIPS shall keep under review the application of the provisions of this Section; the first such review shall take place within two years of the entry into force of the WTO Agreement. Any matter affecting the compliance with the obligations under these provisions may be drawn to the attention of the Council, which, at the request of a Member, shall consult with any Member or Members in respect of such matter in respect of which it has not been possible to find a satisfactory solution through bilateral or plurilateral consultations between the Members concerned. The Council shall take such action as may be agreed to facilitate the operation and further the objectives of this Section.

3. In implementing this Section, a Member shall not diminish the protection of geographical indications that existed in that Member immediately prior to the date of entry into force of the WTO Agreement.

4. Nothing in this Section shall require a Member to prevent continued and similar use of a particular geographical indication of another Member identifying wines or spirits in connection with goods or services by any of its nationals or domiciliaries who have used that geographical indication in a continuous manner with regard to the same or related goods or services in the territory of that Member either (a) for at least 10 years preceding 15 April 1994 or (b) in good faith preceding that date.

5. Where a trademark has been applied for or registered in good faith, or where rights to a trademark have been acquired through use in good faith either:

before the date of application of these provisions in that Member as defined in Part VI; or

before the geographical indication is protected in its country of origin; measures adopted to implement this Section shall not prejudice eligibility for or the validity of the registration of a trademark, or the right to use a trademark, on the basis that such a trademark is identical with, or similar to, a geographical indication.

6. Nothing in this Section shall require a Member to apply its provisions in respect of a geographical indication of any other Member with respect to goods or services for which the relevant indication is identical with the term customary in common language as the common name for such goods or services in the territory of that Member. Nothing in this Section shall require a Member to apply its provisions in respect of a geographical indication of any other Member with respect to products of the vine for which the relevant indication is identical with the customary name of a grape variety existing in the territory of that Member as of the date of entry into force of the WTO Agreement.

7. A Member may provide that any request made under this Section in connection with the use or registration of a trademark must be presented within five years after the adverse use of the protected indication has become generally known in that Member or after the date of registration of the trademark in that Member provided that the trademark has been published by that date, if such date is earlier than the date on which the adverse use became generally known in that Member, provided that the geographical indication is not used or registered in bad faith.
8. The provisions of this Section shall in no way prejudice the right of any person to use, in the course of trade, that person's name or the name of that person's predecessor in business, except where such name is used in such a manner as to mislead the public.
9. There shall be no obligation under this Agreement to protect geographical indications which are not or cease to be protected in their country of origin, or which have fallen into disuse in that country.

The difference between a trademark and a geographic indication is not always apparent. Trademarks are exclusive. The owner of a trademark can prevent other individuals or businesses from using his or her trademark without permission. This right is protected by law and enforceable in court if necessary. A geographical indication is not the property of any one individual or business. Anyone who produces a product in a certain geographic region can use a geographical indication if the location of production lends specific qualities or characteristics to that product.

INDUSTRIAL DESIGNS

If you like the look of a particular piece of jewellery or furniture because of its unique shape, pattern or colour, there is a very good chance that law protects its uniqueness. The owner – not the person who purchased it but the person who created it or had it created on his or her behalf – may have protected the item from unauthorized duplication or imitation by registering an industrial design. This form of intellectual property protection is for the aesthetic features of the article that make it desirable to consumers in contrast to the technical features of an innovative design. In other words, it is based solely on visual appeal.

Industrial designs are generally protected in the countries in which they are issued for a period of five years. Under the TRIPS agreement (Article 26), member states must offer protection for industrial designs for a minimum of 10 years. In many jurisdictions, the applicant can renew the protection, usually to a maximum of 15 years. In order to obtain protection, a design must be 'new' or 'original'. As is the case with patents, such terms are obviously arbitrary and will vary not only from country to country, but will vary from examiner to examiner within an office. Some countries will also recognize certain designs for protection as works of art under copyright law, while others allow for protection of industrial designs under laws intended to address unfair competition.

TRADE SECRETS

The Colonel's secret recipe is secret for a reason: it keeps people coming back for more odd-looking chicken parts in cardboard buckets. If everyone knew the recipe, they might choose to make their own odd-looking chicken parts, potentially destroying a lucrative fast-food franchise. Trade secrets can be virtually anything, including 11 herbs and spices. They can be combinations of chemicals, the names of which we cannot even pronounce yet we consume willingly on a daily basis. Very few people know what is in the Coke formula but it does not prevent them from consuming huge volumes of the stuff. Trade secrets can also be confidential documents relating to pricing strategies or marketing methods. The one common denominator is that the information has commercial value because it is secret and the company or individual with the information has taken steps to keep it secret. Such information is protected as intellectual property under Part II, Section 7 of the TRIPS agreement for example. Trade secrets will be discussed in greater detail in both Chapters 4 and 5.

LAYOUT DESIGNS (TOPOGRAPHIES) OF INTEGRATED CIRCUITS

Electronics technology is so pervasive in our lives that the daily appearance of new gadgets and appliances has become an expectation instead of a phenomenon. In order to feed our hunger for this technology, bright people around the world are developing innovative integrated circuits that perform all kinds of electronic operations. Law protects these topographies. According to information from the WTO:

An 'integrated circuit' means a product, in its final form or an intermediate form, in which the elements, at least one of which is an active element, and some or all of the intercon- nections are integrally formed in and/or on a piece of material and which is intended to perform an electronic function. A 'layout-design' (topography) is defined as the three-dimensional disposition, however expressed, of the elements, at least one of which is an active element, and some or all of the interconnections of an integrated circuit, or such a three-dimensional disposition prepared for an integrated circuit intended for manufacture.

The Treaty on Intellectual Property in Respect of Integrated Circuits (IPIC) protects this type of intellectual property. It is also protected by the TRIPS Agreement. While we will not examine IPIC further, Chapter 4 will explore the TRIPS requirements further.

BREEDERS' RIGHTS

In 1961, the International Convention for the Protection of New Varieties of Plants established the Union internationale pour la protection des obtentions végétales (UPOV). Translated as the International Union for the Protection of New Varieties of Plants, the UPOV convention came into force in 1968, and was revised a number of times up to the 1991 Act, which came into force in April 1998. The purpose of the convention was to establish an international agreement among states that would acknowledge the achievements of breeders of new plant varieties. These breeders would be awarded an exclusive right based on the principles of the convention and their plant varieties would be protected interna- tionally – at least among the signatories of the convention. In order to be eligible for protection, UPOV requires that the plant varieties are:

- distinct from existing, commonly known varieties;
- sufficiently uniform;
- stable;
- new in the sense that they must not have been commercialized prior to certain dates established by reference to the date of the application for protection.

Plant breeders' rights are no different than other forms of intellectual property rights in that they are granted for a limited amount of time before they become part of the public domain. There are also restrictive clauses and controls that are intended to protect the public against abuses. While the rights are protected, other parties are still allowed to use the particular plant variety without permission for both research and for the development of other new plants.

When I look in my garden or hike through the forest with my wife, I ask myself, 'Why do we need all these new plants?' According to UPOV, protection of plants as property provides incentives for both researchers and businesses to continue developing the fields of agriculture, horticulture and forestry. It believes that improved varieties are necessary for improved food production, as well as renewable energy and raw material. As is the case with many types of intellectual property, the upfront investment in this field is substantial and the amount of research that translates into commercially viable products is small. By protecting those plants and seeds that have had a significant return on investment, plant breeders are encouraged to continue down this garden path seeking profitable plants.

The main role of UPOV is to promote international harmonization in the development of plant breeders' rights and to assist with the development of adequate protection within countries seeking to establish legislation in this area. UPOV has also established general principles relating to the examination of plant varieties. And, in case you are wondering how such an organization dealing with intellectual property in the international arena manages to exist independently of the WIPO, wonder no more. The Director General of WIPO is the Secretary-General of UPOV.

THE ENFORCERS

What you cannot enforce, do not command.

Sophocles

Who cares about intellectual property and its protection? Apparently a sufficient number of people to ensure the survival of countless international organizations, councils, associations and other groups dedicated to the global intellectual property regime. In addition to these international entities, there are hundreds of government departments and agencies. Most countries have at the very least one government office devoted to the various aspects of regulating intellectual property. We must not forget the requisite lobby groups, industry associations and trade organizations, all of which are trying to further their specific agendas. There are intellectual property groups dedicated to software copyright issues. There are associations looking out for the interests of musicians and other entertainers. A growing number of organizations are committed to cyberlaw issues and the development of intellectual property rights relating to the Internet. There are also the corporations and their lawyers, other businesses and their lawyers, and individual entrepreneurs, inventors, artists and their lawyers, and more lawyers. Seriously, for something that rarely gets mentioned directly in the course of a business day or a meeting, intellectual property is an industry unto itself.

While there would be enough material for a series of books if all of these groups were given a paragraph or two, this chapter will focus on some of the more influential entities. Throughout the book, you will find references and stories that mention some of the more specialized players in the intellectual property field – perhaps in biotechnology or the film industry, for example – which can lead you to additional information in a specific topic or area of interest. This section of the book will examine key organizations at the international level, particularly the WIPO and the WTO. It will also examine successes at the regional level, represented by the European Patent Office. In addition, you will find a resource list of many government agencies mandated to protect intellectual property at a national level.

Enforcement of laws rarely takes place at an international level. Typically, legal enforcement is a matter of national interest and is symbolic of the autonomous powers of independent states. I cannot think of one government that actively seeks to be lorded over by another country and its legal system. Nevertheless, a number of countries on this planet have decided that they would be better off if they agreed to coordinate basic rules governing the protection of intellectual property. Once the rules where established to their liking, the countries would take responsibility for enforcing the rules within their borders. Such cooperation is admirable in our conflict-loving society. Admirable, but far from perfect because of that Orwellian truth: the countries forming this cooperative are equal; however, some are more equal than others. The power and influence of certain nations extends far beyond the geographic boundaries that define their territory. Consequently, these nations exert considerable pressure on other nations, groups of nations and international institutions to the extent that their role transcends that of active participant in a collaborative process. They call the shots when it best suits their agenda and they act as enforcers not only within their own borders but through a powerful reach that is assisted by the types of international institutions they have created.

This is not a conspiracy theory. It is not meant as fuel for the anti-globalization proponents and it is not intended as a rallying cry for the destruction of the WIPO and the WTO. It is simply recognition that, as well intentioned as these organizations, the people who run them and the member states who vote in them are, the system is fundamentally flawed by the global power imbalance that predates their creation. It is the same problem that plagues most families, let alone international cooperation efforts. Those who make the most money, pay the bills and provide a measure of security and comfort feel that they have additional rights when it comes to setting the rules. How does one address such a dilemma in the global arena? How do we ensure the rules governing international intellectual property protection, for example, are in the best interest of the whole global family?

WIPO

According to WIPO literature, the need for international protection of intellectual property can be traced back to events like the International Exhibition of Inventions, held in Vienna in 1873. Foreign exhibitors refused to participate in the convention fearing that their ideas and inventions would be stolen and commercially exploited in foreign countries. Six short years later, the Paris Convention for the Protection of Industrial Property came into being. It was the first significant international treaty regarding intellectual property protection and helped individuals of one nationality obtain protection of inventions (patents), trademarks and industrial designs in other countries. The Paris Convention was brought into force one year later by 14 member states and an international office was established to deal with the administrative tasks of this new agency.

By 1886, the Berne Convention for the Protection of Literary and Artistic Works brought copyright protection to the international level. It was established to protect everything from poems and operas to paintings and architectural works. A second office was established for the administration of this Convention. Within seven years, however, the two offices had merged to form the United International Bureaux for the Protection of Intellectual Property, better known by its amusing French acronym BIRPI. From seven staff members, this organization eventually grew into the WIPO. In between, BIRPI changed locations in Switzerland, moving from Berne to Geneva in 1960 to be closer to the numerous international organizations located in that city, including the United Nations. A decade later, the Convention establishing the WIPO swallowed BIRPI and the organization took more of the shape we see today. In 1974, WIPO became a specialized agency of the United Nations, thereby committing itself to the intellectual property concerns of the member states of the UN. It was not until 1996, however, that WIPO formalized its relationship with the WTO. The cooperation agreement between these two organizations was a significant acknowledgement of the vital role intellectual property plays in international trade.

Today, WIPO's main objective is to promote the global protection and use of intellectual property rights in a manner that allows all to benefit. An international staff of over 700 people administers this challenging agenda. The organization's main office remains in Geneva. It also has a coordination office at the United Nations Plaza in New York City. Membership in WIPO is open only to nations and, in January 2001, over 90 per cent of the world's countries were members. It serves as a forum for member states to create and/or harmonize rules designed to protect intellectual property rights. This forum comprises nations with well-structured, long-standing laws and regulations as well as nations whose histories relating to intellectual property protection can be measured in years rather than decades and centuries. In 1898, BIRPI was administering four international treaties. Just over a century later, that number has increased to over 20, divided into three distinct types listed below. For each of the conventions or treaties, one or two articles have been cited to not only give you an idea of the content or focus of the agreement, but to familiarize you with the language of the law according to WIPO. The official signed texts of these documents do not have article names however. WIPO has added these in an effort to facilitate the reading of the documents for lay people. A selection of the more common treaties has also been given additional detail in an effort to shed more light on their *raison d'être*. The full version of these texts can be obtained from WIPO or the WIPO Web site (www.wipo.org).

INTELLECTUAL PROPERTY PROTECTION TREATIES

These treaties define the minimum standard of protection offered in a country if that country is a signatory to a particular treaty. In other words, the country has laws and rules in place to meet the requirements of the treaty. Enforcement of those laws, however, is an entirely different matter as we learnt earlier in this chapter and will return to in subsequent chapters. The intellectual property protection treaties include the following:

Paris Convention for the Protection of Industrial Property

This is where it all started. The Paris Convention was first established in 1888 and had been revised seven times by 1979. Its scope is defined in the first of its 30 articles:

Article 1: Establishment of the Union; Scope of Industrial Property

1. The countries to which this Convention applies constitute a Union for the protection of industrial property.

2. The protection of industrial property has as its object patents, utility models, industrial designs, trademarks, service marks, trade names, indications of source or appellations of origin, and the repression of unfair competition.
3. Industrial property shall be understood in the broadest sense and shall apply not only to industry and commerce proper, but likewise to agricultural and extractive industries and to all manufactured or natural products, for example, wines, grain, tobacco leaf, fruit, cattle, minerals, mineral waters, beer, flowers, and flour.
4. Patents shall include the various kinds of industrial patents recognized by the laws of the countries of the Union, such as patents of importation, patents of improvement, patents and certificates of addition, etc.

Berne Convention for the Protection of Literary and Artistic Works

Work on the Berne Convention began in 1886 and by 1979 it had been amended seven times. The text comprises 38 articles, plus an Appendix of six articles specifically addressing developing nations. Article 2 and 2bis document the types of works that are protected and the extent to which they are protected:

Article 2: (Protected Works: 1. 'Literary and artistic works'; 2. Possible requirement of fixation; 3. Derivative works; 4. Official texts; 5. Collections; 6. Obligation to protect; beneficiaries of protection; 7. Works of applied art and industrial designs; 8. News)

1. The expression 'literary and artistic works' shall include every production in the literary, scientific and artistic domain, whatever may be the mode or form of its expression, such as books, pamphlets and other writings; lectures, addresses, sermons and other works of the same nature; dramatic or dramatico-musical works; choreographic works and entertainments in dumb show; musical compositions with or without words; cinematographic works to which are assimilated works expressed by a process analogous to cinematography; works of drawing, painting, architecture, sculpture, engraving and lithography; photographic works to which are assimilated works expressed by a process analogous to photography; works of applied art; illustrations, maps, plans, sketches and three-dimensional works relative to geography, topography, architecture or science.
2. It shall, however, be a matter for legislation in the countries of the Union to prescribe that works in general or any specified categories of works shall not be protected unless they have been fixed in some material form.

3. Translations, adaptations, arrangements of music and other alterations of a literary or artistic work shall be protected as original works
without prejudice to the copyright in the original work.

4. It shall be a matter for legislation in the countries of the Union to
determine the protection to be granted to official texts of a legislative,
administrative and legal nature, and to official translations of such texts.

5. Collections of literary or artistic works such as encyclopaedias and
anthologies which, by reason of the selection and arrangement of
their contents, constitute intellectual creations shall be protected as
such, without prejudice to the copyright in each of the works forming
part of such collections.

6. The works mentioned in this Article shall enjoy protection in all countries of the Union. This protection shall operate for the benefit of the
author and his successors in title.

7. Subject to the provisions of Article 7(4) of this Convention, it shall be
a matter for legislation in the countries of the Union to determine the
extent of the application of their laws to works of applied art and
industrial designs and models, as well as the conditions under which
such works, designs and models shall be protected. Works protected
in the country of origin solely as designs and models shall be entitled
in another country of the Union only to such special protection as is
granted in that country to designs and models; however, if no such
special protection is granted in that country, such works shall be
protected as artistic works.

8. The protection of this Convention shall not apply to news of the
day or to miscellaneous facts having the character of mere items of
press information.

Article 2bis: (Possible Limitation of Protection of Certain Works: 1.
Certain speeches; 2. Certain uses of lectures and addresses; 3. Right to
make collections of such works)

1. It shall be a matter for legislation in the countries of the Union to
exclude, wholly or in part, from the protection provided by the
preceding Article political speeches and speeches delivered in the
course of legal proceedings.

2. It shall also be a matter for legislation in the countries of the Union to
determine the conditions under which lectures, addresses and other
works of the same nature which are delivered in public may be reproduced by the press, broadcast, communicated to the public by wire
and made the subject of public communication as envisaged in
Article 11bis(1) of this Convention, when such use is justified by the
informatory purpose.

3. Nevertheless, the author shall enjoy the exclusive right of making a
collection of his works mentioned in the preceding paragraphs.

Rome Convention for the Protection of Performers, Producers of Phonograms and Broadcasting Organizations

The Rome Convention was completed in 1961 and is intended to supplement, rather than prejudice, the protection of copyright in literary and artistic works. The third of the 34 articles provides the definition for both who is protected and what is protected:

> Article 3: (Definitions: (a) Performers; (b) Phonogram; (c) Producers of Phonograms; (d) Publication; (e) Reproduction; (f) Broadcasting; (g) Rebroadcasting)
> For the purposes of this Convention:
>
> a. 'performers' means actors, singers, musicians, dancers, and other persons who act, sing, deliver, declaim, play in, or otherwise perform literary or artistic works;
> b. 'phonogram' means any exclusively aural fixation of sounds of a performance or of other sounds;
> c. 'producer of phonograms' means the person who, or the legal entity which, first fixes the sounds of a performance or other sounds;
> d. 'publication' means the offering of copies of a phonogram to the public in reasonable quantity;
> e. 'reproduction' means the making of a copy or copies of a fixation;
> f. 'broadcasting' means the transmission by wireless means for public reception of sounds or of images and sounds;
> g. 'rebroadcasting' means the simultaneous broadcasting by one broadcasting organisation of the broadcast of another broadcasting organisation.

Geneva Convention for the Protection of Producers of Phonograms Against Unauthorized Duplication of their Phonograms

The Geneva Convention came into force in 1971 and contains 13 articles. The first article provides the definitions for which it applies and the second outlines the obligations of the contracting parties:

> Article 1: (Definitions)
> For the purposes of this Convention:
>
> a. 'phonogram' means any exclusively aural fixation of sounds of a performance or of other sounds;
> b. 'producer of phonograms' means the person who, or the legal entity which, first fixes the sounds of a performance or other sounds;

c. 'duplicate' means an article which contains sounds taken directly or indirectly from a phonogram and which embodies all or a substantial part of the sounds fixed in that phonogram;

d. 'distribution to the public' means any act by which duplicates of a phonogram are offered, directly or indirectly, to the general public or any section thereof.

Article 2: (Obligations of Contracting States; Whom they must protect and against what). Each Contracting State shall protect producers of phonograms who are nationals of other Contracting States against the making of duplicates without the consent of the producer and against the importation of such duplicates, provided that any such making or importation is for the purpose of distribution to the public, and against the distribution of such duplicates to the public.

Nairobi Treaty on the Protection of the Olympic Symbol

The fact that a 10-article treaty was established in 1981 regarding the protection of the Olympic Symbol is testament to the disturbing power of the International Olympic Committee (IOC), as well as the unhealthy significance we attach to competitive sports. Instead of referencing any particular article, I suggest that you simply remember not to mess around with the Olympic rings and the IOC.

Madrid Agreement for the Repression of False or Deceptive Indications of Source of Goods

The Madrid Agreement for the Repression of False or Deceptive Indications of Source on Goods was established on 14 April 1891 and has been revised four times up to 1958. Act I comprises six articles, while Act II consists of seven articles added in Stockholm in 1967. Article 1 of the first Act outlines the seizure clauses.

Article 1

1. All goods bearing a false or deceptive indication by which one of the countries to which this Agreement applies, or a place situated therein, is directly or indirectly indicated as being the country or place of origin shall be seized on importation into any of the said countries.

2. Seizure shall also be effected in the country where the false or deceptive indication of source has been applied, or into which the goods bearing the false or deceptive indication have been imported.

3. If the laws of a country do not permit seizure upon importation, such seizure shall be replaced by prohibition of importation.

4. If the laws of a country permit neither seizure upon importation nor prohibition of importation nor seizure within the country, then, until such time as the laws are modified accordingly, those measures shall be replaced by the actions and remedies available in such cases to nationals under the laws of such country.
5. In the absence of any special sanctions ensuring the repression of false or deceptive indications of source, the sanctions provided by the corresponding provisions of the laws relating to marks or trade names shall be applicable.

Trademark Law Treaty

The Trademark Treaty Law (TLT) was established in 1994 and comprises 25 articles. Article 2 defines the types of marks covered by the Treaty:

Article 2: Marks to Which the Treaty Applies

1. (Nature of Marks)
   a. This Treaty shall apply to marks consisting of visible signs, provided that only those Contracting Parties which accept for registration three-dimensional marks shall be obliged to apply this Treaty to such marks.
   b. This Treaty shall not apply to hologram marks and to marks not consisting of visible signs, in particular, sound marks and olfactory marks.
2. (Kinds of Marks)
   a. This Treaty shall apply to marks relating to goods (trademarks) or services (service marks) or both goods and services.
   b. This Treaty shall not apply to collective marks, certification marks and guarantee marks.

Patent Law Treaty

In an effort to standardize worldwide efforts regarding patent law, a consensus of WIPO members adopted the Patent Law Treaty (PLT) on 1 June 2001. The PLT applies to both national and regional patent applications and patents, as well as international applications under the Patent Cooperation Treaty (PCT). The PLT is an attempt to get everyone rowing in the same direction by establishing minimum filing date requirements, internationally standardized requirements for applications, including standardized forms, electronic filing basics, and various administrative provisions to simplify the process for everyone involved. This includes inventors, applicants, attorneys, patent office employees – presumably in countries around the world. Does it work? The answer will vary depending on the respondent. WIPO believes that a member state that joins the PLT will benefit by the ease with which national, regional or international applications may be filed. Much of this uniform environment has its foundation in the earlier PCT. The PLT seems to fill in some of the gaps, particularly in the area of formality requirements for national and regional applications and patents. The PLT comprises 27 articles. The third article clarifies the types of applications and patents covered by the Treaty.

Article 3: Applications and Patents to Which the Treaty Applies

1. (Applications)
    a. The provisions of this Treaty and the Regulations shall apply to national and regional applications for patents for invention and for patents of addition, which are filed with or for the Office of a Contracting Party, and which are:
        i. types of applications permitted to be filed as international applications under the Patent Cooperation Treaty;
        ii. divisional applications of the types of applications referred to in item (i), for patents for invention or for patents of addition, as referred to in Article 4G(1) or (2) of the Paris Convention.
    b. Subject to the provisions of the Patent Cooperation Treaty, the provisions of this Treaty and the Regulations shall apply to international applications, for patents for invention and for patents of addition, under the Patent Cooperation Treaty:
        i. in respect of the time limits applicable under Articles 22 and 39(1) of the Patent Cooperation Treaty in the Office of a Contracting Party;
        ii. in respect of any procedure commenced on or after the date on which processing or examination of the international application may start under Article 23 or 40 of that Treaty.
2. (Patents) The provisions of this Treaty and the Regulations shall apply to national and regional patents for invention, and to national and regional patents of addition, which have been granted with effect for a Contracting Party.

Brussels Convention Relating to the Distribution of Programme-Carrying Signals Transmitted by Satellite

The Brussels Convention was completed in 1974. The first article provides, through the use of definitions, the scope of the Convention's coverage. The second of the 12 articles outlines obligations of the contracting states:

Article 1: For the purposes of this Convention

i.   'signal' is an electronically-generated carrier capable of transmitting programmes;
ii.   'programme' is a body of live or recorded material consisting of images, sounds or both, embodied in signals emitted for the purpose of ultimate distribution;
iii.   'satellite' is any device in extraterrestrial space capable of transmitting signals;
iv.   'emitted signal' or 'signal emitted' is any programme-carrying signal that goes to or passes through a satellite;
v.   'derived signal' is a signal obtained by modifying the technical characteristics of the emitted signal, whether or not there have been one or more intervening fixations;
vi.   'originating organization' is the person or legal entity that decides what programme the emitted signals will carry;
vii.   'distributor' is the person or legal entity that decides that the transmission of the derived signals to the general public or any section thereof should take place
viii. 'distribution' is the operation by which a distributor transmits derived signals to the general public or any section thereof.

Article 2

1. Each Contracting State undertakes to take adequate measures to prevent the distribution on or from its territory of any programme-carrying signal by any distributor for whom the signal emitted to or passing through the satellite is not intended. This obligation shall apply where the originating organization is a national of another Contracting State and where the signal distributed is a derived signal.
2. In any Contracting State in which the application of the measures referred to in paragraph (1) is limited in time, the duration thereof shall be fixed by its domestic law. The Secretary-General of the United Nations shall be notified in writing of such duration at the time of ratification, acceptance or accession, or if the domestic law comes into force or is changed thereafter, within six months of the coming into force of that law or of its modification.
3. The obligation provided for in paragraph (1) shall not apply to the distribution of derived signals taken from signals which have already been distributed by a distributor for whom the emitted signals were intended.

WIPO Copyright Treaty

The Internet changes everything – including the world of intellectual property protection. In 1996, WIPO established two treaties to address copyright and related rights that pertain to the digital technologies and the Internet. The WIPO Copyright Treaty (WCT) and the WIPO Performances and Phonograms Treaty (WPPT) are intended to provide a minimum level of rights among member states. This is not accomplished through WIPO directly; rather, the signatory agrees to grant these rights through its own regulatory regime and to grant them on a non-discriminatory basis.

According to WIPO, the WCT protects literary and artistic works such as books, computer programs, music, photography, paintings, sculpture and films. The WPPT (see the next Treaty in this chapter) protects the rights of the producers of sound recordings, such as records, cassettes and CDs. Additionally, the Treaty protects the rights of performers whose performances are fixed in sound recordings. In brief, these two treaties are attempts to give creators basic rights to control and/or be compensated for their creations when the creations are used publicly or by others. Unlike earlier treaties, the WCT and WPPT clarify ownership and rights relating to their creations and how they are made available online to individual consumers. The two treaties also attempt to address 'anti-circumvention' (hacking) and to provide assurance of a reliable online marketplace in which rights management information cannot be deliberately altered or deleted.

Completed in 1996, the WIPO Copyright Treaty (WCT) comprises 25 articles. The first article explains the relation between the WCT and the Berne Convention, mentioned above. Article 2 deals with the scope of copyright protection.

Article 1: Relation to the Berne Convention

1. This Treaty is a special agreement within the meaning of Article 20 of the Berne Convention for the Protection of Literary and Artistic Works, as regards Contracting Parties that are countries of the Union established by that Convention. This Treaty shall not have any connection with treaties other than the Berne Convention, nor shall it prejudice any rights and obligations under any other treaties.
2. Nothing in this Treaty shall derogate from existing obligations that Contracting Parties have to each other under the Berne Convention for the Protection of Literary and Artistic Works.
3. Hereinafter, 'Berne Convention' shall refer to the Paris Act of July 24, 1971 of the Berne Convention for the Protection of Literary and Artistic Works.
4. Contracting Parties shall comply with Articles 1 to 21 and the Appendix of the Berne Convention. (See the agreed statement concerning Article 1(4)).

Article 2: Scope of Copyright Protection

Copyright protection extends to expressions and not to ideas, procedures, methods of operation or mathematical concepts as such.

WIPO Performances and Phonograms Treaty

Completed in 1996 and consisting of 33 articles, the WPPT is the second of the Internet Treaties and is also divided into five chapters. These chapters address general, common and administrative provisions, as well as rights of the producers of phonograms and the rights of performers. For example, Article 5 defines the moral rights of performers and Article 12 outlines the rights of producers to distribute works.

Article 5: Moral Rights of Performers

1. Independently of a performer's economic rights, and even after the transfer of those rights, the performer shall, as regards his live aural performances or performances fixed in phonograms, have the right to claim to be identified as the performer of his performances, except where omission is dictated by the manner of the use of the performance, and to object to any distortion, mutilation or other modification of his performances that would be prejudicial to his reputation.
2. The rights granted to a performer in accordance with paragraph (1) shall, after his death, be maintained, at least until the expiry of the economic rights, and shall be exercisable by the persons or institutions authorized by the legislation of the Contracting Party where protection is claimed. However, those Contracting Parties whose legislation, at the moment of their ratification of or accession to this Treaty, does not provide for protection after the death of the performer of all rights set out in the preceding paragraph may provide that some of these rights will, after his death, cease to be maintained.
3. The means of redress for safeguarding the rights granted under this Article shall be governed by the legislation of the Contracting Party where protection is claimed.

Article 12: Right of Distribution

1. Producers of phonograms shall enjoy the exclusive right of authorizing the making available to the public of the original and copies of their phonograms through sale or other transfer of ownership.
2. Nothing in this Treaty shall affect the freedom of Contracting Parties to determine the conditions, if any, under which the exhaustion of the right in paragraph (1) applies after the first sale or other transfer of ownership of the original or a copy of the phonogram with the authorization of the producer of the phonogram.

GLOBAL PROTECTION TREATIES

These treaties were designed to ensure that a single international registration and filing exercise is all that is required to be effectively registered or filed with any of the national signatories to the treaty or agreement in question. The Global Protection Treaties are an excellent example of the type of role at which WIPO can excel, provided it takes into consideration the constraints (such as technological limitations) that developing nations continue to face when they attempt to participate in the international intellectual property regime. The Global Protection Treaties include the following:

Patent Cooperation Treaty

The Patent Cooperation Treaty (PCT) originated in Washington on 19 June 1970, and was amended in September 1979, and again in February 1984. This is a lengthy treaty, comprising 69 articles. The associated regulations under this treaty are the most recently amended of all the WIPO regulations, having come into force as of 1 March 2001. Including the March changes, they have been amended 22 times since 1970. The Treaty itself was amended twice since 1970: in 1979 and again in 1984. Article 9 defines who qualifies as an applicant and Article 15 looks at the parameters related to international searches.

Article 9: The Applicant

1. Any resident or national of a Contracting State may file an international application.
2. The Assembly may decide to allow the residents and the nationals of any country party to the Paris Convention for the Protection of Industrial Property which is not party to this Treaty to file international applications.
3. The concepts of residence and nationality, and the application of those concepts in cases where there are several applicants or where the applicants are not the same for all the designated States, are defined in the Regulations.

Article 15: The International Search

1. Each international application shall be the subject of international search.
2. The objective of the international search is to discover relevant prior art.
3. International search shall be made on the basis of the claims, with due regard to the description and the drawings (if any).

4. The International Searching Authority referred to in Article 16 shall endeavor to discover as much of the relevant prior art as its facilities permit, and shall, in any case, consult the documentation specified in the Regulations.
5. a. If the national law of the Contracting State so permits, the applicant who files a national application with the national Office of or acting for such State may, subject to the conditions provided for in such law, request that a search similar to an international search ('international-type search') be carried out on such application.
   b. If the national law of the Contracting State so permits, the national Office of or acting for such State may subject any national application filed with it to an international-type search.
   c. The international-type search shall be carried out by the International Searching Authority referred to in Article 16 which would be competent for an international search if the national application were an international application and were filed with the Office referred to in subparagraphs (a) and (b). If the national application is in a language which the International Searching Authority considers it is not equipped to handle, the international-type search shall be carried out on a translation prepared by the applicant in a language prescribed for international applications and which the International Searching Authority has undertaken to accept for international applications. The national application and the translation, when required, shall be presented in the form prescribed for international applications.

Budapest Treaty on the International Recognition of the Deposit of Microorganisms for the Purposes of Patent Procedure

The Budapest Treaty was established in 1977 and amended in 1980. Apparently, some ground rules were required to keep track of all the microorganic property that travelled internationally. The fifth of the 20 articles in this Treaty addresses the dangers inherent in the transportation of microorganisms.

Article 5: Export and Import Restrictions

Each Contracting State recognizes that it is highly desirable that, if and to the extent to which the export from or import into its territory of certain kinds of microorganisms is restricted, such restriction should apply to microorganisms deposited, or destined for deposit, under this Treaty only where the restriction is necessary in view of national security or the dangers for health or the environment.

75

Madrid Agreement Concerning the International Registration of Marks

The Madrid Agreement (not to be confused with the Madrid Agreement for the Repression of False or Deceptive Indications of Source on Goods) was established in 1891 and has undergone seven revisions between its inception and 1979. It comprises 18 long articles, including Articles 4 and 4bis, which establish how an international registration is to be treated under this Agreement. The references to Article 3 and 3ter refer to the contents of the application of the registration and requests for territorial extensions respectively.

Article 4: (Effects of International Registration)

1. From the date of the registration so effected at the International Bureau in accordance with the provisions of Articles 3 and 3ter, the protection of the mark in each of the contracting countries concerned shall be the same as if the mark had been filed therein direct. The indication of classes of goods or services provided for in Article 3 shall not bind the contracting countries with regard to the determination of the scope of the protection of the mark
2. Every mark which has been the subject of an international registration shall enjoy the right of priority provided for by Article 4 of the Paris Convention for the Protection of Industrial Property, without requiring compliance with the formalities prescribed in Section (4)D of that Article.

Article 4bis (Substitution of International Registration for Earlier National Registrations)

1. When a mark already filed in one or more of the contracting countries is later registered by the International Bureau in the name of the same proprietor or his successor in title, the international registration shall be deemed to have replaced the earlier national registrations, without prejudice to any rights acquired by reason of such earlier registrations.
2. The national Office shall, upon request, be required to take note in its registers of the international registration.

Protocol Relating to the Madrid Agreement Concerning the International Registration of Marks

This Protocol was signed at Madrid on 28 June, 1989 and comprises 16 articles dealing with the international registration of marks. Article 4bis clarifies what happens when a national or regional registration is replaced by an international registration. The reference to Article 3ter concerns requests for territorial extensions.

Article 4bis: Replacement of a National or Regional Registration by an International Registration

1. Where a mark that is the subject of a national or regional registration in the Office of a Contracting Party is also the subject of an international registration and both registrations stand in the name of the same person, the international registration is deemed to replace the national or regional registration, without prejudice to any rights acquired by virtue of the latter, provided that
   i. the protection resulting from the international registration extends to the said Contracting Party under Article 3ter(1) or 3ter(2),
   ii. all the goods and services listed in the national or regional registration are also listed in the international registration in respect of the said Contracting Party,
   iii. such extension takes effect after the date of the national or regional registration.
2. The Office referred to in paragraph (1) shall, upon request, be required to take note in its register of the international registration.

Lisbon Agreement for the Protection of Appellations of Origin and their International Registration

The Lisbon Agreement came into effect in 1958. It was amended in 1967 and 1979 and comprises 18 articles. The key definitions are found in Article 2.

Article 2: (Definition of Notions of Appellation of Origin and Country of Origin)

1. In this Agreement, 'appellation of origin' means the geographical name of a country, region, or locality, which serves to designate a product originating therein, the quality and characteristics of which are due exclusively or essentially to the geographical environment, including natural and human factors.
2. The country of origin is the country whose name, or the country in which is situated the region or locality whose name, constitutes the appellation of origin which has given the product its reputation.

Hague Agreement Concerning the International Deposit of Industrial Designs

The Hague Agreement has received five full or partial reincarnations between 1934 and the Geneva Act version in 1999. The 14th of the 34 articles outlines the effects of international registration with regard to the international deposit of industrial designs:

Article 14: Effects of the International Registration

1. (Effect as Application Under Applicable Law) The international registration shall, from the date of the international registration, have at least the same effect in each designated Contracting Party as a regularly-filed application for the grant of protection of the industrial design under the law of that Contracting Party.
2. (Effect as Grant of Protection Under Applicable Law)
   a. In each designated Contracting Party the Office of which has not communicated a refusal in accordance with Article 12, the international registration shall have the same effect as a grant of protection for the industrial design under the law of that Contracting Party at the latest from the date of expiration of the period allowed for it to communicate a refusal or, where a Contracting Party has made a corresponding declaration under the Regulations, at the latest at the time specified in that declaration.
   b. Where the Office of a designated Contracting Party has communicated a refusal and has subsequently withdrawn, in part or in whole, that refusal, the international registration shall, to the extent that the refusal is withdrawn, have the same effect in that Contracting Party as a grant of protection for the industrial design under the law of the said Contracting Party at the latest from the date on which the refusal was withdrawn.
   c. The effect given to the international registration under this paragraph shall apply to the industrial design or designs that are the subject of that registration as received from the International Bureau by the designated Office or, where applicable, as amended in the procedure before that Office.
3. (Declaration Concerning Effect of Designation of Applicant's Contracting Party)
   a. Any Contracting Party whose Office is an Examining Office may, in a declaration, notify the Director General that, where it is the applicant's Contracting Party, the designation of that Contracting Party in an international registration shall have no effect.
   b. Where a Contracting Party having made the declaration referred to in subparagraph (a) is indicated in an international application both as the applicant's Contracting Party and as a designated Contracting Party, the International Bureau shall disregard the designation of that Contracting Party.

CLASSIFICATION TREATIES

These classification treaties create systems intended to organize intellectual property-related information, such as inventions, trademarks or industrial designs into structured retrieval systems. While it sounds rather unimportant – some kind of make work project – these classification systems help organize massive amounts of data. For example, WIPO data illustrate that between 1980 and 2000 the number of groups in the International Patent Classification for biotechnology rose from 297 to 718. The classifications for medicines increased from 839 to 1,966. All told, WIPO's International Patent Classification defines over 70,000 technology categories. These treaties include the following.

Strasbourg Agreement Concerning the International Patent Classification

The 17 articles of the Strasbourg Agreement concerning the International Patent Classification are the culmination of work that established the Treaty in March 1971. It was amended in 1979 and is intended, in the words used in the text to the Contracting Parties of the Treaty itself, to 'establish closer international cooperation in the industrial property field, and to contribute to the harmonization of national legislation in that field'. Article 4 defines how the classification is to be used.

Article 4: Use of the Classification

1. The Classification shall be solely of an administrative character.
2. Each country of the Special Union shall have the right to use the Classification either as a principal or as a subsidiary system.
3. The competent authorities of the countries of the Special Union shall include in
   i. patents, inventors' certificates, utility models and utility certificates issued by them, and in applications relating thereto, whether published or only laid open for public inspection by them, and
   ii. notices, appearing in official periodicals, of the publication or laying open of the documents referred to in subparagraph (i) the complete symbols of the Classification applied to the invention to which the document referred to in subparagraph (i) relates.
4. When signing this Agreement or when depositing its instrument of ratification or accession:
   i. any country may declare that it does not undertake to include the symbols relating to groups or subgroups of the Classification in applications as referred to in paragraph (3) which are only laid open for public inspection and in notices relating thereto, and
   ii. any country which does not proceed to an examination as to novelty, whether immediate or deferred, and in which the procedure for the grant of patents or other kinds of protection does

not provide for a search into the state of the art, may declare that it does not undertake to include the symbols relating to the groups and subgroups of the Classification in the documents and notices referred to in paragraph (3). If these conditions exist only in relation to certain kinds of protection or certain fields of technology, the country in question may only make this reservation to the extent that the conditions apply.

5. The symbols of the Classification, preceded by the words 'International Patent Classification' or an abbreviation thereof to be determined by the Committee of Experts referred to in Article 5, shall be printed in heavy type, or in such a manner that they are clearly visible, in the heading of each document referred to in paragraph (3)(i) in which they are to be included.

6. If any country of the Special Union entrusts the grant of patents to an intergovernmental authority, it shall take all possible measures to ensure that this authority uses the Classification in accordance with this Article.

Nice Agreement Concerning the International Classification of Goods and Services for the Purposes of the Registration of Marks

The Nice Agreement concerning the International Classification of Goods and Services for the Purposes of the Registration of Marks was established in 1957, revised a decade later and again a decade after that. The most recent amendment to the 14-article Treaty occurred in 1979. Article 2 describes the legal parameters of the classification system.

Article 2: Legal Effect and Use of the Classification

1. Subject to the requirements prescribed by this Agreement, the effect of the Classification shall be that attributed to it by each country of the Special Union. In particular, the Classification shall not bind the countries of the Special Union in respect of either the evaluation of the extent of the protection afforded to any given mark or the recognition of service marks.

2. Each of the countries of the Special Union reserves the right to use the Classification either as a principal or as a subsidiary system.

3. The competent Office of the countries of the Special Union shall include in the official documents and publications relating to registrations of marks the numbers of the classes of the Classification to which the goods or services for which the mark is registered belong.

4. The fact that a term is included in the alphabetical list in no way affects any rights which might subsist in such a term.

Vienna Agreement Establishing an International Classification of Figurative Elements of Marks

The Vienna Agreement was completed in 1973 and amended in 1985. It comprises 17 articles, the 12th of which defines the conditions for becoming a party to the Agreement.

Article 12: Becoming Party to the Agreement

1. Any country party to the Paris Convention for the Protection of Industrial Property may become party to this Agreement by:
   i. signature followed by the deposit of an instrument of ratification, or
   ii. deposit of an instrument of accession.
2. Instruments of ratification or accession shall be deposited with the Director General.
3. The provisions of Article 24 of the Stockholm Act of the Paris Convention for the Protection of Industrial Property shall apply to this Agreement.
4. Paragraph (3) shall in no way be understood as implying the recognition or tacit acceptance by a country of the Special Union of the factual situation concerning a territory to which this Agreement is made applicable by another country by virtue of the said paragraph.

Locarno Agreement Establishing an International Classification for Industrial Designs

Signed in 1968 and amended in 1979, the Locarno Agreement establishing an International Classification for Industrial Designs comprises 15 articles, as well as a lengthy annex of codes defining classes and subclasses of the international classification. This annex came into force in January 1994 and comprises 33 classes (01 to 32 for specific groups and 99 for miscellaneous). These include anything from brushware (Class 04) to Transport and Hoisting (Class 12) to everybody's favourite, Arms, Pyrotechnic Articles, Articles for Hunting, Fishing and Pest Killing (Class 22). Article 1 explains how all of this has come about.

Article 1: Establishment of a Special Union; Adoption of an International Classification

1. The countries to which this Agreement applies constitute a Special Union.
2. They adopt a single classification for industrial designs (hereinafter designated as 'the international classification').
3. The international classification shall comprise:
   i. a list of classes and subclasses;

    ii. an alphabetical list of goods in which industrial designs are incorporated, with an indication of the classes and subclasses into which they fall;

    iii. explanatory notes.

4. The list of classes and subclasses is the list annexed to the present Agreement, subject to such amendments and additions as the Committee of Experts set up under Article 3 (hereinafter designated as 'the Committee of Experts') may make to it.

5. The alphabetical list of goods and the explanatory notes shall be adopted by the Committee of Experts in accordance with the procedure laid down in Article 3.

6. The international classification may be amended or supplemented by the Committee of Experts, in accordance with the procedure laid down in Article 3.

7. a. The international classification shall be established in the English and French languages.

    b. Official texts of the international classification, in such other languages as the Assembly referred to in Article 5 may designate, shall be established, after consultation with the interested Governments, by the International Bureau of Intellectual Property (hereinafter designated as 'the International Bureau') referred to in the Convention Establishing the World Intellectual Property Organization (hereinafter designated as 'the Organization').

ADMINISTRATIVE AGREEMENTS

The Agreement of Trade Related Aspects of Intellectual Property Rights (TRIPS) and the Agreement Between the World Intellectual Property Organization and the World Trade Organization are primarily administrative agreements between the two organizations. The former will be discussed in greater detail in this chapter and has been mentioned throughout this book. The latter will not be examined as it is more of a joint declaration between these two international intergovernmental agencies to cooperate in areas of mutual interest. Interestingly, WIPO is distinctly unique when it comes to specialized agencies within the United Nations. Not only does it fulfil its role as an international intergovernmental organization, it also offers intellectual property registration services to the public. The traditional task of these specialized agencies is to serve the interests of its members. In WIPO's case, membership comprises around 177 nations, or more accurately, government representatives from 177 nations. However, anyone can use WIPO's Global Protection Services (GPS) for registering patents, trademarks and industrial designs. The patent protection falls under the PCT, allowing an applicant the opportunity to register for patent protection in any or all of the over 100 countries that are signatories to the PCT. Likewise, trademark protection can be sought in all countries that are member states to the Madrid Agreement concerning the International Registration of Marks and its Protocol, and industrial design protection can be applied for and received for all of the signatories to the Hague Convention for the International Registration of Industrial Designs. In 1999, WIPO received over 74,000 international applications under the PCT alone. These WIPO-based intellectual property systems are aligned as much as possible with the procedures and rules that exist in national and international (European Community, for example) systems.

The GPS is certainly a step in the right direction and if the cost and complexity can be continually reduced, it will actually be beneficial to those member states from the developing world. Ultimately, it will be useful to the least developed nations as well. Cost and operating ease aside, the foundation for the system – a fair and equitable intellectual property regime – must also exist for all member states to truly benefit. In the interim, WIPO is working on an indirectly related goal: the worldwide patent. As the name implies, the patent approval would have worldwide coverage. Depending who you are and how you feel about the direction that intellectual property protection is taking, this is either a blessing or a nightmare.

For those who are interested in knowing more on a country-by-country level rather than a treaty-by-treaty level, WIPO also offers a Guide to Intellectual Property Worldwide on its Web site. This Guide provides valuable information on intellectual property through individual country profiles on WIPO member states. The profiles include basic legislation, membership of international treaties, administrative structures, governmental and non-governmental bodies for information and enforcement, educational institutions and industrial property statistics. The Web site also includes contact addresses for obtaining additional information for a particular country. WIPO has attempted to fashion a tool for diverse users, including officials working in the field of intellectual property, lawyers, teachers, students, researchers, creators or owners of intellectual property, or the general public.

World Intellectual Property Office, 34 chemin des Colombettes, PO Box 18, CH–1211, Geneva 20, Switzerland.
http:www.wipo.int

New York Coordination Office, 2 United Nations Plaza, Suite 2525, New York, New York 10017, USA.

WTO

It is probably a testament to the value of intellectual property in our business world that the international organization dedicated to the promotion of international trade is still compelled to dedicate a substantial chunk of its time and resources to the topic of intellectual property. As we continue to attach more importance to names, brands, designs, entertainers and technology, intellectual property will become even more valuable as an asset. It is currently one of the greatest competitive advantages a company possesses and one that is transformable into profits. It is not surprising that the WTO focuses on intellectual property. Many of the trade issues that will occur in the future will be primarily concerned with the protection of intellectual property.

The WTO was the offspring of the Uruguay Round of trade negotiations that concluded in 1994. Established in 1995, the WTO is the premier international institution concerned with the rules governing trade among nations. Its headquarters in Geneva employs a staff of over 500 to administer to the concerns of its membership. As of December 2001, the WTO comprised 143 member states. The organization seems to be a constant source of news and a sponge for endless criticism. It is the most visible target of hatred for diverse opponents to international trade and globalization. The WTO has been blamed for virtually every social and economic problem in the world over the last few years. In reality, it is no different from many other international institutions. It is powerful because it is guided primarily by the interests of the powerful nations, regardless of the voting democracy that exists within its framework. It is inefficient because it is bureaucratic in the worst meaning of the word. And it implements both good and bad policies because it is managed by fallible beings from nations around the world.

The TRIPS Agreement

The TRIPS Agreement celebrated its seventh birthday in January 2002 and is still considered the most comprehensive multilateral agreement relating to intellectual property. A product of the WTO and its member states, TRIPS covers copyright and related rights, trademarks, geographical indications, industrial designs, patents, layout-designs of integrated circuits and undisclosed information, which is commonly referred to as 'trade secrets'. This book will examine some of the more contentious areas of the TRIPS Agreement, its history and the original objectives that lead to its current status. In doing so, we will refer to certain sections and look at specific articles from the Agreement without turning this chapter into a legal text.

The goals of the Agreement are rooted in the Uruguay Round of negotiations and subsequent related efforts in the mid- to late-1980s. The WTO lists these goals as 'the reduction of distortions and impediments to international trade, promotion of effective and adequate protection of intellectual property rights, and ensuring that measures and procedures to enforce intellectual property rights do not themselves become barriers to legitimate trade'. Article 7 of the Agreement attempts to capture the essence of this, as well as create a balance between diverse needs. It is aptly titled 'Objectives' and states, 'The protection and enforcement of intellectual property rights should contribute to the promotion of technological innovation and to the transfer and dissemination of technology, to the mutual advantage of producers and users of technological knowledge and in a manner conducive to social and economic welfare, and to a balance of rights and obligations.'

Clearly, the focus of the TRIPS Agreement is the protection of intellectual property in the context of promoting international trade. WTO literature refers to the 'rule-based trade system' that is intended to provide more stability and predictability with respect to trade disputes over intellectual property rights in the international trade environment – or at least that part of the environment that the WTO member states comprise. According to the WTO, the Agreement covers five broad issues:

- The application of basic principles of the trading system and the application of other intellectual property agreements.
- The provision of adequate protection to intellectual property rights.
- The manner with which countries adequately enforce those intellectual property rights in their own territory.
- The manner by which members of the WTO settle disputes relating to intellectual property.
- The type of special transitional arrangements that will exist during the period when the new system is introduced.

Without going into inordinate detail for each of these issues, we can explore the elements that are most relevant to our topic. The first issue suggests that the TRIPS Agreement is founded upon basic principles that governed earlier trade agreements such as the General Agreement on Tariffs and Trade (GATT). At the top of the list is non-discrimination and the concepts of most-favoured nation status (equal treatment for all trading partners within the WTO) and national treatment (equal treatment for your own population as well as foreigners) illustrate this basic principle very well. The second issue, which focuses on the rules for protecting intellectual property, has its foundation in the WIPO Treaties. In particular, the WTO refers to the Paris Convention and the Berne Convention; however, it has also added new standards for protection or adopted more stringent versions of existing standards in some areas where the WIPO standard was considered inadequate. The TRIPS Agreement clearly states that governments must be able to enforce intellectual property laws and must institute penalties that are deterrents to further violations of the law. Clearly, a nation does not meet the requirements of the Agreement simply by passing the laws. That is the easy part. The Agreement includes some general principles that apply to all intellectual property protection procedures.

TRIPS also contains provisions relating to civil and administrative procedures and remedies and other requirements that facilitate the enforcement of rights by those who hold the rights. In addition to the enforcement aspect of this third issue, the signatory must also establish fair and equitable procedures for dealing with intellectual property violations. The fourth issue concerning disputes between WTO members is addressed by the WTO's own dispute settlement procedure. Any challenges regarding the TRIPS obligations of another member must be taken up within the organization's channels. The fifth issue deals with the time periods that member states were given to ensure that their laws conform to the TRIPS Agreement. When it came into effect in 1995, developed nations were given one year to meet the minimum standards. Developing countries and certain transitional economies were allowed a five-year time period for conformance. The least developed nations have until 2006 to meet the requirements of the Agreement.

In terms of its content, the TRIPS Agreement addresses three components of intellectual property protection: standards, enforcement and dispute settlement. While we have addressed enforcement and dispute settlement briefly, the concept of standards may be examined more closely.

Standards

Like many international Agreements, TRIPS sets out a minimum standard of protection by which all member states must abide. As mentioned above, a time limit is set for these nations to reach this minimum level of protection. Some nations may have already surpassed this standard, while others are struggling to find the funds and the expertise to implement even the most basic system of intellectual property protection. The latter is often a dilemma in developing nations and is discussed in detail in Chapter 9. These members have a less restrictive, but no less challenging, time frame in which to meet the minimum standards of TRIPS. By establishing a minimum standard, the WTO members maintain reasonable autonomy to establish more stringent rules and regulations. Additionally, the manner in which the members implement the provisions of the Agreement within their own legal systems is left almost entirely to their discretion.

The TRIPS Agreement addresses the specific areas to be protected (patents, for example), the specific rights that are to be conferred, as well as any possible exceptions, and the duration for which the protection lasts. As mentioned above, all signatories to TRIPS must also be in compliance with all the intellectual property obligations covered by the WIPO's main conventions, the Paris Convention (dealing with industrial property) and Berne Convention (dealing with literary and artistic works). These conventions are incorporated into TRIPS by reference and as such, become obligations of the Agreement. Additionally, TRIPS incorporates provisions that extend beyond these other agreements to address new areas or reinforce weak sections of the other conventions.

The TRIPS Agreement comprises seven parts:

- general provisions and basic principles;
- standards concerning the availability, scope and use of intellectual property rights;
- enforcement of intellectual property rights;
- acquisition and maintenance of intellectual property rights and related *inter-partes* procedures;
- dispute prevention and settlement;
- transitional agreements;
- institutional arrangements and final provisions.

As this book is primarily concerned with the types of protection afforded to different types of intellectual property, the second part of the agreement (standards) is our main focus. For the sake of brevity, however, I will not cite the relevant articles of Part II. Some of these were employed in Chapter 3 to illustrate the types of intellectual property rights that currently exist and for which the TRIPS Agreement provides protection. Rather, the articles will be mentioned in reference to the corresponding intellectual property type.

Copyright and related rights

Articles 9 through 14 are intended to cover to wide range of creations that could possibly be covered by copyright protection, as well as terms of protection and rental rights. There is the obvious reference to compliance with the Berne Convention and additional clauses for both computer programs and compilations of data (Article 10) and protection for performers, producers of phonograms and broadcasting organizations.

Trademarks

Articles 15 through 21 deal with numerous aspects of trademark protection, including the types of things that can be protected (Article 15), the rights conferred upon trademark owners (Article 16) and the term of protection (Article 18). Trademarks, unlike patents and copyrights, can be renewed indefinitely.

Geographical indications

Articles 22, 23 and 24 address the various protection issues for geographical indications. Interestingly, Article 23 is entirely devoted to additional protection for geographical indications for wines and spirits. We seem to have a hard time agreeing on the labelling of genetically modified foods but we want international agreements to ensure the 'quality' of our alcoholic beverages.

Industrial designs

Articles 25 and 26 define the requirements for protection and the protection of industrial designs respectively. For example, an owner of an industrial design has the right to prevent a third party from making, selling or importing a copy of the industrial design or, as the article states, 'substantially a copy' if the act has been undertaken for commercial purposes. Article 26 also ensures a minimum protection period of 10 years for industrial designs.

Patents

Patents are covered by Articles 27 to 34 of the TRIPS Agreement. Patentable subject matter (Article 27) includes 'any inventions, whether product or processes, in all fields of technology, provided that they are new, involve an inventive step and are capable of industrial application'. Interestingly, there is no reference to the Paris Convention for the Protection of Industrial Property in this section of the Agreement. It would appear that the Berne Convention was mentioned under copyrights in order to define a difference between it and the TRIPS copyright section. Presumably, no such reference was required for patents.

Layout-designs (topographies) of integrated circuits

Articles 35 through 38 address the protection of layout-designs of integrated circuits. First, members to the agreement must comply with relevant articles and sections of the Treaty on Intellectual Property in Respect of Integrated Circuits (IPIC). In addition, they must comply with the scope of protection (Article 36), certain exceptions (Article 37) and the term of protection (Article 38) which must be at least 10 years from the date of filing an application for registration, or where registration is not required, from the date of the first commercial exploitation of the layout-design.

Protection of undisclosed information

Trade secrets and other valuable intellectual assets are covered by Article 39 of the TRIPS Agreement. This section builds on the protection defined in the Paris Convention and defines what constitutes undisclosed information. We will explore the topic of trade secrets and related intellectual property in greater detail later in this book when we examine the value of innovation and the necessity to protect it. The third clause of Article 39 is another example of the power of the pharmaceutical and agricultural chemical interests in the global decision-making sphere. While all of the other requirements are universal, this clause is dedicated to the protection of test data relating to new chemical entities.

Control of anti-competitive practices in contractual licences

Article 40 addresses the possibility that licensing practices may be anti-competitive and may adversely affect trade. In short, it requires that all members to the agreement play fair and ensure that intellectual property rights within their borders do not promote abusive licensing practices that restrain either foreign or domestic competition. The most prominent example of this in recent memory has been the Microsoft debacle with the US Department of Justice.

As I alluded to at the beginning of this chapter, delving deeper into the WTO or the content of the TRIPS Agreement will have to be the subject of another book. Any reader interested in pursuing additional information can access the WTO Web site (www.wto.org) or contact: World Trade Organization, rue de Lausanne 154, CH–1211, Geneva 21, Switzerland.

THE EUROPEAN PATENT OFFICE

It is not uncommon for US business people to forget the extent to which the nations of Europe have integrated many of their governmental and administrative functions. While this book will not be looking at specific national intellectual property offices, the European Patent Office (EPO) is worth exploring in greater detail. Considering that the first patent law was passed by the city of Venice in 1474 and that the Statute of Monopolies in England came into effect in 1624, Europe has provided the foundation for the modern intellectual property laws that proliferated in the late 19th century.

The EPO grants European patents for all of nations that are contracting parties to the European Patent Convention (EPC). This Convention was signed in 1973 and came into force four years later. The EPO is the executive agency of the European Patent Organisation, an intergovernmental body that was established as a result of the same Convention. Its membership comprises the EPC contracting states: Austria, Belgium, Cyprus, Denmark, Finland, France, Germany, Greece, Ireland, Italy, Liechtenstein, Luxemburg, Monaco, Netherlands, Portugal, Spain, Sweden, Switzerland, Turkey and the United Kingdom. From an outsider's perspective, the EPO does an excellent job of representing the countries of Europe and providing a coordinated approach to the protection of inventions. Its model, as defined by the EPC, has influenced many patent systems around the world. The beauty of the EPC is its ability to grant protection in several or all of the contracting states by pursuing a single patent grant procedure. As a result, all applicants from the diverse contracting countries listed above encounter the same rules governing the treatment of patents. In its efforts to support European innovation and competitiveness, the EPO has grown to include 5,000 employees from over 20 countries, providing services in three official languages (English, French and German). In 2000, the Office received an estimated 140,000 patent applications and 34,000 file inspections.

NATIONAL INTELLECTUAL PROPERTY AGENCIES

Here is an alphabetical list, by country, of some organizations that may be of interest if you want to find out more about intellectual property laws and other issues on a national level. Wherever possible, both the general address and the Web site address have been provided.

Australia
IP Australia, Ground Floor, Discovery House, 47 Bowes Street (PO Box 200), Woden ACT 2606
www.ipaustralia.gov.au

Brazil
The Brazilian Industrial Property Office (INPI)
www.inpi.gov.org

Canada
Canadian Intellectual Property Office (CIPO), Industry Canada, Place du Portage 1, 50 Victoria Street, 2nd Floor, Hull, Quebec, K1A 0C9
www.cipo.gc.ca

China
State Intellectual Property Office of the People's Republic of China (SIPO) No. 6, Xitucheng Road, Haidian District, Beijing 100088
www.cpo.cn.net

France
Institut National de la Propriété Industrielle, Accueil Du Public, 26 bis, rue de Saint Pétersbourg, 75800 Paris cedex 08
www.inpi.fr

Germany
Zweibrückenstr. 12–80331, Münich, Germany
www.dpma.de

India
Intellectual Property & Knowhow Informatics Division, National Informatics Centre
Ministry of Information Technology, Government of India, 'A' Block, CGO Complex, New Delhi 110 003, India
http://pk2id.delhi.nic.in

Italy
Ufficio Italiano Brevetti e Marchi
www.minindustria.it
or the European Patent Office, D–80298 Münich, Erhardtstr. 27
www.european-patent-office.org

Japan
Japan Patent Office, International Affairs Division, General Administration Department 3–4–3 Kasumigaseki, Chiyoda-ku Tokyo 100–8915
www.jpo.go.jp

Mexico
Instituto Mexicano de la Propriedad Industrial (IMPI)
Periférico Sur 3106, Col Jardines del Pedregal, Delegación Alvaro Obregón, Código Postal 01900, México, DF
www.impi.gob.mx

Russia
Russian Agency For Patents and Trademarks (ROSPATENT), Federal Institute of Industrial Property, bld. 30–1, Berezhkovskaya nab., Moscow, G–59, GSP–5, Russia, 123995
www.rupto.ru

Spain
Oficina Española De Patentes Y Marcas c/ Panamá, 1, 28071 Madrid, España
www.oepm.e

United Kingdom
The Patent Office, Concept House, Cardiff Road, Newport, South Wales, NP10 8QQ, UK
www.patent.gov.uk

United States
General Information Services Division, US Patent and Trademark Office, Crystal Plaza 3, Room 2C02, Washington, DC 20231
www.uspto.gov

THE NEW CURRENCY

If you steal from one author, it's plagiarism; if you steal from many, it's research.

Wilson Mizner

In Chapter 2 we discussed the historical events that gave rise to the advantages of 'brainpower' in the industrial world. As we moved forward into a technological revolution, this form of corporate fuel has only increased in significance. Now we find that companies are devoting as much attention to their capabilities in the area of innovation, strategy and creativity as they devote to their financial assets. All these assets are linked. Some analysts suggest that the value of intellectual property worldwide, for example, is worth more than the value of global production. Additionally, these types of assets are often more stable than money for an international business and become a reliable form of currency in the international marketplace. This would explain the overwhelming desire by businesses and individuals to protect these assets. In some cases, confidential information is being protected in order to sustain a competitive advantage. The fewer people exposed to this information, the better. In other instances, the protection of a highly visible mark (ie a brand name) or industrial design is top priority. The business relies on extensive public recognition of its mark or design in order to attract consumers or customers, yet it must also uncover and eliminate any unauthorized use or reproduction of its intellectual property.

From the early stages, these businesses must define what they are trying to protect. Not all of their intellectual assets qualify as intellectual property. In addition, definitions of intellectual property can also be troublesome because they are not universal. For example, the WIPO offers the following statement defining intellectual property rights:

> *The rights relating to literary, artistic and scientific works; performances or performing artists, phonograms, and broadcasts; inventions in all fields of human endeavor; scientific discoveries; industrial designs; trademarks, service marks and commercial names and designations; protection against unfair competition; and all other rights resulting from intellectual activity in the industrial, scientific, literary, or artistic fields.*

In contrast, certain national definitions, and even definitions in bilateral and multilateral agreements, may be less encompassing or may rely on different terminology. The North American Free Trade Agreement (NAFTA) refers to 'copyright and related rights, trademark rights, patent rights, rights in layout designs or semiconductor integrated circuits, trade secret rights, plant breeders' rights, rights in geographical indications and industrial design rights'. Does this imply the same intellectual property as the WIPO definition? There does appear to be ample room for interpretation in these two definitions. Of course, these are only two examples and both are using English to define the concept. If you start adding Russian, Chinese and Portuguese definitions you may find even greater latitude for interpretation.

Such concerns may seem rather minor to businesses competing in the marketplace. Regardless of intellectual property definitions, an entrepreneur or business still has to rely on their intellectual assets, whether they are patentable creations from research and development efforts, trademarks resulting from the marketing department's innovative branding efforts, copyrights for software produced by computer programmers or some innovative approach that falls outside the realm of intellectual property. This can include manufacturing processes and marketing strategies and business alliances. Many of these businesses feel that there are neither guarantees nor assurances that their treasures are protected. This is not pure cynicism. In some ways, the firm is at the mercy of chance every time it conducts business. The potential for intellectual property crime greatly exceeds the resources available to catch the criminals. Enforcement action is the weakest link in the intellectual property protection chain. Prosecution, as we will learn, poses serious challenges as well. Many businesses are learning that they must take the initiative to protect their valuable assets. The worth of a company and its very existence may depend on it. Consequently, information becomes a precious commodity to be shared or exchanged discreetly. Understanding the power of information is critical to understanding why intellectual assets are often more valuable than cold, hard cash.

INFORMATION AND POWER

Information is power. This is not an original concept. A study of virtually any historical event – military conquest, religious persecution, political upheaval and industrial monopoly – will reveal that information was a critical factor in the event's development and outcome. For example, reconnaissance concerning the location and number of enemy troops can result in an alternative battle strategy and a surprising victory. Suppression of information can maintain fear in people's lives and keep them subject to a tyrannical dictator or religious zealot. As worn and tired as it may be, the mantra 'information is power' seems to be especially true in the knowledge economy that we are now experiencing. Still, it is not always evident whether the power is obtained by sharing the information or hoarding the information. Current evidence would suggest that retaining the information until you are in a position to profit from it is the best course of action. And the intellectual property regime supports that notion, with 20-year patents and copyright protection extending past the death of the copyright owner.

Yet there exists a type of information that is extremely valuable and that requires protection. It falls outside of the scope of intellectual property and the individuals privy to the information do not necessarily own it, nor have they created it. They profit by ensuring that the information is not made readily available to others or is manipulated sufficiently to render it questionable. Is this type of 'information hoarding' an asset to a business? If you pose this question to executives at one of the giant tobacco firms that made billions by spending millions on the suppression of scientific data regarding the dangers of cigarettes, the response would vary. A decade or two ago, the answer may have been an overwhelming 'yes'. Keeping information from others is valuable for business. Over the last couple of years, the groundbreaking legal judgements against these firms have caused considerable uproar and may eventually bring the tobacco giants to their knees. Of course, information suppression is not exactly the same as protecting a trade secret but its value to the cigarette manufacturers was analogous to Coca-Cola's secret formula, for example. The cigarette manufacturers had little or no protection from intellectual property laws with regard to their products; rather, they relied on less ethical means of manipulation coupled with the willingness of addictive personalities to ignore their emotional issues in favour of cigarettes. The result was huge profits year after year. I am not certain were the statement 'information wants to be free' originated, but it seems so appropriate in so many instances.

I recently read that with every new discovery in medicine, countless people live longer lives due to the fact that the knowledge has been freely shared. This appears to be a very common belief and one that is accepted with little controversy. That knowledge has been shared, more often than not, in the form of expensive, patent-protected drugs and the accompanying messages from the pharmaceutical firms. The intellectual property laws assist these companies in protecting their investments in research and development by giving them a monopoly period to exercise their patent rights and reap the benefits of their innovation. The drug companies even share research data with the medical community – free information – on how the drugs work and possible side effects that patients may experience. Yet, they do not share the possibility that the drugs can kill you, or that they may suppress whatever symptoms you are experiencing at the time without ever healing you, or that they may make your condition worse, resulting in the need for more powerful patented drugs, or that they may create long-term health problems in some other organ or system in your body. Whether the drug makers do not know, do not care or simply suppress this information does not matter. It is absolutely frightening that they gamble with peoples' lives for profit. Western society has become so dependent on and trustful of the medical community that it rarely looks past the advice given by the family doctor, pharmacist or the advertisements in the media. All these people are far more intelligent that the general public, right? Yet, the source of all this information is the same. That is the power of information. And that is how easily most people give their power away. The knowledge is readily available if you look hard enough to find it and if you know what you are looking for. Doctors and pharmacists, for example, are not trying to harm patients and generally have the best of intentions when it comes to helping people. Nevertheless, many of them accept what they are told about new drugs and medications. These messages come from the same sources that lobby to have natural herbs and health products banned or labelled as poison because they have not been backed by laboratory tests to prove their safety. Instead, these roots, leaves, berries and barks have centuries of use by people who were more in touch with the healing properties of nature's gifts. Even natural products that have clinical evidence to back their claims are often prevented from advertising such claims.

These contentious issues surrounding drugs and modern medicine will be discussed in other chapters as well. The point in raising them here is to consider how valuable information and knowledge is under many different circumstances. Corporate knowledge can and does include the ability to misinform or partially inform others. The skills required to deflect negativity about a product or service or turn it into an advantage are invaluable. Whether it is ethical or not is another matter, and it is certainly not one that is addressed by intellectual property law. As the business world becomes increasingly competitive, companies will use every asset at their disposal to ensure their future success. Unfortunately, success today often pushes the boundaries of criminal activity, public opinion or both. The line is very fine indeed.

MICROSOFT: INTELLECTUAL PROPERTY WARRIOR

Microsoft has used its financial and intellectual assets brilliantly for the last two decades to manipulate, bully and frighten adversaries, competitors and lawmakers. In addition to its recent anti-competition trials, the company has taken aim at the open source computer operating systems movement, such as Linux. One of Microsoft's main weapons in this fight is intellectual property. The software giant has expressed publicly that the open source movement jeopardizes property rights and could undermine the software industry. In May 2001, the *Ottawa Business Journal* reported that Craig Mundie, President of Microsoft, expressed concerns that open source software creates greater degrees of security risks, software instability and incompatibility and could force valuable corporate intellectual property into public hands. Loosely translated, it would appear that Microsoft's business model is profitable because it keeps its Windows operating system as proprietary as possible, allowing software developers access to source code to develop new products or fix program bugs. Subsequently, Microsoft reaps huge financial rewards and maintains an incredible (dare we say monopolistic?) competitive advantage in the industry. The switch to an open source philosophy in which copyright and ownership are non-issues is, according to Mundie, impractical for businesses like Microsoft. Loosely translated again, it might be insane for Microsoft, considering how successful they have been in fending off attack after attack. The company uses its intellectual property rights to full advantage at every opportunity.

Microsoft has never been a stranger to intellectual property issues. In the early 1980s, Bill Gates wrote letters to local computer clubs lambasting members for copying programs that he and Paul Allen had spent thousands of hours developing. Now Microsoft is quite likely the biggest target for software pirates around the world. The company grew in tandem with the technology that makes copying digital media and programming code simple. We must keep in mind that the problems are not related to inadequate laws. Intellectual property protection in this sphere has been reasonably good until recently. Novels, movies, software and other works covered by copyright have been reasonably secure under existing laws. However, that 'ease of replication' issue raises its ugly head again. As the reproduction technology is becoming more effective, software, movies and other desirable copyrighted material have come under greater risk. As a result, there are more calls to 'beef up' protection for these types of property, particularly from the individuals and entities most threatened by the technology. This creates a challenge for both lawmakers and enforcement agencies. Determining the best approach for dealing with legislative, enforcement and prosecution issues is a complicated task.

PROSECUTING INTELLECTUAL PROPERTY CRIMES

David Goldstone (2001), team leader of the United States Department of Justice's Intellectual Property Team and a trial attorney for the Computer Crime and Intellectual Property Section of the Department, illustrates a number of the issues relating to the prosecution of intellectual property crimes. Initially, he points out that there are certain characteristics about intellectual property cases that help prosecutors in their evaluations of the case. These include:

■ Intellectual property crimes always have a direct victim, namely the intellectual property holder. The crimes also undermine the intellectual property system as a whole in addition to fraud that may have been perpetrated on the individual or entity that bought or received a counterfeit good, for example, or a pirated work.

■ The direct victim of intellectual property crime is, in most cases, defenceless against intellectual property theft because there is rarely direct contact with the victim when the crime is perpetrated. This is clear when you consider how easy it is to commit copyright violations of written works or software programs, for example.

■ Intellectual property rights in virtually all countries are the creation of the state and are usually enforced at the federal level and administered or coordinated by federal agencies. This is evidence of their significance at the national or federal level.

■ Growth in the area of electronic commerce and digital communications demands effective intellectual property protection to safeguard the rights of those conducting business and sharing information in cyberspace.

■ In the case of the United States, revisions to Sentencing Guidelines in May 2000 more accurately reflect the seriousness of intellectual property crimes and the severity of the losses resulting from these crimes.

The last point is not surprising. Rather, it seems long overdue in the United States. Goldstone suggests that the Department of Justice has recognized the importance of intellectual property to the national economy and has designated crimes of this nature as a 'priority' for federal law enforcement. This first occurred in 1999, when Deputy Attorney General, Eric Holder, announced that the US economy was increasingly dependent on the production and distribution of intellectual property and was currently the world leader in the creation and export of these types of assets. Consequently, the Department of Justice, the Federal Bureau of Investigation (FBI) and the United States Customs Service agreed that the investigation and prosecution of these crimes was paramount. As a world leader in so many areas of science, technology, communications, manufacturing, arts, entertainment, health and medicine, the United States has a vested interest in promoting stringent intellectual property protection around the world. As we learnt earlier in this book, this is a phenomenon of the last century or so. Prior to this time, the United States was 'relaxed' in its approach to intellectual property rights on its soil. If it was ambivalent about the rights of its own nationals, it was downright apathetic regarding the rights of foreign inventors and creators. Now, it has become the watchdog of the global economy and it has been one of the most frequent users of the WTO's dispute resolution mechanism. In the last few years, the United States has argued with Argentina over patents and exclusive marketing rights for pharmaceutical products. It has taken Canada to task over patent protection terms. It has success-fully argued that Denmark change its legislation to authorize *ex parte* search and seizures in civil intellectual property rights enforcement proceedings. The Danish government enacted legislation in March 2001 to ensure it meets the requirements of the TRIPS Agreement. US pressure sparked Ireland into action in order to meet its TRIPS obliga-tions. As a result, the Irish government enacted, passed and imple-mented copyright legislation that raised the penalties for copyright infringement. And in March 2001, Greece and the United States resolved a three-year long dispute over television piracy. Greece had failed to adequately enforce intellectual property laws that would have prosecuted television stations that were broadcasting US copyrighted works without authorization. Prior to the United States' intervention, a large number of small and medium-sized Greek television stations had infringed on US copyrights for television programmes and movies. These stations were neither held criminally liable nor closed down by authorities. According to the Office of the United States Trade Representative, since the initiation of the case in April 1998, the level of television piracy in Greece has decreased significantly. Yet the watchdog still has to deal with considerable intellectual property problems at home as well. As intellectual property production increases, so does the criminal activity directed at the property.

Goldstone (2001) provides some interesting guidelines for deter-mining the seriousness of an intellectual property crime as well. While his list in not all-inclusive, he cites the following factors in the bulletin:

■ whether the counterfeit goods or services present potential health or safety issues (eg counterfeit medications or airplane parts);

■ the scope of the infringing or counterfeiting activities (eg whether the subject infringes or traffics in multiple items or infringes upon multiple industries or victims), as well as the volume of infringing items manufactured or distributed;

■ the scale of the infringing or counterfeiting activities (eg the amount of illegitimate revenue and any identifiable illegitimate profit arising from the infringing or counterfeiting activities based upon the retail value of the infringed item);

■ the number of participants and the involvement of any organized criminal group;

■ the scale of the victims' loss or potential loss, including the value of the infringed item, the size of the market for the infringed intellectual property that is being undermined (eg a best-selling software package or a famous trademark), and the impact of the infringement on that market;

- whether the victim of the crime or victims took reasonable measures (if any) to protect against crime; and
- whether the purchasers of the infringing items were victims of a fraudulent scheme, or whether there is reasonable likelihood of consumer mistake as a result of the subject's actions.

There are some valuable factors in this list and some inevitable holes. As an author of a business management book, can I reasonably expect federal authorities to pursue unauthorized copying of my work by a university student or by some individual reformatting portions of it for sale on the Internet? I would think not, no matter how much I argued and how unjust the infringement was in my mind. Assuming I could accurately track down the culprit, I might be able to stop the infringement with a 'cease and desist' approach or some other legal threat. If the entire book was replicated by someone else and was being offered for sale, no doubt the magnitude of the offence against the book publisher and myself would spark a little more interest from law enforcement agencies. Clearly, other titles by the publisher or other book publishers may also be threatened by this piracy scheme.

What reasonable measures could I, or my book publisher, have taken to protect the work from criminal activity in such an instance? The book is protected by copyright and the rights are clearly stated as part of the book. With a book or other written works, there is not much that can be done to enhance the level of protection. The same is true for clothing and fashion items, sporting goods and many other forms of intellectual property. Intellectual assets such as Web sites are not even immune from counterfeiting activities. These are difficult crimes to prosecute even when they are discovered. They are even more difficult to deter. David Goldstone's report is available on the Department of Justice's Web site at http://www.cybercrime.gov.

On a lighter note, law.com published its favourite trademark cases of 2001 on its Web site (www.law.com). As frivolous as these disputes may seem, they illustrate the seriousness with which rights holders will go to protect their marks from outright theft, imitation, abuse and mockery. Every perceived abuse is a potential loss in revenue and the losses can quickly mount if the abuse is condoned. For example, Mattel Inc is the trademark holder of Barbie, the 42-year-old, anatomically disproportionate doll that has contributed to emotional and self-image problems for countless young girls. The toy manufacturing giant is appealing a decision that allowed an artist to feature Barbie in a series of unflattering photographs with vintage kitchen equipment. The judge ruled that the 'art project' was non-commercial and fell within the realm of fair use. In another case, a company called Aubryn International Inc struck a deal with a man named Jack E Daniels for water rights to a large acreage in Gorman, California. Aubryn began producing and selling 'Jack Daniel's' bottled water. The more widely known distillery of the same name, Jack Daniel's Properties Inc, felt it had a trademark dilution case and sued Aubryn. The water vendor counter-sued, claiming libel as well as a charge against the distillery for filing a frivolous lawsuit. This case had not been settled at the time of writing this book. Finally, the following example symbolizes the incredible power and disturbing influence that the entertainment industry has in our society. Despite the fact that there is no possibility of confusion, Lucasfilm Ltd, the company founded by George Lucas, creator of *Star Wars* and owner of the intellectual property relating to the films and spin-off toys, games and other paraphernalia, challenged a maker of medical devices for using the term 'light saber'. Minrad is a maker of laser-guided biopsy equipment such as syringes and needles. While the case was settled for undisclosed terms, it is a reminder that Lucas will 'use the Force', if need be, to protect his intellectual assets.

Other examples and additional valuable information can be found on the law.com Web site, one of the many useful Internet resources for intellectual property information. A compilation of these sites is found in Chapter 8.

PROTECTING TRADE SECRETS AND OTHER INTELLECTUAL ASSETS

Michelle Cook and I recently wrote about Dr Mauri Gronroos and his thoughts on protecting trade secrets (Cook and Cook, 2000). Trade secrets are intellectual assets, but they are not as easily defined or cate-gorized as other forms of intellectual property. Consequently, infringe-ments against confidential information and other trade secrets are not always indisputable. The precautions taken by an individual or a firm to establish both the significance of the asset and the efforts to protect it are critical for claiming an infringement and establishing a case that will hold up under scrutiny. Gronroos has put together a checklist to help businesses in this regard:

1. It is unimportant what the secret is. It can be a formula, pattern, method, process, piece of information or object. What is critical, however, is that a trade secret is economically important as long as it is kept secret. This means that if the trade secret becomes commonly known, the owner (usually a company or an entrepreneur) loses its competitiveness against the competitors.
2. Inform all employees about the nature of your business. Emphasize the fact that the success of your operations depends on certain confidential information, such as trade secrets. Tell them what things are secret, for example 'our price calculations'. Ensure that everybody has understood this. Do not rely on spoken information but give the statement in print, in the internal rules or the quality manual. Consider a signed document that confirms all employees are familiar with the rules of the manual. Stress the fact that an authorized disclosure will lead to prosecution.
3. Ensure that the trade secret is only shared with those employees who need it to fulfil their work tasks.
4. Mark clearly all documents that contain confidential (secret) material.
5. Keep confidential material apart from all other documents in your plant or office.
6. Restrict the access of unauthorized people to the space where you keep your confidential material.
7. Make a non-disclosure agreement with the employees who are exposed to confidential material. Without such an agreement, a former employee is free to disclose or use all your confidential information. Thus, former employees (or employees about to quit) are the biggest hazard to your secrets. Be sure that the scope of the agreement is not too broad. The agreement should only cover the actual secrets by name, for example, the moulding method, profitability calculations, future strategies, upcoming products, etc. Do not forget to make non-disclosure agreements with everybody outside the company who might get in touch with your confidential material, such as suppliers and customers. The latter group is very crucial because many buyers have a tendency to rotate your quotations around in order to squeeze the price.
8. Always prosecute a violator immediately. Be prepared to give full evidence that the disclosure of your trade secret has financially harmed you and that you had taken all possible measures to protect your secrets. The World Trade Organization's TRIPS Agreement speaks about 'reasonable steps' to keep one's information secret. The term is, however, very vague and it is strongly recommended that you go beyond this.
9. Last but not least, remember that the defence of the offender usually, if not always, argues with two claims: first, 'your secret was not secret at all but already widely known'; second, 'you never told or acted as if the information should be kept secret'. Be prepared to answer these arguments.

In addition to Dr Gronroos' excellent checklist, I have also come across an interesting list compiled by R Mark Halligan (2001). Halligan is an attorney with Welsh and Katz and one of the foremost authorities on trade secrets in the United States. Using a manufacturing firm as an example, he has created a very thorough checklist for the purpose of conducting a trade secret audit. This checklist includes the following:

- technical information/research and development;
- proprietary technology information;
- proprietary information concerning research and development;
- formulas/compounds;
- prototypes;
- processes;
- laboratory notebooks;
- experiments and experimental data;
- analytical data;
- calculations;
- drawings – all types;
- diagrams – all types;
- design data and design materials;
- vendor/supplier information;
- research and development reports – all types;
- research and development know-how and negative know-how (ie what does not work);
- production/process information;
- cost/price data;
- proprietary information concerning production/processes;
- special product machinery;
- process/manufacturing technology;
- specifications for production processes and machinery;
- production know-how and negative know-how;
- quality control information;
- quality control procedures;
- quality control manuals;
- quality control records;
- maintenance know-how and negative know-how;
- sales and marketing information;
- proprietary information concerning sales and marketing procedures;
- sales forecasts/data;
- marketing and sales promotion plans;
- internal sales call reports;
- competitive intelligence information;
- counterintelligence information/procedures;
- proprietary information concerning customers;
- proprietary customer lists;

- customer needs and buying habits;
- know-how concerning the management of customer confidence;
- the proprietary customer development cycle;
- proprietary sales and marketing studies and reports;
- internal financial information;
- internal management information;
- proprietary financial information / projections;
- internal financial documents;
- budgets;
- forecasts;
- computer printouts;
- product margins;
- product costs;
- operating reports;
- internal profit and loss statements (closely held companies);
- proprietary administrative information;
- internal administrative information;
- internal organization;
- key decision makers;
- strategic business plans; and
- internal computer software.

As Halligan points out in the article, this list is not exhaustive. However, I suspect it surpasses the lists of most companies when they consider what assets to protect. Some of the items on the list may not apply to all types of businesses but they may serve as a reminder about another aspect of the business that can be included in the audit. Halligan also states that protecting confidential business information and trade secrets is not a one-time event. This is an ongoing and dynamic process because 'A company's portfolio of trade secrets is constantly changing. Information may become obsolete and therefore no longer commercially valuable. Meanwhile, new information may be created that is extremely valuable but not yet properly protected'. According to Halligan, a systematic approach to protecting one's business and intellectual assets will reap large rewards in a couple of ways. First, Halligan believes that the value of these intangible assets will increase. Second, a company will have a greater likelihood of success in the event that it must pursue legal action to protect its trade secrets because it will have been organized and prepared in advance.

By using the tools of Gronroos and Halligan, any business can be well positioned to protect all of its inventions, confidential documents, strategic plans, and other forms of innovation under most circumstances. Starting within the operation is an excellent point of departure for protecting these forms of intellectual property. However, additional complications arise when a business starts to look to new ventures and international growth.

INTELLECTUAL PROPERTY PROTECTION STRATEGIES

There are as many ways to conduct business as there are types of businesses. Consequently there is no single approach to success when a firm is exploring opportunities in new markets. It becomes more challenging when the type of business that is conducted is intellectual property intensive. Add to this challenge the possibility that unknown entities will be involved in the expansion effort and paranoia begins to creep in. Some of the general strategies for dealing with this situation are presented below.

Zero exposure

This is a slightly misleading term because it is impossible to insulate your company completely from external threats and still manage to conduct business. Zero exposure refers to an entirely defensive posture with regard to risking your intellectual property. Some critics advocate this strategy as a means to reduce to the greatest degree the likelihood of your intellectual property being stolen. And, if it is stolen, your recourse in terms of legal action and compensation are maximized. For example, a Canadian small appliance firm with a patent for an innovative vacuum cleaner technology begins to sell its product in the Canadian market. The owners of the firm are confident that they understand Canadian laws for both intellectual property rights and fair business practices. They also have faith in the system and the protection it affords them. They do not have such confidence beyond their borders and feel that their best option is to limit their exposure to the Canadian jurisdiction. In other words, they have chosen not only to research, develop and manufacture their technology in Canada, they have chosen to sell it solely in Canada.

There are obvious drawbacks, however. If you are an ambitious entrepreneur with a great product and a competitive growth strategy, you will not limit yourself to the Canadian market alone, regardless of how big and lucrative it seems. Just south of the border, you have ten times the population with considerable buying power and a very similar culture. Not to mention, there are numerous bilateral trade agreements that further reduce all sorts of risks related to conducting business in the United States. Perhaps even more obvious is the fact that this strategy does not protect your intellectual property from potential exploitation in any other market, including the United States. If your product can be purchased and transported beyond the Canadian border (and most can), you have not controlled your exposure. This strategy is entirely useless for a software firm, for instance. If the computer program can be purchased online and down-loaded directly to a buyer's computer, there are no limitations. The purchaser could be a rival who simply copies the program and dupli-cates it for sale overseas.

The zero exposure strategy only serves to reduce the potential for access to your intellectual property in some very limited cases. I have no doubt that there are many examples of companies finding a prof-itable little corner of the world in which to sell their products and services without the risk of having their intellectual property stolen. In my mind, this is what business is all about. Yet, so many companies want to take on the world because they believe they have the next big thing or a product to help people or, on the negative side of that coin, an opportunity to exploit the fears and desires of humanity. Limiting your business opportunities to one market will eventually limit your growth. You may be the only business doing what you do in Brazil, for example, but success cannot be kept secret. Your monopoly will not last for long even if you operate in a country where foreign investment is discouraged. Local competition will eventually grow and markets are becoming increasingly transparent. Arguably, there is no such thing as a domestic market any longer and this, too, is a reason why intellectual property protection has become an international concern rather than simply a national issue. While it may have been an option 30 or 40 years ago, the zero exposure strategy is not realistic in the modern world.

Controlled exposure

A controlled exposure strategy is commonly employed by businesses that wish to benefit from the opportunities that lucrative foreign markets offer while at the same time increasing the chance that any infringements of intellectual property will still be addressed through a credible and just process. Controlled exposure requires additional planning on the part of the firm that wishes to implement the strategy. It also introduces greater risk in exchange for greater market potential. Briefly, the firm or the owner of the intellectual property must research and analyse which foreign markets are attractive for the product or service in question, including the track record of the country or region in matters of intellectual property protection. There are a number of nations around the world that offer substantial protection for intellectual property. What is important in this analysis is not that the laws exist but that they exist and are enforced for both domestic and foreign firms conducting business in the country or region in question.

Obviously, there are some natural choices that would require less diligent efforts. As mentioned above, the Canadian firm with the vacuum cleaning technology would probably reap more rewards than encounter problems if it developed a well-planned expansion strategy into the United States. Likewise, businesses from nations that are part of the European Union will have fewer barriers and fewer intellectual property threats to address if they conduct business within that community because of the regional system that has been established. However, stepping outside of that safety net to enter the Russian marketplace, for example, increases the risk substantially. While this added layer of security and familiarity is a definite motivation for pursuing new markets with great ideas and inventions, caution must still be exercised when choosing strategic partners, foreign distributors and even when dealing with foreign government officials.

A US computer manufacturer with a unique and innovative design sought a strategic partner in Asia to manufacture and assemble the components of its distinctive laptop. Excited about the prospects of negotiating the contract and beginning production, the representatives of the computer firm provided considerable detail about their strategy, far beyond what was required to contract with a manufacturer of housings and components. To their surprise the deal fell through before it was completed. To their shock and dismay, the potential partner took the information that had been shared and began to replicate the innovative computer and market it. They had no recourse in this country with regard to intellectual property rights and were not prepared to take it through political channels due to the time and expense. Fortunately for the US firm, its representatives had not given away all the details of their design and strategy and some of the critical, confidential information that they felt was necessary for success was not exchanged. Nevertheless, it was a difficult and expensive lesson to learn and it slowed down the company's progress.

On the bright side, it prepared its representatives for future negotiations with potential partners and opened their eyes to the reality of protecting intellectual assets in all circumstances.

Full exposure

This is a strategy that very few companies can afford to implement. It requires deep pockets and an existing international reputation. Industry leaders like Microsoft and worldwide brands like Nike and Reebok can ride their reputations and consumer popularity to virtually every market on the globe, provided that consumers in that market can afford to buy their wares. For these corporate giants, the battle to protect their copyrights, trademarks and other intellectual property is never-ending; however, the costs of fighting piracy combined with the revenues lost to piracy are far less than the profits that they amass by getting the world addicted to their goods and services. A company like Microsoft will endure the pirated copies of Windows and other programs in China in the short term in anticipation of the staggering long-term returns on its investment in this billion-consumer marketplace. As capitalism and the entrepreneurial spirit continues its creeping progress and Chinese laws and enforcement activities reflect international standards, the intellectual property protection environment in China will become more secure. Entry into the WTO will accelerate progress in some areas. Those companies with a foothold will have a definite competitive advantage. As the standard of living increases and the population get a taste for all the modern conveniences, they will likely seek out the familiar names of domestic firms as well as foreign businesses that have invested in the country for years.

DUE DILIGENCE

Due diligence may sound like legal jargon to many entrepreneurs and business people, but it can mean the difference between profitable and rewarding international business experiences and loss of control over your intellectual property. To be diligent in the context of protecting your intellectual assets means that you have taken reasonable care or attention to the matter. Consequently, your efforts are adequate to avoid a claim of negligence. Simply put, due diligence means watching out for your own best interests, something that many firms do very well in many areas of their business yet fail to address in others. A firm can be duly diligent by uncovering and verifying everything it can about anyone with whom it chooses to conduct business. See Cook and Cook (2000) for competitive intelligence tools and techniques that are very useful for this purpose.

Businesses work extremely hard to develop their patents into profitable products. They spend a great deal turning their trademarks into valuable commercial brands and they invest considerable time and effort into their copyrights and industrial designs. It makes sense that they would devote sufficient time and effort to ensure that their valuable creations are as secure as possible when they venture into unfamiliar territory. If you do not know who or what you are dealing with, how can you expect to proceed with confidence? How can you ensure success for your business? Due diligence can provide the answers to these questions. Consider this: you would probably think it insanity to leave your spouse or your children in the hands of strangers. It makes sense to take this view when conducting business and protecting your intellectual property.

There are many methods that are useful for uncovering the business history of a potential partner, whether it is an entire company, its leadership, or an individual. If you undertake this type of work or hire another party to conduct it on your behalf, you must ensure that the approach is legal and ethical. If you are attempting to determine whether your potential partner is trustworthy, yet you are devoid of integrity and break the law without a second thought, you deserve to be caught and punished. Resorting to such tactics is ridiculous when so much information is available in the public domain.

With a little creativity and effort, for example, a thorough background check on the principals of a company can be documented. This check may reveal whether the individuals have left a path of success or destruction in their wake. Additionally, company financial documents as well as legal records from outside sources may be accessible to determine if the partners in question have a history of litigation. When conducting such searches, it is important to determine the reliability of the information you have uncovered. For example, a Web-based source should be verified with a primary source, such as an industry expert with whom you speak or a former customer or client of the target you are researching. It is not uncommon to find a profile of a company or a businessperson that is absolutely glowing; in these cases, seek out additional intelligence to confirm or refute its authenticity. References and related leads can be highly valuable sources of information as well. Following up on leads you have on a potential partner may lead to dead ends or send you in circles. This will be your first clue that something is amiss.

Protecting your intellectual property and your rights in new markets must extend beyond due diligence with potential partners. Government agencies and judicial systems should be considered suspect until proven otherwise, and must be checked for evidence of corruption as well. Wherever possible, the company that is risking its intellectual property should choose to conduct its contracts and legal negotiations under the jurisdiction of its own legal system. This is another valuable safeguard when working with new partners in international markets and developing strategic alliances with foreign firms. For example, the sporting goods firm in Münich can insist that its strategic alliance with a clothing manufacturer in Seoul be subject to German or European intellectual property protection laws. While this is hardly a guarantee of security, it does provide a company with the foundation from which to pursue breaches relating to its intellectual property rights.

Global markets are becoming increasingly competitive and the untapped potential of huge consumer markets in China and other parts of Asia, as well as Latin America, is no longer a secret. Despite the economic instability and political unpredictability in such regions, the lure of big profits in the future is driving continued investment. More and more firms are willing to risk their intellectual assets for a piece of the action. In doing so, they pave the way for increased attention to intellectual property rights in these regions and contribute to a more secure environment for the companies that follow. Is the gamble worth it? Many firms are answering in the affirmative and continue to move forward, relying on a combination of planning and fate to strike it rich. It would be premature to predict the success rate of such strategies, considering the numerous internal and external challenges the international environment creates for businesses and their intellectual assets. These challenges only serve to compound the intellectual property risk, as we shall find out in the next chapter.

ROGUE NATIONS AND FALSE CREATIONS

Do not pursue what is illusory – property and position: all that is gained at the expense of your nerves decade after decade and can be confiscated in one fell night.

Alexander Solzhenitsyn

Consider the following tale of a company that had the bulk of its talented employees lured away by a larger competitor that felt threatened by the smaller firm's successes and capabilities. The competitor used the automated telephone directory to find out the names of the employees and then contacted them personally to make them offers that seemed too good to be true. Indeed, the offers were too good to be true. The smaller firm was decimated by the departures of so many of its key people and never recovered completely from the loss of so much intellectual capital. The competitor captured as much of this capital as it could from the new employees and kept a few key people; however, most of those it lured away from the smaller company were let go within a very short span of time.

It may be difficult to accept that all of your business accomplishments could be taken from you in a matter of months, weeks, days or even hours. This is the reality of a business world in which so much of one's success hinges upon having the right people, the right product and the right promotion at the right time. All or any of these 'right' components can be removed with relative ease in the absence of necessary precautions. This includes intellectual property and the protection of your rights. If it is this easy to lose seemingly dedicated employees, imagine how easy it is for someone to copy your Web site and start selling your products online in order to obtain credit card numbers. Imagine how easy it is for that software program you developed to be copied by someone on the other side of the world, who then shares it with a number of friends. The illegal copies multiply at an alarming rate far beyond the speed with which legal copies leave the retail outlets. Does Adidas really know how many companies are illegally manufacturing running shoes, soccer balls and golf shirts under their brand name? And how many government offices or universities around the world can actually claim to be free of pirated software or plagiarized reports and studies?

In this chapter, we will examine the extent to which theft, piracy and other infringements of intellectual property rights occur at all levels in society. The protection of intellectual property is not an international objective. It is not even a priority for much of the world. Many people do not even know what intellectual property means or why it is important. Consequently, many people steal it unknowingly or under the guise of sharing something that they believe is valuable with others who could benefit from it. They are correct of course – it is valuable. That is the reason it is afforded protection by the law. Others are well aware of this and they willingly engage in criminal behaviour because the potential financial gain is gripping. And, in many instances, their crimes go undetected or unpunished. Such is the nature of intellectual property enforcement.

There is no single standard against which intellectual property rights and related protection can be measured. According to Harvard Law Professor, William Fisher, intellectual property protection in the international environment varies by context. It varies by type and it varies by country. Says Fisher:

> If you take patent protection for pharmaceuticals as one example with a lot of current interest on the international scene, formal protections internationally are quite good, meaning that the large majority of the countries in the world – over 140 are members of the World Trade Organization – are obliged either already or very soon because of the TRIPS Agreement to institute effective patent protection for pharmaceuticals, among other things. So, as a matter of formal

law the shields are very substantial but formal law is different from the law in action and is different from getting the law enforced. They are offsetting pressures.

Fisher points out that in some countries the judicial apparatus does not exist to provide effective patent protection, while in other areas the judicial apparatus exists but the humanitarian cost of enforcement of intellectual property rights has produced quite serious resistance. A prime example that Fisher provides is the AIDS drug controversy. Despite the power of the TRIPS Agreement, the international protection for pharmaceutical rights is going down in the face of widespread human tragedy. Like many individuals, Fisher supports the current direction and refers to existing provisions in the TRIPS Agreement that provide 'appropriate escape hatches' as he labels them, in times of public health crises to permit countries to suspend patent protection for drugs necessary to respond to epidemics on the scale of the AIDS tragedy. He quickly points out, however, that an executive at a pharmaceutical company would likely find this very disturbing. Patents and compassion do not blend well in the pharmaceutical industry.

A CANADIAN EXAMPLE

Governments that should know better still find themselves in hot water when it comes to intellectual property protection. Following the tragic events of the terrorist attacks on the United States on 11 September 2001 the world was treated to an outbreak of biological terror as anthrax spores were deliberately spread through various US locations. At the time of writing this book, the bulk of the verifiable anthrax attacks were confined to the east coast of the United States; however, hoaxes were turning up around the world. Canada received its fair share of hoaxes and, consequently, the government took steps to prepare the nation for the possibility of a genuine threat. One of these steps included a C $1.5 million (approximately US $1 million) purchase of an antibiotic drug used for combating anthrax infections. Health Canada, the federal ministry responsible for the purchase, entered into agreement with Apotex, a leading Canadian developer and manufacturer of generic drugs. In its haste to protect Canadians from a threat that had not yet materialized, government officials failed to recognize and honour that the patent for Cipro, the drug in question, belonged to Bayer AG and it had the exclusive rights to produce and manufacture the antibiotic. Apotex was not even licensed by Bayer to produce the drug, yet it was going to supply Health Canada at a price estimated at 30 per cent less than that of Bayer. Needless to say, the German pharmaceutical giant was incensed to learn that the Canadian government had not only ignored Bayer's patent, but also the national laws in place to protect companies from such an infringement. As the story became public, Health Canada backpedalled furiously to contain the damage and make amends to both drug manufacturers and to preserve the country's reputation as a nation that respects patent law and other forms of intellectual property. They claimed that Bayer was contacted and the company indicated that it could not fill the order. Consequently, officials from the department turned to Apotex. There are provisions in Canadian law authorizing the government to override patent laws in urgent situations. These provisions require that the government notify both the patent holder and the federal patent office. This did not happen. In fact, Bayer claims it was not even contacted by Health Canada regarding the order for Cipro.

In the end, no one was sued, everyone was paid, and Health Canada had an abundance of Cipro, just in case. On the surface it appears that the best was made of a bad situation. Yet, in this example, everyone loses. The taxpayers potentially pay for the double order of anthrax antibiotics when a single case of the infection has yet to be recorded in Canada. Apotex looks like it willingly infringes on other firms' patents by assuming that the federal government contract followed legal procedures. Bayer AG is potentially branded as a firm more concerned with its corporate image and patents than the welfare of people who buy its numerous products. And companies seeking to invest in Canada may wonder if the country's reputation for a fair and stable business environment is actually warranted. They may question whether their innovative products and services are protected under its intellectual property regime.

There are conditions under which a government can and will break a patent monopoly, as the Canadian government recklessly attempted above. In these other cases, the necessity for doing so seemed a little more apparent. Because it is a rare occurrence, few patent holders, let alone the general public, realize that the government can legally override their individual rights as patent holders. The government can also pay off a patent holder when it wants to claim the invention for its own uses. For example, if a scientist in Arizona invented a process that would render human beings invisible, the military might find this technology both intriguing and threatening. As the scientist attempts to patent her discovery, officials might approach her seeking to buy the technology and the patent for the government. In cases where the technology is considered critical to national welfare, this can happen. The scientist and the government will negotiate a 'fair compensation' for the process. In other words, the government will make an offer and the scientist will accept it or go to court to obtain a better settlement. In addition, she may be offered a very lucrative job to continue her work for a new and powerful employer: the government of the United States.

In other circumstances, such as war, patent monopolies can be broken to ensure that national security is not compromised. In the First World War, the United States government had to pressure the Wright-Martin Aviation Company to license their technology to a rival firm in order to guarantee that an adequate supply of aeroplanes would be available for the war effort. More recently, the leadership of countries around the world has been 'violating' drug patents in order to increase the supply of inexpensive medicines to combat disease and illness among their people. This type of violation is different because it extends beyond national boundaries. Most of the violators are developing nations and most of the patents belong to US or European multinational corporations. In these cases, it is possible that both national patent law and international intellectual property treaties are being ignored in an effort to respond to a national crisis.

WHY NATIONS CONDONE INTELLECTUAL PROPERTY THEFT

The example above clearly illustrates that there was no ill intention on the part of the Canadian government to rob the German firm of its intellectual property. Nor was there any conspiracy with the Canadian supplier to disadvantage the foreign patent owner. It was simply a poor policy decision implemented during a moment of panic. Yet, there are a number of reasons why nations do sponsor intellectual property theft and a number of ways in which they do it. Whether it is belligerent and outright refusal to participate in the international system of rights and protection, or turning a blind eye to criminal activities in the business community, the impact on the marketplace is severe. Briefly, here are some of the reasons why nations steal:

■ Rogue nations: simply put, there are countries within our global community that are magnets for lawlessness and crime. Typically, they are controlled by military despots who terrorize the people and strip the country of any wealth it may have. That includes any foreign investment and intellectual assets associated with the investment. In other cases, rogue nations are embroiled in so much civil conflict that matters of intellectual property rights are far less important than finding inexpensive suppliers of guns, missiles and ammunition. Additionally, there is no central authority to take up the challenge of implementing and enforcing the type of legal system required to protect not only intellectual property rights but rights of any kind.

- Fence sitters: the government leaders of these nations nod approvingly in the right places when the topic of intellectual property rights is raised. They speak in the affirmative on the significance of protecting intellectual assets. They confirm their commitment to protecting foreign businesses that wish to invest in their economies. When all the platitudes and promises have been delivered, however, nothing is done to stem the software piracy and the patent and copyright infringements. In some cases, these nations are contracting parties to the World Intellectual Property treaties or the TRIPS Agreement, which afford them certain rights and privileges they might not otherwise have. Some of these nations are seeking membership into these clubs and they have gone through the motions of establishing laws that cannot be enforced or will not be enforced for reasons we will explore in more detail below and in later chapters.

- Parasites: these nations have flourishing markets as a result of their ignorance of intellectual property rights. Cracking down on illegal business practices in their towns and cities in order to protect the trademark rights of a sporting goods firm in Germany, for example, is not a good short-term economic strategy for these countries. Long-term vision is not a strong characteristic of these governments.

- Protesters: some nations are struggling to reach new levels of economic stability and self-sustaining growth. While they have received considerable foreign aid from individual nations or through World Bank or International Monetary Fund programmes, the imposed conditions for this aid has become as burdensome as the economic troubles they strive to overcome. In certain instances, these nations speak out and take action against the inequality they see in international systems, such as the intellectual property regime. They recognize it as a barrier to their economic and social growth and just another way to keep them from reaching the level of comfort, security, stability and influence of the wealthy developed nations. Consequently, they actively and flagrantly oppose certain rules and codes of conduct established by international institutions.

These are just a few of the reasons why intellectual property crime flourishes on a national level. Clearly, they are not the only reasons. Intellectual property crime in the United States, for example, is a widespread problem yet the country does not fit into any of the descriptions above. The difference is this: despite the extent of intellectual property crime that occurs in the United States, the government has made concerted efforts in the area of legislation, enforcement and prosecution of intellectual property crimes. In addition to its domestic efforts, the United States is the self-appointed global watchdog, determined to draw attention to the deficiencies of other nations and protect the intellectual assets of US firms conducting business abroad. In contrast, little effort to protect intellectual property is being made in these other nations. It may be for one of the reasons listed above, a combination of them or some other reason altogether. In all of these examples, however, motivation and enforcement stand out as weak links.

THE ECONOMICS OF INTELLECTUAL PROPERTY THEFT

Certain types of intellectual property are very difficult to steal. It would not take too long for BMW to discover that an automotive plant in Chile was churning out luxury sedans identical to the German cars. Few people would know what to do with a highly specialized (and easily identifiable) optical networking component that was protected by a patent. And a singer would not be able to claim originality to a song from another artist's best-selling CD recording. Other types of intellectual property are simply not that lucrative, or are too obscure or complex to merit attention from prospective thieves. Software, on the other hand, is different. There exists powerful formal copyright protection in the form of the international agreements we have examined in this book, as well as improved protection in nations aspiring to join the WTO. Nevertheless, these are simply laws on the books. In practice, as Fisher (1999) observes, 'The enforcement mechanisms vary dramatically. So software piracy rates remain extremely high in much of Eastern and Southeast Asia. They remain quite high in

Latin America, and reasonably high in Eastern Europe.' But Fisher reminds us that that has little to do with the laws in these countries that protect software against replication. Rather, it has to do with enforcement mechanisms. It also has to do with motivation. An economy that flourishes as a result of illegal activity is still flourishing, no matter how shortsighted and ethically disturbing such an approach may seem. Clamping down on activities that are fuelling spending and providing jobs is not a popular policy decision even if it helps pave the way for future growth through legitimate businesses and foreign investment. Weak-willed government officials and law-enforcement agencies turn a blind eye to infringements of intellectual property rights such as street vendors selling brand-name clothing and jewellery imitations or manufacturing facilities that clone computers or small appliances. These are sources of income for people who would otherwise be unemployed. They spend the money they make from pirating the goods of rich foreign firms on local goods, such as housing and food. Their activities may even be a source of supplementary income to officials who are bribed to refrain from enforcing the laws.

It has almost become a way of life. People in the United States brag about the Gucci bag they bought in Hong Kong for US $5 and the Rolex watch they purchased for US $10 in Barbados. In fact, they could have saved the travel expenses and found similar deals on the streets in most of their big cities. They may even have been able to order comparably priced replications over the Internet. As governments fight long and hard for enhanced protection in foreign nations so that local businesses can safely and successfully compete in new markets, the general public continues to undermine those governments' efforts. And, as more money and law enforcement resources are diverted into protecting the intellectual assets of powerful corporations at home and abroad, these same people will wonder why their taxes are increasing yet again. Intellectual property infringements know no boundaries. It is neither an issue of poverty or wealth nor is it an issue of criminals or lawmakers. Anyone can play this game, and most people do.

INTERNATIONAL ENFORCEMENT MECHANISMS: POWER OR PUSHOVER?

How effective are the international institutions at dealing with these rogue nations? As Mauri Gronroos points out, the WTO is very powerful and has a large arsenal of weapons with which to retaliate against nations that fail to enforce the international intellectual property rights. He is quite optimistic that issues such as piracy can somehow be brought under control. He also believes that global capabilities to enforce intellectual property protection will be enhanced by a shift in status of one of the greatest offending nations. Gronroos told me, 'The job will be significantly easier now because China will be taken in the WTO. Russia is still outside but after these two oases of piracy are full members, the law enforcement will be possible.' Gronroos also seems to suggest that the 'ignorance is bliss' approach of the past is no longer excusable. 'The developing nations have actually become familiar with the fact that the innovations of the West will be protected by the intellectual property rights,' he says. 'And these rights must be respected – or else.'

When developing nations have something to offer the West, as do both China and Russia, this 'fair is fair' approach is workable and both sides can make concessions for a greater good. Russia is troublesome in this regard because criminal activity runs rampant through most industries and sectors and determining who has the power to make change and who is simply a mouthpiece is not easy. Still, the West tolerates these challenges because some of these nations still see significant market potential in Russia, with its large consumer base, natural resources and relatively skilled and diverse labour force. And Russia may want to be a superpower again; and its leaders recognize that foreign investment is required to generate the economic conditions that lead to such a dream. Becoming an international pariah as a result of lawlessness is not the road Russia wants to follow.

In contrast, developing nations that heed the 'or else' approach to intellectual property protection are in a bind if they have little to offer to foreign investors other than solid intellectual property laws. If there are no resources to exploit, shortages of skilled labourers and the country is geographically or environmentally 'challenged', it will simply be ignored by foreign investors. It is very difficult to attract multinational corporations to the desert, for example, if there is no oil or natural gas to be found. It is a sad reality that many countries will remain economically depressed as a result of their geographic location and their 'marketability'. Yet others, with considerably more advantages, continue to violate international laws that they have committed to uphold.

According to the Office of the United States Trade Representative (USTR), some recent offenders on the national and regional level include:

■ The European Union: failure to provide national treatment for the protection of geographical indications, specifically in the area of agricultural products and foodstuffs.

■ Ukraine: alleged offences in the area of optical media piracy, as well as the failure to implement adequate and effective intellectual property laws.

■ Brazil and Taiwan: failure to take effective enforcement action that would create a deterrent against commercial piracy and counterfeiting.

■ Argentina, Hungary and Israel: inadequate protection of the confidential test data of pharmaceutical and agricultural chemical companies.

■ India and the Dominican Republic: insufficient term protection for patents.

■ Former Soviet republics such as Armenia, Azerbaijan, Belarus, Kazakhstan, Tajikstan, Turkmenistan and Uzbekistan: failure to adequately protect pre-existing works.

■ Philippines: inadequate intellectual property enforcement, particularly in the availability of *ex parte* search remedies.

In addition to this list of complaints, the USTR has problems with the alleged lax border enforcement that many of the United States' trading partners have in dealing with pirated and counterfeit goods. Undoubtedly, there are complaints against the United States as well. 'Uncle Sam' is simply more vocal than many other nations.

CORPORATE OFFENDERS

While this chapter has focused primarily on the role of nations in advancing intellectual property protection or hindering it, the topic would be incomplete without addressing the role of other key entities; namely, the corporation and the individual. Often these two entities are linked. The corporation or business blatantly abuses intellectual property rules for its own profit, and enlists the assistance of employees or outsiders to meet its objectives. There are also businesses that operate in the grey area of intellectual property law, pushing the boundaries and exploring the shady edges of what is legal and what is not. And, finally, there are businesses that simply do not know that they are breaking the law. While ignorance is not an excuse, not all businesses are in the position to know the detailed provisions of intellectual property law that pertain to their operation. If you do not know the limits of the law, you may pay a high price indeed.

Fisher cites the case of Two Pesos, a Mexican restaurant that was ordered to pay a substantial sum for damages to Taco Cabana, a rival restaurant. The rival claimed that Two Pesos had appropriated its layout, décor and overall 'theme'. As Fisher describes, all the features in question were non-functional, yet they contributed to a distinctive overall image. After five years of legal battles, the courts decided that Two Pesos had acted wrongfully in appropriating Taco Cabana's image without permission. Fisher's essay provides wonderful background and interesting historical facts to help the reader understand how, in the United States, the appearance of a restaurant can be owned.

Threats from within

Employees and former employees are arguably the greatest threat to businesses trying to safeguard their intellectual property. Consider Lucent Technology's dilemma in May 2001, when two of its scientists were arrested for allegedly delivering trade secrets to Datang Telecom Technology Company Ltd, a Chinese government-owned company. The men were working on a Lucent project called PathStar that was developing low-cost voice and data services for use by Internet service providers. Lucent had the two employees arrested for stealing company equipment as well as intellectual property. Had they caught the offenders prior to the transfer of Lucent's assets, minimal damage would have incurred. Having caught the men, Lucent still must evaluate the damage. Once the exchange has taken place, how many people have access to the secrets? How quickly can they be duplicated, re-engineered, understood and even presented as original? Even if Datang Telecom is both punished and prohibited from benefiting from the stolen technology, what measures are in place to prevent it resurfacing elsewhere in a slightly modified form?

One of the most celebrated cases of trade secret theft in recent years was discussed in Cook and Cook (2000). A General Motors Corporation executive held covert discussions with Volkswagen during his tenure at the US automotive manufacturing giant. After some time, he accepted a lucrative offer to join Volkswagen. However, he also agreed to obtain confidential business plans from General Motors and bring them to his new employer. This was accomplished with the assistance of General Motors employees, who delivered other trade secrets to Volkswagen and eventually joined the German automaker as well. Needless to say, this case went to court and the executive was charged with theft of trade secrets.

Both the Lucent and Volkswagen cases are blatant examples of intellectual property theft that span national borders. Newsworthy cases such as these are becoming increasingly common in an increasingly competitive business environment. Corporate espionage continues to flourish despite strict laws and punishments. The penalties under the United States' Economic Espionage Act, for example, are severe; however, many businesses and individuals continue to employ illegal and unethical means to undermine the competition. The lure of profits is addictive. Unquestionably, the bulk of corporate intellectual property theft is less exciting. It falls under the category that might be referred to as 'victimless crimes'. This is a misnomer because all crimes victimize someone. As we discovered in Chapter 2, these corporate infringements on intellectual property can be related to software piracy or other forms of copyright abuse. They may be prompted by nothing more than ignorance or apathy but they are still damaging to other businesses. If a consulting firm was operating in an environment in which it could not collect on 30 per cent of its consulting services because of theft, it would definitely be seeking support and a change in the status quo.

Despite the risks that we have discussed in this chapter, businesses from around the world are compelled to seek new markets for the their products and services. Consequently, they are prepared to bear the risk of competing and partnering internationally. It would appear that the vast majority of companies have found the experience rewarding on a cultural, social, and financial level. They have yet to be intimidated by the occasional horror story of another company devastated by the intellectual property abuses it has suffered in foreign markets, resulting in the loss of its intellectual property, the failure of its international expansion efforts or the destruction of its business. Ignorance is no excuse in today's competitive and risky markets. Preparation is critical to ensure that intellectual property and all other valuable components of your business are protected when your firm ventures into unknown territory.

TEACHERS, STUDENTS AND COPYRIGHT ABUSES

Organizations and people in the academic world often escape unscathed despite flagrant abuses of copyright. And it is not simply the students who are breaking the law. Plagiarism is an insidious problem in schools, and the Internet has simply made it easier for students to copy the work of others and submit it as their own. This has spawned Web sites that actually advertise their writing services to students. However, professors and teachers are often offenders as well. Janeen McCarthy, Donna Lerch, Lynn Gilmore and Shellie Brunsman, graduate students in the Curriculum, Technology, and Education Reform (CTER) Masters of Education programme at the University of Illinois Urbana-Champaign, conducted an informal and anonymous survey of teachers at the kindergarten to sixth grade level. The survey was part of their white paper entitled 'Educator's Guide to Intellectual Property, Copyright and Plagiarism' (available online at http://lrs.ed.uiuc.edu/wp/copyright/wpindex.html) and involved teachers from four elementary schools (20 to 40 teachers per school) in Springfield, Illinois during 1999.

From experience, I would suggest that the responses and attitudes captured in this survey have been representative of the general view of intellectual property in most education programmes, with the possible exception of law and journalism programmes at post-secondary institutions. They are worth repeating here and, as McCarthy et al point out, 'Obviously, teachers think one way, and act another – and feel justified in doing so'. The survey generated the following responses:

1. Do you have a basic knowledge of copyright law? Yes 74%. No 26%.
2. Have you ever knowingly broken copyright law? Yes 64%. No 36%.
3. Have you ever copied something that you thought should not have been, but were not sure? Yes 89%. No 11%.
4. Do you think copyright laws should be changed? Yes 75%. No 25%.
5. Do you think that teachers should set a good example for their students by strictly adhering to copyright laws? Yes 70%. No 30%.
6. Do you think that schools and teachers should not have to follow copyright laws as much as the general public, since we are non-profit, and under-funded? Yes 78%. No 22%.
7. Have you had any instruction in how copyright law effects the Internet? Yes 4%. No 96%.
8. Do you think teachers should receive more education about ethics and laws in college? Yes 74%. No 26%.
9. Have you heard of a school or teacher being prosecuted for copyright infringement? Yes 9%. No 91% (Most of the 'yes' clarified that it was a church).
10. Have you ever copied software instead of purchasing it? Yes 46%. No 54%.

The authors draw out additional conclusions from their research into this area. They believe that many teachers rationalize their misuse of copyrighted material by pleading that a lack of funding prevents them from getting new and original copies of material. They argue that they are not benefiting financially from photocopying the material of others for distribution in classrooms. And ultimately, no one appears to get caught with regard to this type of copyright infringement and the students benefit from getting more materials from which to learn. The authors suggest that the situation has 'Created an ethical paradox that teachers feel unprepared to address.' Are they, without question, law-abiding role models for students? Or must they question, bend, or ignore laws that prevent them from passing on knowledge to their students in an effective means?

Perhaps they are not trying hard enough to find an alternative that does not involve theft. I clearly recall sitting in a lecture hall as my professor reeled off the texts required for his course. He indicated that numerous sections of each book were relevant and it was apparent that they would have to purchased and read in their entirety. Except for one. The professor named the book and the required sections and proceeded to tell the class that, by his calculations, we would each save five dollars by obtaining the book from the library and photocopying the relevant chapters instead of purchasing it at the campus bookstore. I am convinced that this is not an isolated incident. If the educators are not prompting it, the students are often taking this route on their own.

Academics are not above the law when money is involved. A recent scandal involving one of the United States' most respected historians illustrates this clearly. Stephen Ambrose built his reputation as a history professor and author of academic texts pertaining to various presidents of the United States. These works were recognized for extensive citations and footnotes and acknowledged as valuable historical contributions by the small yet influential community that reads such books. Less than a decade ago, Ambrose added popular historical fiction to his repertoire and became a publishing success in the mainstream market. His novels earned him millions of dollars, fame and opportunities he might otherwise have missed. These types of works are intensive, and many authors require a few years to adequately research and write their manuscripts, to ensure historical and factual accuracy. Ambrose was able to produce them in about half the time of his rivals. Clearly, he could have been more organized and quicker at getting his thoughts on paper. Yet it also became obvious that he had taken passages from the works of other authors and injected them into his text. In many instances the passages were substantial and virtually identical to the original prose used in the earlier work. One passage in his novel *The Wild Blue*, which was published in 2001, described the difficulties encountered by three-person crew boarding their cramped stations inside an aircraft. The words of the passage are almost identical to those used by Thomas Childers in his novel *Wings of Morning*, written six years earlier. As a result of this discovery, people have begun analysing his books for other copyright infringements and have found additional cases of plagiarism. Once may have been excusable but it appears that this habit had become part of the writing process for Ambrose.

While there may have been colleagues and peers who were bitter or envious of Ambrose's transformation from esteemed history professor to multi-million dollar book industry and celebrity, few would argue that their criticisms in this scandal were unfounded. A research fellow from Harvard's Kennedy School summed it up succinctly in an article in Canada's *Globe and Mail* newspaper ('The fall of Ambrose Inc', 17 January, 2002): if his students submitted work that included the passages of others and these passages were not cited, the students would be called to task and would have to rewrite the paper. More importantly, they would be reported to the Dean of the school.

As is often the case, the lure of profits overcame common sense and respect for the rights and property of others. We mistakenly hold professors, doctors, scientists, lawyers and other professionals in a higher esteem because we have attached artificial values and significance to their particular professions. Society assumes these people are more intelligent and infallible. In reality, they are human beings capable of making the same mistakes and committing the same crimes as anyone else. Intellectual property is so pervasive in our society, it is easy to 'borrow' a witty statement for a magazine column, or cut and paste a philosophical argument from someone's Web site into a term paper on St Augustine and Thomas Aquinas.

A few years ago, I wrote an article on the topic of records management and document management. I was addressing the need for advance planning and preparation when combining your technology (databases, data warehouses, data mining software, etc) with the needs of the users. I referred to a poorly planned and excessively complicated system as a 'data graveyard' that would not be used by anyone. Shortly after its publication, I was contacted by a gentleman who was a director of a successful records management company. He complimented me on my article and the way in which it simply expressed some of the issues he was trying to explain to potential clients. He especially liked the 'data graveyard' reference and asked if I had come up with it on my own because he would like to use it in his presentations. My first reaction was to respond that it was 'original material' and to thank him for the consideration of asking my permission before using it. He certainly was not obliged to do so, considering it was a two-word expression. The more I thought about his question, the less certain I became that it was original. It was possible that I had read it somewhere else or had heard someone use it in conversation. In response, I told him that I believed it was original but had absolutely no proof. No one, including the author of this humble book, can claim to be 100 per cent original when it comes to creativity, whether it is written expression, a musical composition, a software program, or an industrial invention. But at the very least, we must make an honest attempt to give credit where credit is due.

INTELLECTUAL PROPERTY THEFT QUIZ

How many of us can claim to be squeaky clean when it comes to intellectual property rights? I would guess that most people have infringed on someone else's rights in some way, intentionally or not. If you answer 'yes' to any of these questions, you have infringed upon the intellectual property rights of someone else.

1. Have you ever recorded a favourite CD or tape on to a blank audio-cassette as a gift for someone else?
2. Have you recorded, distributed or sold movies that you duplicated from a videotape, DVD or cable / satellite service?
3. Have you bought an imitation Gucci bag or Rolex watch?
4. Does your office buy one single-user software package and install it on a number of computers?
5. Do you copy your friend's computer software?
6. Do you 'borrow' interesting or witty paragraphs from other writers without giving them credit?
7. Have you photocopied and distributed the copyright protected written works of others?
8. Have you submitted an essay or term paper for a course that contained copyright protected ideas and expressions of someone else, yet claimed the work as your own?
9. Do you manufacture a product in one location yet make claims of origin to draw on the prestige of another part of the world (ie genuine 'Tuscany' tiles, manufactured in Vietnam)?
10. Have you put the logos of your favourite sports teams and images of your favourite sports stars on your Web site as a means to attract other fans to your site?

THOUGHTS ON THE FUTURE OF THOUGHT

All truly wise thoughts have been thought already thousands of times; but to make them truly ours, we must think them over again honestly, till they take root in our personal experience.

Johann Wolfgang von Goethe

In his novel *1984*, George Orwell presented a frightening view of the future, complete with mind-controlling institutions and a complete lack of personal freedoms, including thought, speech and movement. Fortunately, we have not sunk quite to that level yet, despite all the upheavals the world has experienced since Orwell copyrighted his material. Looking back to 1984, the year he chose to prophesize his futuristic nightmare, we were oblivious to cyberlaw or global software piracy. The WIPO had been a specialized agency of the United Nations for a mere decade. Another decade would have to pass before the WTO would come into existence.

While it would be a stretch to describe our current state of affairs as 'Orwellian', we do seem to be subject to many more laws, more international institutions with power and influence over the ways in which we conduct business and conduct our personal affairs. It is not all that surprising that some people struggle against the systems we have in place to govern our activities, protect us against crime, ensure we are contributing to society and establish the boundaries for many of our actions. It is not surprising that some people question the degree to which they are free and the extent to which they are exercising free will.

In this chapter, we are going to explore these broad concepts within our narrow scope, namely intellectual property. As we have read already in this book, intellectual property laws such as the Digital Millennium Copyright Act in the United States have been portrayed as unconstitutional and dangerous threats to freedom of speech. The influence of powerful nations and powerful corporations contribute to both the exploitation and encouragement of developing nations. In many cases, the verdict is still out. It is premature to judge the impact that the current intellectual property system is having on individuals, cultures, societies, nations, regions and the natural environment. We can gaze into our crystal ball, however, and explore some of the big issues that loom on the horizon. We can also look at the pressing issues that grab the headlines today and analyse how they relate to intellectual property concepts. There are few global and national issues, for example, that do not have some kind of direct or indirect relationship to the ideas we are addressing in these pages.

THE FUTURE OF THE
INTERNATIONAL INSTITUTIONS

What can we say about the leading international institutions and their agendas for the future? Harvard Law Professor William Fisher describes the WIPO's role as one devoted to coordinating, enforcing and educating about international intellectual property agreements. In contrast, the WTO has a much wider set of responsibilities in terms of lowering barriers to international trade in lots of dimensions and intellectual property is just one of them. In an interview Fisher told me that, 'Both organizations, in my view, are going too far too fast in protecting intellectual property rights.'

There is considerable evidence to support Fisher's opinion. It is in the best interest of WIPO to continue pushing for additional intellectual property rights and wider coverage, if only for the sake of self-preservation. Bluntly, if we had all the laws in place and everyone was adhering to them the need for WIPO might be questionable. As simplistic as this explanation is, it has merit. The ultimate goal of many organizations should be their own extinction after a job well done. Unfortunately this is not the case and the proliferation of specialty associations, non-governmental organizations and international institutions continues. WIPO has a seemingly endless supply of new and exciting projects, many of which are technology focused or incorporate technology into the delivery of the solution. This is admirable; however, it pulls valuable resources away from less glamorous challenges that remain unresolved. An extraordinary number of treaties have been implemented or amended to protect virtually anything with a price tag. Yet the fundamental definitions of intellectual property and the concepts around intellectual property rights are neither universally accepted nor understood.

WIPO could change its focus, proceed with caution and resolve the fundamental problems of the intellectual property regime it has built before undertaking new and exciting projects. But, who has the authority or influence to make this request? Who would make it, even if they did have the authority or influence? Wealthy, industrialized nations have a considerable stake in an ever-expanding, technology-driven intellectual property system based on definitions and concepts that originated with them. Their agenda drives the system, providing a continuous stream of new areas for WIPO to explore.

The WTO suffers from many of the same symptoms as WIPO. Its agenda is driven primarily by the largest trading nations in the world. Not surprisingly, these are the most industrially developed and economically wealthy countries. Despite the 'one vote per nation' fairness of the WTO, democracy of this nature can be easily overcome by favours and influence. As a result of the WTO's single-minded objective to increase (and improve, in all fairness) global market opportunities and international commerce, all related aspects of international trade are coloured by this objective. The TRIPS Agreement is a prime example. Intellectual property rights must be upheld... so that trade can grow in a secure environment. Intellectual property must be protected... because it is a financially valuable commodity to be traded around the world. In fact, the emphasis on the 'trade' aspect of intellectual property diminishes other aspects: cultural exploitation, threats to the natural environment and dangerous commercial products or services that have been misrepresented or inadequately tested. The speed with which the WTO and WIPO are pushing intellectual property rights must decrease. Already, we are seeing evidence from those who are ready to push back.

FUTURE DISPUTES AND CONTROVERSIES

There is always one certainty that comes from having an intellectual property system: disputes. As long as people continue to claim rights to objects, expressions, sounds, and computer code, other people will object to those claims. Alternatively, they will ignore the claims and use the property or expressions without permission. Intellectual property disputes will increase in direct proportion to the amount of intellectual property that is claimed and protected. The following areas are likely candidates for controversy.

Agriculture and biotechnology

Mauri Gronroos sees big and bitter disputes looming on the horizon. He points to the so-called Farmer's Right dilemma to highlight the problems that must be solved in the future. This issue revolves around a farmer's right to save post-harvest seeds from crops that were grown using genetically modified seeds. Such seeds are purchased from multinational seed corporations like Monsanto. When I contacted him, Gronroos posed the following questions: 'When the farmer reaps the harvest and saves some seed to sow them again, should he [or she] pay some royalties to the inventor of the super seed, in other words to the multinational corporation? If he [or she] is not obliged to pay, can he [or she] sell some of the seed to his [or her] neighbour?'

It is frightening enough to see how efficiently these seed companies are spreading their genetically modified, patent-protected seeds around the world. The rate of proliferation will accelerate out of control if farmers start to actively distribute seeds for profit. It is small consolation, but this is one issue over which I hope the seed companies triumph. By limiting the distribution channels, companies like Monsanto will make a greater direct profit but the slower rate of proliferation provides more time for farmers and the general public to educate themselves regarding the risks of genetically modified crops. The number of contentious issues regarding agriculture, biotechnology, genetic modification and related patents grows daily. This hotspot is unlikely to resolve itself, considering the mounting pressure from the public for more knowledge regarding the ways in which businesses are manipulating nature. The backlash will continue to grow and when protests reach a critical mass, the revolt against these firms will have dire economic consequences. Not only will their products and services be shunned, the return on investment of their research

131

and development dollars will be negligible. Finally, their intellectual assets, including their intellectual property, will decrease significantly in value.

This is a long-term scenario, in my mind. The biotechnology industry in all its many forms remains a key asset in national port-folios. Yet, there appears to be a wave travelling through the global community at this time. Some nations in Europe and, to a lesser extent, in the United States are now facing the dilemma of supporting and investing in these 'industries of the future' as engines of economic growth while responding to the public's growing unease over many facets of the industry. These nations have been riding the wave and are now on its crest, waiting to see if they are going to crash or continue riding it safely to dry land. In other parts of the world, nations are craving investment to establish domestic biotechnology industries. Countries like Argentina see biotechnology as an opportunity not only to benefit from technology transfer from other nations, but to establish their own competitive advantage based on domestic strengths such as a continued reliance on agriculture for local employment and exports.

A second example is the growing acceptance of Eastern medicine and health practices in other parts of the world. This creates consid-erable opportunity for Asian medical, biotechnology and pharmaceu-tical firms. The body of knowledge on Traditional Chinese Medicine (TCM) is greatest in China. A major component of TCM is the use of Chinese herbs. As the market for these effective treatments expands beyond China, the opportunities to capitalize on this growth also expand. Local firms will look for ways in which to isolate particular components of different plants, create synthetic versions of them, and manufacture tablets, capsules and beverages containing the key ingre-dients. Foreign firms will invest in Chinese companies and hire Chinese experts in order to tap into the knowledge base and intel-lectual assets that, until recently, remained exclusive to China. As agri-cultural science and biotechnology grow in China, the decision-makers and the Chinese people will become more exposed to the ways in which biotechnology can protect their crops from pests, increasing yields and supplying more food to a nation that struggles to feed its population. The country will increase its output of intellectual property and local business revenues will benefit from foreign sales and international licensing agreements. The perceived benefits of biotechnology and the ways in which it can alleviate many economic, social and health-related challenges will become very much apparent, as it has in many nations. The pitfalls and dangers of certain biotechno-logical activities will likely fall on deaf ears or be suitably suppressed in order for the industry to gain a foothold. These nations are feeling the swell of a wave under them and are eagerly anticipating the excitement of the ride. The possibility of drowning is never considered at this stage.

Internet disputes and WIPO's Digital Agenda

In the next chapter, we are going to explore the incredible impact the Internet has had on just about every aspect of our lives, including the way we understand and respect intellectual property. As we learnt in Chapter 3, domain names have become, in many cases, as important as trademarks for firms conducting business over the Internet. Consequently, domain names have also been targets for hackers and other criminals seeking to exploit the success of legitimate online operators. Online dispute resolutions mechanisms will grow in popularity and increase in influence as businesses and individuals seek methods to protect their online intellectual assets. More and more Internet-related disputes will be handled in this manner, replacing the costly and lengthy courtroom deliberations of the past. The Internet Corporation for Assigned Names and Numbers (ICANN), a non-profit, private-sector corporation formed in 1998, will continue to be a driving force in this area.

ICANN is involved in the 'management' of the many technical and administrative issues relating to the Internet. This is not to be mistaken for 'managing' the Internet; however, the organization wields considerable influence. It was a driving force behind the development of a Uniform Dispute Resolution Policy (UDRP), which came into existence in 1999. In fact, ICANN approved WIPO as the first dispute resolution provider under the UDRP that same year. The first case was decided in January 2000. In 1999, ICANN also formed the Intellectual Property Constituency (IPC) to address pressing intellectual property issues relating to the Internet. Current discussions and position papers can be found on the IPC Web site at http://ipc.songbird.com.

Around the same time that ICANN was putting the finishing touches on the UDRP, the WIPO International Conference on Electronic Commerce and Intellectual Property was held. In September 1999, the Director General of WIPO used the conference to launch the Organization's Digital Agenda. Comprising 10 main elements, the Digital Agenda is intended to address the present and future influences of the Internet and electronic or digital technologies on the sphere of intellectual property. The Agenda, according to WIPO's public information in the summer of 2001, included:

1. Expanding the participation of developing countries through the use of WIPONET (a global intellectual property information network developed by WIPO) and other means for access to intellectual property information; participation in global policy formulation; and opportunities to use their intellectual property assets in electronic commerce.

It has taken technologically advanced nations like the United States, the United Kingdom, Canada and Japan over a decade to become sufficiently wired to reap the benefits of the Internet. Some critics would suggest that electronic commerce is still in its infancy. This is an admirable goal and with a generous time frame, we may see it come to fruition; however, it is premature to discuss intellectual property assets in e-commerce in countries where traditional infrastructure such as highways, let alone information highways, are sadly lacking due to insufficient resources. Many of these countries could use help standing on their own two feet before they are taught to surf. While there is insufficient space in this book to go into detail, WIPO has produced a 'Primer on Electronic Commerce and Intellectual Property Issues' (WIPO, May 2000). This document is over 100 pages and can be obtained directly from WIPO. At the time of writing this book, it was listed on WIPO's Web site at http://ecommerce.wipo.int.

2. Promoting the entry into force of the WIPO Copyright Treaty (WCT) and the WIPO Performances and Phonograms Treaty (WPPT) before December 2001.

Known jointly as the Internet Treaties, the purpose of the WCT and the WPPT is to update and improve upon the protection that already exists in the area of copyright and related rights. In particular, they address areas such as digital technologies that would not have been relevant a few decades ago. They were concluded in 1996, however, which in 'cybertime' is the equivalent of a couple of decades at least. Undoubtedly, these treaties will see frequent updates and modifications over their useful lives.

3. Promoting adjustment of the international legislative framework to facilitate electronic commerce through the extension of the principles of the WPPT to audiovisual performances; the adaptation of broadcasters' rights to the digital era; and progress toward a possible international instrument on the protection of databases.

This agenda item comprises necessary housekeeping and updating elements. Necessary does not necessarily mean important, although there are certainly influential forces driving these types of changes.

4. Implement the recommendations of the Report of the WIPO Internet Domain Name Process and pursue compatibility between identifiers in the real and virtual worlds by establishing rules for mutual respect and eliminating contradictions between the domain name system and the intellectual property system.

This 150-page report that will celebrate its third birthday in April, 2002. Also known as 'Management of Internet Names and Addresses: Intellectual Property Issues', it tackles very interesting subject matter. As mentioned earlier in this book, domain names are becoming as valuable as trademarks, yet they are not viewed as intellectual property. The report looks at issues such as notoriety, famous and well-known marks, resolving international conflicts through uniform dispute resolution mechanisms and the introduction of new generic top-level domain names.

5. Developing appropriate principles with the aim of establishing, at the appropriate time at the international level, rules for determining the circumstances of intellectual property liability of Online Service Providers (OSPs), compatible within a framework of general liability rules for OSPs.

What responsibility does an OSP have for hosting material that infringes on intellectual property rights? What responsibility does the postal service have for delivering illegal material sent through the mail? This is another highly contentious area in cyberlaw. Debates will likely be fierce as decisions in this area come into force.

6. Promoting adjustment of the institutional framework for facilitating the exploitation of intellectual property in the public interest in a global economy and on a global medium through administrative coordination and where desired by users, the implementation of practical systems in respect of: the interoperability and interconnection of electronic copyright management systems and their metadata (ie the information about the copyrighted material stored in these systems); the online licensing of the digital expression of cultural heritage; and the online administration of intellectual property disputes.

If this means that WIPO is encouraging the development of a universally accessible and affordable system for accessing information on copyrights; increasing protection in the area of cultural heritage through quick and efficient licensing schemes; and encouraging dispute resolution online as a way to reduce time and expenses, I am all for it. If this item means something else, I am not certain how to explain it.

7. Introducing and developing online procedures for the filing and administration of international applications for the Patent Cooperation Treaty (PCT), the Madrid System and the Hague Agreement at the earliest possible date.

Online procedures will certainly streamline the application and filing procedures for these important agreements. Coupled with reduced costs and greater online accessibility around the globe, WIPO will have a model international system for administering international conventions.

8. Studying and, where appropriate, responding in a timely and effective manner to the need for practical measures designed to improve the management of cultural and other digital assets at the international level, by, for example, investigating the desirability and efficacy of: model procedures and forms for the global licensing of digital assets; the notarization of electronic documents; and the intro-duction of a procedure for the certification of web sites for compliance with appropriate intellectual property standards and procedures.

The wording used in this item suggests that the 'study' is a mere formality and that these initiatives are clearly desired. It will be inter-esting to follow the development of these issues, which appear both desirable and useful.

9. Studying any other emerging intellectual property issues related to electronic commerce and, where appropriate, develop norms in relation to such issues.

The catch-all clause that ensures that WIPO can manage any unforeseen intellectual property and e-commerce issues that arise in the digital world: when business is being conducted at cyberspeed, one cannot be expected to think of everything in advance.

10. Coordinating with the other international organizations in the formulation of appropriate international positions on the horizontal issues affecting intellectual property, in particular: the validity of electronic contracts; and jurisdiction.

WIPO does not act unilaterally in the creation and implementation of intellectual property policy: additionally, decisions made with respect to intellectual property have implications in other related areas. This agenda item acknowledges this reality and captures two of the many 'sub-issues' that will be affected by WIPO's Digital Agenda.

INTELLECTUAL PROPERTY ALTERNATIVES

Does the future hold an alternative to intellectual property rights when it comes to the creations of modern humankind? Of course. There are glimmers of hope all the time. Linux, the open source operating system, is a great example of how a truly commercial invention – software to rival Microsoft's Windows and other less competitive computer operating systems – can be developed and shared without the constraints of copyright protection. In fact, Linux has not even known the constraints of a corporate entity.

A gentleman by the name of Dr Richard Jefferson has drawn strength from the Linux example to forge ahead in one of the most controversial and commercially lucrative areas of science: agriculture. It is important to set the stage for Dr Jefferson's story, which was reported in the Economist.com's *Technology Quarterly* ('Grassroots innovator', 6 December, 2001). While it is often forgotten or simply lumped in with biotechnology (ag-bio being the trendy way to describe the relevant sector), the agriculture industry is a massive commercial undertaking. For those accustomed to rural areas filled with sprawling farms and fields of green corn stalks or golden wheat blowing in the wind, describing agriculture as an industry seems almost blasphemous. Yet it has become a lucrative industry under the firm grip of both biotechnology firms and more 'traditional' agricultural corporations.

As I alluded to earlier in this chapter, biotechnology has become the industry of the future for many economies and many governments have poured significant funds into programmes that support the commercialization of biotechnology research, economic development schemes designed to attract biotechnology investment and a certain amount of biotechnology research and development. Many of the firms benefiting from these programmes and incentives are working in the area of agriculture. Consequently, much of the innovation occurring in agriculture is the result of corporate science, with the clear aim of future profits. The type of research that was conducted 30 years ago – partnerships between government researchers and local experts such as farmers – receives very little funding in contrast to the money poured into projects with a primarily economic goal. As the Economist.com article accurately points out, if your business does not have making money as one of its goals, you will not be in business for long. Biotechnology businesses are very similar to pharmaceutical companies. There is a significant upfront investment in research and development, with the hope of a huge pay-off in the not too distant future. Consequently, such businesses will focus their efforts and resources on the projects that will have the greatest return on investment. These are likely to be projects that can be made commercially viable in rich markets. The benefits of ag-bio to the poorest African nations, for example, does not register high on the strategic plans of executives in leading biotechnology firms, nor does it alter the policies of the governments that pursue biotechnology as an economic growth engine. The will to sacrifice commercial gain in order to focus on helping those who currently are not in a position to help themselves is simply not strong enough yet. As the author of 'Grassrooots innovator' succinctly remarks, 'biotech firms are not charities'.

With all this background in place, let's return to the heart of the issue – intellectual property and specifically, to the way intellectual property rights are distributed between the 'haves' and the 'have nots' of our world. In this book, we have examined the ways in which intellectual property rights such as patents protect creators so that they have a fair opportunity to benefit from their innovations and creativity. Throughout this book, we also see how patent rights and other intellectual property rights can be used to exploit, monopolize and bully individuals, businesses, cultures, heritages and the natural world. Biotechnology firms and pharmaceutical companies are often accused of the last of these. For example, the 'haves', who include the wealthy businesses and research centres in technologically advanced countries in the United States, Europe and Asia, have spared no effort to secure legal rights to diverse genes, plant varieties and related 'property' for the purpose of commercializing whatever they can develop and market. The result has been a complex and confusing legal morass that actually stifles development in the field.

Dr Jefferson, founder of the Centre for the Application for Molecular Biology to International Agriculture (CAMBIA) in Canberra, Australia, is looking for ways not only to liberate research and development from the patent-crazed corporate giants in the industrialized centres, but to return agricultural innovation to the experts in the fields: growers and plant breeders in local areas. As the article states, Jefferson believes in what he refers to as 'meta-technologies' as a solution for breaking through the barriers erected by the current intellectual property regime. This is the approach that is analogous to Linux in the software world. He envisions these meta-technologies as a viable alternative to the current agri-business structure. Jefferson has used CAMBIA and his own extensive expertise and innovation as the foundation for this alternative system. Among these technologies is 'transgenomics', which uses the genetic diversity residing within a plant to alter aspects of the plant. These strains can then be crossbred with unaltered plants to examine whether any new and valuable traits appear. While this still appears to be humankind messing with nature, it sounds considerably safer than the standard biotechnology approach of combining genes from different species of plants to see what might happen. The latter approach is far more unpredictable. For example, soybeans are a fairly wholesome food; however, genetically modified soy can contain genes from the petunia. While this probably has something to do with making the soy plant more resistant to pests, the petunia is a member of the nightshade family. Nightshades are often linked to severe (and usually undiagnosed) pain in humans and other animals. Working within the genetic makeup of one plant seems less likely to result in plants that are affectionately described as 'frankenfoods'.

Dr Jefferson has plans to develop apomixes as well. Apomixis is plant reproduction without the need for pollination or the asexual transformation that occurs in plants that create new plants out of themselves. Apomixis results in the production of a seed, which is superior to asexual plant reproduction because it is not as vulnerable to plant diseases. Furthermore, it would allow for the creation of a hybrid seed that, unlike those of companies like Monsanto, could be reproduced by the plant naturally and used year after year. Farmers would no longer be in the grips of seed companies, forced to buy new hybrid seeds every year. The Economist.com article refers to a Boston Consulting Group study that determined that apomixes technology could save cassava and potato growers as much as US $3.2 billion annually. And the bonus is that Jefferson believes that every plant has the capacity for apomixes. Consequently, there is no need to introduce foreign material into existing plant species. Rather, a genetic shift within the plant may be sufficient to create the seeds in this manner.

Jefferson and like-minded colleagues in the field signed a declaration in which they vowed to keep apomixes in the public domain. The technology and methodologies were not going to become intellectual property, thereby allowing the work to be widely used without the complications of licensing agreements or other hindrances. Regardless of how you feel about biotechnology or the trends in agriculture today, it is fairly apparent that this is a step in the right direction. In terms of intellectual property as well, this appears to be a bold and timely approach to agricultural and biotechnological research. Somehow, these people are still making a living without tying the hands of other researchers or monopolizing potentially valuable discoveries. The difference may be in how one defines the word 'valuable'. Certainly, the CEO of a biotechnology company must include monetary value and profit as part of his or her definition. It appears that people like Dr Jefferson include the capacity to ease global problems with minimal restraints and maximum cooperation as part of their definition of value.

FESTO: CHALLENGING THE POWER OF PATENTS

Future alternatives to the current intellectual property regime are not limited to options outside the legal system. Sometimes monumental change can manifest from within. Legal decisions can shake the foundations upon which the power and influence of intellectual property resides. While this book was being completed, the case of Festo Corp v Shoketsu Kinzoku Kogyo Kabushiki Co, was going before the United States Supreme Court. This case has patent attorneys, businesses and other patent holders riveted to its developments and has illustrated the divisiveness in the patent community on the topic of future patent rights. The brief version of the story is that Festo USA, a New York-based manufacturing company and affiliate of the German firm Festo Corp, has been in the courts for over 13 years charging that the Japanese company named above copied Festo's patented cylinder, which is used in robotics. This sounds fairly basic and not particularly controversial; however, I am guessing that thick, rambling legal books will be written about the outcome of this case.

In November 2000, the US Court of Appeals for the Federal Circuit attempted to clarify the 'doctrine of equivalents', which was established in 1854 and allows a patent holder to enforce a patent against another party when the patent holder can provide evidence for the following:

- The 'infringing' patent or process performs substantially the same function as the 'legitimate' patent.
- The 'infringing' patent or process functions substantially in the same way as the 'legitimate' patent.

■ The function of the 'infringing' patent achieves substantially the same result as the 'legitimate' patent.

The language sets up numerous possibilities for interpretation so it is hardly surprising that the task of determining equivalents has plagued courts in the United States for years. The Festo case has become significant because the decision of the Federal Circuit Court narrowed the doctrine of equivalents in many patent scenarios. In other circumstances, it eliminated the doctrine completely. Opponents of the decision claimed that it reversed close to 150 years of patent law. Additionally, they claimed the decision would stifle future creativity and make it virtually impossible for attorneys to pursue patents and patent protection for their clients. Proponents of the decision supported the interpretation's clarity. In their opinion, it will actually promote research and creativity and discourage litigation.

Prior to the Festo case, it was common practice for patent applicants to amend their claims at different points in the patent process. For example, the language in the claim may have been unclear, or the patent examiner may have objected to certain aspects of the claim. In Festo's case, a re-examination of one of its patents by the United States Patent and Trademark Office revealed a claim for a feature that was not part of the actual patent being re-examined. The original patent was issued in 1973 and language relating to the patent description was in German – the translation to English was partially responsible for the inaccurate description. Festo made changes to the description by eliminating one claim and adding another, which the examiner allowed because it had not been previously addressed under the 'prior art' section of the application. In making the change, Festo lost its right to claim that the Japanese company's 'substantially' similar devices infringe on Festo's patent. This is just one example of the common amendments that would not be protected based on the recent interpretation. But it is the example that is rocking the intellectual property world. Opponents of the Circuit Court decision believe that anyone wishing to 'copy' the patent can now review the patent filings and prosecution history to uncover minor changes to the application and use it to modify their own product or process and easily obtain a patent. As a result, the whole process of offering protection and encouraging further research and innovation is undermined.

The implications of the US Court of Appeals' decision are staggering. Arguably, hundreds of thousands of patents – perhaps over 1 million – not only became unenforceable, their value as intellectual assets virtually disappeared. It was not surprising that the decision was appealed and Festo headed to the Supreme Court. Still, many companies were pleased with the ruling including corporate giants like Ford and IBM. The latter, as we learnt earlier in the book, is concerned with its ability to benefit from cross-licensing agreements and other lucrative extensions of its patent pool. IBM and other corporate giants will also benefit from decreased litigation and the costs associated with defending themselves against charges of infringement. The decision seems to favour those companies with substantial cash and intellectual property. Smaller companies and individuals are less excited about the prospects of change. The significance of a patent or patents for these entities is often greater with respect to the overall survival of the business. Companies are formed on the basis of the intellectual property that the founders possess. As we have discovered, intellectual assets are one of the key criteria start-ups use to attract both working capital and additional skilled employees. If the value of patents is decreased, as opponents of the Federal Circuit decision claim, the value of any companies that rely heavily on their intellectual property will also diminish. Van Dyke and Pedersen (2002) cite as an example the biotechnology industry:

> For example, a major component of corporate valuations in the biotech and pharmaceutical industries is their patent portfolio. These industries have come to rely heavily upon the doctrine of equivalents for adequate protection of their inventions. Thus, most biotech companies favor over-ruling Festo. In its amicus brief, Chiron, a biotech company that owns more than 3,000 patents, notes that 'Festo provides a road map for a would-be copyist to avoid infringement by substituting a known, interchangeable amino acid at one position in a claimed protein'. The biotech industry maintains that such interchangeability in its technology demands the doctrine of equivalents for adequate protection.

This type of support for the doctrine is also found among the academic research community. Major universities are concerned that multibillion dollar funding for their research programmes will decrease significantly as a result of a devaluation of their patentable discoveries. The doctrine of equivalents may have sufficient support at the Supreme Court level as well. In the mid-1990s, that Court ruled in favour of the doctrine of equivalents in a case known as Warner-Jenkinson. The judges will likely find it difficult to back a decision by the Federal Circuit which conflicts with their own ruling less than six years ago. In addition, foreign firms and other interested parties have criticized the interpretation, arguing that many nations have used the doctrine of equivalents, as developed by the United States, as a foundation for their own intellectual property laws. Others suggest that the decision flies in the face of international treaty mandates respecting both international trade and intellectual property. In its efforts to make a controversial issue less controversial, the Federal Circuit Court has raised the level of controversy to new heights. It will be interesting to follow the progress and, regardless of the outcome, there is no assurance that the issue will extinguish quietly and quickly. Such is the power of the patent.

QUESTIONING THE RIGHT TO INTELLECTUAL PROPERTY RIGHTS

The future may also bring about a greater focus on what may be perceived as a fringe argument: namely, that the concept of intellectual property 'rights' is both flawed and has little legitimacy. Consequently, the assumption that we are obliged to protect copyrights or patents, for example, is incorrect. On this basis, for example, developing nations would have legitimate reasons for disputing intellectual property claims originating in developed nations. Dean Baker, Co-Director of the Center for Economic and Policy Research (CEPR), discusses this view in a recent article. The CEPR is based in Washington, DC and was established to promote democratic debate on important economic and social issues. HDR 2001 refers to the *Human Development Report 2001* published by the United Nations Development Programme. Baker strongly opposes the use of the term 'rights' by policy analysts and believes that United Nations Development reports cannot approach intellectual property issues from a neutral perspective when adopting such terminology. With regard to the obligation to protect intellectual property rights, Baker (2001) states that:

> It has become standard, even for economists, to refer to copyrights, patents, trademarks and other claims to intellectual property as 'rights'. This characterization implies that these forms of property have value apart from their social purpose in promoting innovation and creativity – in the same way that the rights to freedom or expression or freedom of religion

*have value independent of any resulting economic gains.
There is no obvious basis for this contention.*

Baker draws attention to the fact that the reference to intellectual
property in the United States Constitution does not appear in the Bill
of Rights, but in the section that defines the power of Congress
(Section 8). The wording declares that Congress will have the power
to 'promote the progress of science and useful arts, by securing for
limited times to authors and inventors the exclusive right to their
respective writings and discoveries'. As Baker points out, 'In short,
the United States Constitution explicitly describes the purpose of any
intellectual property as the promotion of innovation and creativity,
not as an individual right.'

Whether you buy into this perspective or not, it adds a colourful
dimension to the intellectual property debate. It is difficult to argue that
patents, for example, are not a form of protectionism, as Baker suggests,
and as we explored earlier in this book. Yet, this is the case with other
forms of intellectual property or anything for that matter, when rights
are assigned to it. The question is, 'Does this form of protectionism
serve a higher good or is it ultimately more harmful to progress?'

FUTURE INNOVATION, HIGH STAKES AND MARKET INSTABILITY

We can ponder whether the protectionism offered by patents or other
forms of intellectual property are harmful to progress. In addition to
that question, it is critical to analyse an environment in which the
financial stakes are so high that a single innovation can destabilize an
entire market. New inventions can, and do, wipe out older creations. It
happens all the time and it is simply an element of progress; however,
there are realms in which innovation is occurring so rapidly, every new
creation or improvement threatens all that came before it. As exciting
as this may seem, it is a disturbing trend that must be corrected. It is
exacerbated by another disturbing trend: many people seem to need
the latest version of everything and automatically assume that as soon
as something new is available, it must be better, faster, more powerful,
more fashionable than all similar products that appeared earlier. They
cannot live without it. While this book exposes many of the problems
we contribute to the intellectual property dilemma we face, it is not
intended to delve into our emotional and psychological problems.

Consequently, we will focus on the potential destabilization of existing markets resulting from rapid and unanticipated innovation.

Technological innovation

The current generation has witnessed a technological revolution unparalleled in recorded history. While people still own and use radios, few families gather in the kitchen to hear the news and listen to their favourite comedy show. Today, they stretch out in the family room and watch television or a movie on their VCR. The anti-social teenager locks his or her bedroom door and surfs the Internet, downloads music and e-mails similarly anti-social teenagers. Television did not cause the extinction of the radio, but it drastically changed the popularity and importance of the radio in many households. Computers have not hurt television sales, yet. However, there is greater crossover potential for these media. Television businesses are interested in computers and computer entrepreneurs see wonderful possibilities for marrying their technologies with the television concept.

For every technology survivor, there are many others that slip into obscurity. Beta technology could not overcome the incredible marketing and promotion strategy of VHS proponents even though Beta was considered to be a superior video format. Now, videotape manufacturers are threatened by DVD technology. Prices for DVD players have reached a point that opens up a much larger market opportunity for businesses with these products. They are no longer the exclusive toys of wealthy consumers. There are a number of responses videotape-related businesses can take. They can crumble as their market share continues to erode and join vendors of eight-track tapes on the unemployment line. They can jump on the bandwagon and get involved in DVD technology by manufacturing it, selling it, or improving upon it. Or they can strike out into new territory, looking for the next big thing that will replace digital disk media because it will be replaced. Guaranteed. The point is, the technology used for VCRs and audiotapes for the last 10 years has been valuable intellectual property and the source of considerable profits for the companies and individuals holding the various technology patents. With the advent of widespread DVD use (or some other technology for watching movies), VCR-related intellectual property is not quite so valuable any more. And all peripheral businesses that cling to this technology as a source of income will experience a decline.

For centuries, people used to plant and harvest their fields using the same methods, eat the same foods, wear the same style of clothes made of the same fabrics, and live in the same style of houses built from the same materials. In 2002, a new and improved product comes out every day. Brand X clothing is trendy when only last year it was 'worn by geeks' and interestingly, sold at half the price. Technology exaggerates this rapid-fire change that we accept as normal. How much processor speed do I need to write this book on my laptop? Apparently I could have accomplished this task on a Commodore 64 that was 'state-of-the-art' in the early 1980s. Yet, I have a much more modern, fully loaded, powerful computing device full of patented components and copyright protected software. Tomorrow, however, a computer hardware company may announce a development in microchip technology that renders the products of the current monopolies in that industry obsolete. The product will be patent protected and the company will become the new industry giant through licensing agreements and direct sales to computer makers. Everyone will want its technology, yet a whole industry is rocked to its foundations because they did not expect the change. Contracts that they had secured with the former monopoly will be competitive disadvantages for businesses as they try to capitalize on the marketing potential of this new technology.

In 2001, Internet and telecommunications industries took a beating in the markets. The Canadian stock market took a huge tumble as world-leading telecom and fibre optics companies fell from their seemingly invincible positions. Some of the largest stock drops and employee lay-offs in Canadian history ensued. Similar events took place in the United States, and across Europe and Asia. Many of these companies had spent the preceding year accumulating incredible amounts of intellectual assets and intellectual property through huge mergers and acquisitions. In their efforts to capture all of the talent, innovation and potential breakthroughs that could give them an advantage, they were blinded to the fact that the market for their fibre optic technologies and networking devices had dried up. Instead of selling product, they were busy buying 'assets', which they could no longer unload. Instead, they unloaded employees and their salaries. They unloaded subsidiaries that they had just purchased. And they unloaded market value as financial analysts and shareholders punished them. In addition to all the carnage that the newspapers report, it would be fascinating to know just how many great projects were terminated as a result of this gross mismanagement. Arguably, there were a few potentially useful innovations that will never see the light of day unless some unemployed engineer can raise sufficient capital to resurrect it. Of course, he or she will need to own the intellectual property rights...

Our current approach to both business and consumption will continue to fuel this instability in many markets. Some business people thrive on this risk and love the high stakes. This is the epitome of competition, in their mind. Combined with rampant consumerism, the environment in which we work and live is nothing short of volatile. It is not surprising that stress-related diseases are the greatest killers in the industrialized world. Such an environment will contribute to the volatility of intellectual property as well. This may be the reason that so many businesses are willing to exploit natural and cultural resources, people, and inadequately tested scientific discoveries. They want to make a quick profit from their intellectual property before the business environment changes again. This short-sightedness will ultimately be their downfall.

CHOOSING OUR DESTINY

While it is not my nature to dwell on the negative, it would appear that a catastrophe of epic proportions – a global war or a planetary-wide natural disaster – would be required to halt or decrease international trade. Its unrelenting growth is not likely to be contained through sudden changes of heart among influential leaders of economically wealthy nations. The pull of the material gain is simply too compelling and it has become an expectation for the people who back these leaders. Fair enough. Let international trade continue to grow and let us find a way to make it more equitable. And, if we are prepared to acknowledge that increased international trade will continue to involve valuable intellectual assets of individuals and businesses from around the world, we ought to be prepared to afford these people some claim to their ideas, including the ability to profit financially from them. If we wish to categorize these as 'rights' and call some of them 'intellectual property', perhaps we should ensure that the categories are universally accepted and based on criteria other than the desires of the powerful stakeholders.

Returning to the initial concept of trade, if we recognize that international commercial transactions and global trade will continue to be targeted by criminals seeking a quick buck at the expense of others, we must accept that some kind of order or code of conduct needs be established. We have opted for laws: national laws, regional laws and international laws. We have opted for treaties and conventions and agreements among nations because the human race cannot agree upon a single ethical approach to concepts such as theft, fairness, harm, welfare, progress, right and wrong, to name a few. But laws have their limitations as we have seen in other chapters in this book and in the news reports we hear every day. In the world of intellectual property rights, for example, some of the criminal activity is state sponsored, or flourishes as a result of regulatory neglect. Although continued work in the area of international agreements, increased incentives to join international trade organizations, and more effective enforcement measures at an international level may help alleviate some of the criminal activity, it is unlikely to filter through the whole system to heal the root of such a problem. The law is limited when we speak of rights. For now, however, it is our tool of choice.

It is possible that the implementation of a world court with international legal authority to hear alleged abuses of intellectual property rights would have greater success than the current dispute resolution mechanisms offered by the WTO and national justice systems. However, the likelihood of a true world court being established is slim, considering the threat it would pose to the autonomy that nations currently believe they enjoy. With such divisiveness among people and countries, worldwide solutions to intellectual property issues are a distant hope. Likewise, there seems to be little threat of George Orwell's *1984* on the horizon. We still possess an abundance of freedoms, including the freedom to think and create. In some parts of the world this is more apparent than others, but the trend is encouraging. Slowly, almost imperceptibly, we are functioning more like a global community as opposed to warring factions that can only prosper at the expense of others. Once we figure out that we can all prosper, intellectual property issues and everything else for that matter will fall into place.

INTERNET RULES: INTELLECTUAL PROPERTY AT CYBERSPEED

The choice between an Internet without copyrights or copyrights without the Internet is a false choice.

David Boies, Napster Attorney

While I will try to write the remainder of this chapter without any further reference to Napster, the words of David Boies are intriguing. Indeed, many arguments regarding piracy and the Internet seem to fall into the 'all or nothing' category. There is the Wild West approach that suggests the Internet is beyond the reach of law, order and control and that is its strength. In contrast, there are those who will not rest until the Internet is entirely regulated – and regulated in a manner of their liking. Boies simply reminds everyone that there are always alternatives, even in the complex environment of digital media and the Internet.

The global appeal of the Internet continues to increase. This is not surprising considering how pervasive the World Wide Web has become. According to the ITU World Telecommunication Indicators Database, it took a mere four years for the Web to reach 50 million users. In contrast, the telephone took 74 years, radio took 38 years, personal computers and television took 16 and 13 years respectively. A report by TeleGeography Inc reported that, while the United States continues to dominate this information and communication medium in terms of overall users, the rest of the world is gaining ground. In the late 1990s, Internet use in the United States was growing at an annual rate of 30 per cent. In 2001, growth in Canada and the United States slowed to 16 per cent and 15 per cent respectively. Another company researching the subject, Emarketer, predicted that by the end of 2001, 108 million residents in Europe will be active Internet users. This is an increase of 50 per cent from 2000. The Asia-Pacific region is growing more quickly, with 143 million users in 2001. This figure is double the number of users from 2001. Half of the 4.6 million Internet users in Africa are located in South Africa, as much of the continent is limited in terms of the financial resources and infrastructure needed for most necessities, let alone Internet development. In the Middle East, 4.2 million Internet users surf the Internet in 2001, compared to 1.9 million in 2000. It is therefore no surprise that the primary language of users is also shifting away from English. An estimated 45 per cent of users in 2001 claim English as their first language – a 6 per cent decrease from 2000. Japanese and Chinese language users are the second and third largest groups. Jupiter Research forecasts that, by 2005, the Asia-Pacific will comprise one third of Internet users, surpassing the number of US users.

In terms of business, the value of global electronic commerce has been estimated by the Organization for Economic Co-operation and Development (OECD) at US $330 billion for 2001–2002 and is predicted to reach US $2 or 3 trillion by 2005 at the latest, according to Forrester Research. Where there is commerce, there is intellectual property. And where there is intellectual property, there is the potential for theft and a need for protection.

There are countless Internet issues relating to intellectual property and we could fill volumes on this subject alone. In this chapter, we will focus primarily on criminal activity loosely defined as piracy, as well as a law in the United States that, at the time of writing this book, is setting a disturbing precedent for regulating and enforcing activities related to the digital world. An examination of these two issues will undoubtedly bring up a number of other concerns, questions and frustrations. With some luck, we will shed additional light on these issues and realize that the answers can be found beyond what Boies defines as the 'false choice'. There is a saying – 'If you always do what you have always done, you will always get what you have always got' – and although I have no idea of its origin, I consider it relevant for most things, save intellectual property protection and the Internet. The Internet has revolutionized business and the result has been new models and methods for improving customer management, information management, supply chain management, inventory control, and numerous other aspects of running a business. The face of the global economy has been completely changed. Communication has been revolutionized by the Internet, providing vast stores of information to huge populations of people at a rate that is difficult to comprehend. Peripheral technologies, which have roots in some Internet-related task, have blossomed to serve a multitude of uses beyond the Web. These spheres – economic, communications, technology – and many more did not fight the Internet; rather, they were swept up in its irresistible potential. Law, in contrast, is never swept up in the irresistible potential of anything. Law fears the irresistible potential and seeks to control it. And, by always doing what it has always done (in this case, attempting to control and regulate the Internet using traditional legal means), it is not getting what it always got in the past. The Internet by nature demands new approaches to what are essentially age-old problems. They just happen to be problems exacerbated by a freedom of information the magnitude of which has never been encountered in what we commonly refer to as recorded history.

The Internet cannot be a free for all and it appears that most people accept this reality without reservation. Generally speaking, most of the world seems to like life to be orderly and predictable. There is nothing wrong with that and there is nothing wrong with applying law to cyberspace. In fact, it is necessary and desirable, for the same reasons that we accept law in other spheres of our life. If human beings functioned entirely from an awareness of universal goodness and compassion then quite possibly the concept of human-made law would be rendered useless. There are those who would argue that human function in this manner at any time in history is nonsense. To these critics, humanity has always required intervention by itself to protect itself from itself. This describes virtually all the societies inhabiting the earth and it certainly describes the heavily regulated and legally protected modern societies of the Western World. In short, we cannot be trusted to do the right thing or the honest thing or the loving, caring, respectful and peaceful thing. For all its greatness, the Internet also makes it easier for us to be untrustworthy. Laws or not, only we can change that.

INTERNET PIRACY

According to a survey conducted by the Software and Information Industry Association (SIIA) and KPMG LLP, software piracy on the Internet is a booming business and a significant problem. The SIIA is a trade association that represents the software and digital content industry and provides government relations, business development and intellectual property protection services to over 800 software and information companies. The survey, released in November 2001 and available at the time of this book's publication on the SIIA Web site (www.siia.net), was conducted to gather data regarding the acquisition and use of software and digital content via the Internet. Analysis of the data revealed that nearly 30 per cent of the 1,004 business people surveyed could be, in the words of the SIIA and KPMG, 'classified as pirating software through a variety of electronic methods'. The survey also revealed that over half of the respondents were unaware of any corporate policies in place governing intellectual property. Of the respondents 54 per cent indicated that they did not know whether distributing information from online sites (such as subscriber services) was permissible and 23 per cent stated their belief that such distribution was permitted. As Barbara Carbone, National Industry Director for KPMG LLP's Software and Services Practice, states in her comments on the survey, 'The business community needs to do a better job of educating its employees about Internet use, or risk fines, lawsuits or other incidents that can arise from conducting business in a digital workplace.'

Clearly, the Internet is not all fun and games. It is not even that idyllic, untamed communication wonder that we so often dreamt it would be. It is serious business and it gets more serious – and more complex – every day. The Internet is the largest receptacle of ideas in the world, and these ideas are continually tapped into, borrowed, or blatantly stolen by others without a second thought. Complete books have been copied on to the Internet for the use of all, without any compensation to the author or publisher of the original work. Software is downloaded, copied and distributed among friends or co-workers without a thought given to the investment of time and money made by the developer. And, as the survey mentioned above indicates, the redistribution of subscription business content (paid databases, for example) is a frequent activity.

All told, this illegal activity results in billions of dollars of lost revenues for thousands of businesses and individuals. Remember, we are only discussing Internet-related piracy in this chapter. If you include non-Internet-related theft of intellectual property, the numbers are mind-boggling. For this very reason, there is no shortage of work for lawyers – corporate lawyers, government lawyers, association lawyers and others – in finding ways to protect their clients or track down and persecute offenders. As the SIIA so succinctly describes the situation on its Web site, piracy not only stifles commercial and academic creativity, the expense and time involved in pursuing legal action is also a significant burden. Many companies already struggle with the costs associated with conducting business. Expensive litigation to protect their own creations and ideas can drain needed funds from additional research, product development or other operational costs.

Determining the best way to protect intellectual property in cyber-space is a thankless job. The likelihood of pleasing anyone, let alone the majority of the stakeholders, is slim because there are few clearly defined issues. For example, the majority of people can agree that it is a crime to rob a bank. However, is it wrong to develop a software program that exposes the limitations of another product? Is it wrong to sell the software program? Is it a criminal offence? Consider the case of Dmitry Sklyarov, a Russian cryptanalyst jailed in the United States when he arrived to discuss his work at the DEF CON computer security convention in Las Vegas in July 2001. He was arrested at the request of Adobe, the software company he embarrassed by 'breaking the code' that Adobe had offered as an encryption tool for electronic books (e-books). Adobe's encryption in one particular e-book reader was based on a well-known and apparently simple code called rot13, which substitutes each letter with the letter that follows 13 places after it in the alphabet. Adding insult to Adobe's injury, the company that employed Sklyarov sold his decryption program over the Internet. Sklyarov was arrested for distributing software that breaks the simplistic codes used in some cryptography software.

Critics of Sklyarov portray him as a hacker exploiting technology and encouraging lawlessness on the Web. To many others, however, he simply exposed inferior products that actually increased the possibility that both writers and publishers of books would be victimized by unauthorized duplications of their copyrighted works. Although Adobe later regretted its approach to the situation and requested the release of Sklyarov, the wheels of justice had already rolled too far. Bruce Perens, co-founder of the open source initiative and a leading

Linux developer, summed up the situation wonderfully in an article (title unknown) for ZDNet (2 August, 2001). He states, 'It's ironic that a Russian had to come to the US to be arrested for what are essentially thought crimes: allowing people access to books, and exercising his free-speech right by blowing the whistle on inferior products.' The law under which Sklyarov was arrested was introduced to protect copyright owners who feared the loss of their intellectual property in the Internet age. This law is called the Digital Millennium Copyright Act.

THE DIGITAL MILLENNIUM COPYRIGHT ACT

One of the most contentious pieces of intellectual property legislation ever passed by the United States, the Digital Millennium Copyright Act (DMCA), has spawned a small industry of protesters and there is at least one anti-DMCA Web site that is quite organized and professional. The Act, which was passed in October 1998, was intended to implement the treaties signed by the United States at the WIPO's Geneva conference in 1996. The DMCA goes beyond the minimum standards typically outlined in WIPO treaties and this is partially responsible for the backlash from many groups, including scientists and academics. According to the UCLA Online Institute for Cyberspace Law and Policy, an excellent online resource for information on law and policies affecting the Internet, the Act:

■ Makes it an offence to circumvent anti-piracy measures built into most commercial software.
■ Outlaws the manufacture, sale or distribution of code-cracking devices used to illegally copy software.
■ Permits the cracking of copyright protection devices in order to conduct encryption research, assess product interoperability and test computer security systems.
■ Provides exemptions from anti-circumvention provisions for non-profit libraries, archives and educational institutions under certain circumstances.
■ In general, limits Internet service providers (ISPs) from copyright infringement liability for simply transmitting information over the Internet. Service providers, however, are expected to remove material from users' Web sites that appears to constitute copyright infringement.

- Limits liability of non-profit institutions of higher education – when they serve as online service providers and under certain circumstances – for copyright infringement by faculty members or graduate students.
- Requires that 'webcasters' pay licensing fees to record companies;
- Requires that the Register of Copyrights, after consultation with relevant parties, submit to Congress recommendations regarding how to promote distance education through digital technologies while 'maintaining an appropriate balance between the rights of copyright owners and the needs of users'.
- States explicitly that 'nothing in this section shall affect rights, remedies, limitations or defenses to copyright infringement, including fair use'.

This appears to be fairly reasonable if not admirable. Yet the interpretations of the law have raised questions that go to the very heart of the United States, such as freedom of speech. Entire professional communities and associations have criticized its very existence.

So who is backing the DCMA? Some of the biggest industries in the United States and their lawyers for a start. For quite some time, Hollywood, the film industry in general, and the music industry have feared the Internet and its open, information-sharing environment. Not surprisingly, the opponents of the DCMA often regard the legislation as a custom-made legal hammer for these powerful industry groups. Mark Cuban, Internet visionary, co-founder of Broadcast.com and current owner of the National Basketball Association's Dallas Mavericks, posted interesting comments to an Industry Canada Web site. The government was trying to capture public opinion to proposed changes to Canada's Copyright Act (as reported in *eBusiness Journal*, November 2001). Cuban stated that, 'One only has to look at the results of the DMCA in the US to see that the primary result has been litigation. Lots and lots of litigation against those companies who are the most progressive and innovative filed by those who stand to gain the most from the status quo.'

This is not a new phenomenon. Over a decade ago, many 'Internet experts' were predicting that the information highway would be the fast track to widespread illegal trade and, therefore, a significant menace to capitalist-centric societies. Rather than crushing corporate society as we know it, the Internet has given birth to a number of different business models. Most 'traditional' businesses tried on one of these models to take advantage of the benefits of the Internet. Many were eager, others tentative; however, most learnt to live with the

Internet even if they did not love it. Others chose to fight the Web and its open environment, seeing it as a threat to their established way of making money. Hollywood and the music industry are prime examples. The sheer popularity of their products – films, videos, CDs and tapes, for example – make them prime targets for unscrupulous online distribution systems. In an article by K K Campbell in *Backbone Magazine* (November 2001), the author points out that lawyers, rather than market forces, were responsible for shutting down offending cyber services like Napster. Mark Cuban echoes this sentiment. He believes that laws such as the DMCA has and will continue to kill all Internet media. And, as long as organizations like the Recording Industry Association of America (RIAA) wield considerable power, there will not likely be a quick resurrection. The RIAA is a trade group that represents the US recording industry. It works to protect its stakeholders' (primarily US recording artists) intellectual property rights worldwide, as well as the First Amendment rights of artists. Yet, according to Cuban, 'There is a reason why almost the entire Internet radio and video industries have died. The DMCA is a death ray controlled by the RIAA and they are using it indiscriminately to kill off anyone who could potentially confuse the music industry. They are not even doing things that are in their own best interest. They care most about control.' In his comments to Industry Canada, Cuban points out that it is associations representing large copyright holders rather than individuals that have complained about lost music sales. Yet, music sales were growing prior to the passing of the DMCA, while they have declined since its enactment.

Cuban shares a story of frustration from his days at Broadcast.com, regarding a negotiation with the RIAA of a price for a compulsory licence in 1999. He started Broadcast.com in 1995, quickly creating one of the Internet's leading audio and video destinations, which was acquired by Yahoo! in August 1999. Compulsory licences are also known as statutory licences and can be granted to third parties by copyright holders when certain conditions are met. These conditions are set out by law, as is the fee, or statutory rate that is paid for the licence. According to the RIAA, the most common use covered by statutory licences is non-interactive webcasting or Internet radio. The RIAA considers this licensing system to be fair and efficient since it does not require the third party using the recording to approach each copyright owner for a licence.

According to Cuban, the RIAA wanted to charge Broadcast.com 0.5 cents per song. Cuban calculated that, at 12 songs per hour, he would be charged six cents per hour per user, which did not seem like much until one considers that Internet advertising is sold on the basis of 'cost per thousand' users or impressions. Cuban again calculated that one thousand users listening for an average of one hour would amount to a 'cost per thousand' of US $60. The going Internet rate at the time was US $20. 'The RIAA told me that they were just trying to be fair', said Cuban, 'and that if the market changed, they would change their pricing, which of course was nonsense. Today the market for advertising is dead and I have yet to see the RIAA attempt to change their pricing.' Cuban adds that this approach, coupled with the fact that music broadcasters are still responsible for royalties dating back three years, creates a no-win situation for these types of businesses. 'I said it during the discussions I was involved in back in 1998. If the DMCA survives longer than its predecessor, the DCA (which was two years), the industry will be dead. And it died this year [2001].'

Cuban looks beyond the existing businesses to the future of broadband and multimedia and he believes the scenario is not bright as long as the DMCA is enforced. Says Cuban, 'It [the DMCA] has killed development, investment and creativity because there are no rewards and the prospects of the RIAA suing you is the ultimate sledgehammer that no entrepreneur or investor wants to face.' As a result, he believes that the growth of both multimedia and broadband, which needs multimedia as a primary application, has been destroyed in the United States. Ultimately, the creativity that remains in this field may find homes in other countries that present fewer constraints for investors and entrepreneurs. Whether such an environment will continue to exist in Canada, for example, or European or Asian nations remains to be seen.

The movie industry has been slightly more buffered from the perceived threats of the Internet and digital media, although video-sharing sites are up and running. As K K Campbell illustrates, the large movie studios do have some advantages over the music industry because of the nature of their product. Movie piracy is not particularly lucrative when the movies are not new. The delayed release strategy that movie studios use for videos and their Web sites makes movies less attractive to potential pirates. Additionally, the massive files sizes of movies still require 20 to 40 minutes to download, even with high-speed Internet connections. Most people can get to the local video store and back in that time. And movie files can incorporate programs that erase the file within a set period of time, although these may simply challenge hackers. As Campbell points out, 'if it can be digitized, it can be pirated'.

Cuban has entered the HDTV business but he has not escaped the powerful influence of the entertainment industries. He does not believe that their approach to protecting their interests is protecting them at all. Rather, it is a reflection of their inability to cope with new technology and use it to their advantage. He feels the public at large are honest, so the issue of protection does not stem from the potential threat of theft but the technological ignorance of these industries. With regard to his HDTV business, Cuban states, 'The movie industry has so intimidated the consumer electronics industry, the only way to get a viable VCR for HDTV is to go on eBay because every manufacturer of DVHS (VHS for HDTV) has stopped production of their units. It is ridiculous. All this to give the movie industry the feeling of being powerful... it has zero business protection for them at all.'

A fair examination of the DMCA would not be complete without an impartial legal perspective. William Fisher, Professor of Law at Harvard University sheds some light on the law from that perspective. He told me that, 'the aspiration of the DMCA was to stop piracy or what is characterized as piracy through the clarification of copyright law and through legal reinforcement of encryption of their copy protection technology. That was its goal and it has surely been unsuccessful in that regard. Piracy of the sort that the DMCA was aimed at continues to flourish – just one example is the use of the Internet for peer-to-peer copying of music. It is now at an all-time high, higher than the peak usage of the Napster system. Over three billion songs are copied each month now.' Fisher adds that a large proportion of that traffic is in the United States, home of the DMCA. Fisher has observed that the negative side effects of the DMCA are revealing themselves in freedom of speech issues, as well as academic research or creativity. He uses the example of the Felten case to illustrate the problems with the DMCA.

FELTEN, COPYRIGHTS AND FREEDOM OF SPEECH

In the autumn of 2000, the Secure Digital Music Initiative (SDMI) ran a contest inviting participants to hack six different digital watermarking techniques that had been developed by different software companies. They asked participants to adhere to specific rules regarding what they could do and what they could say after the competition was concluded. Professor Edward Felten's Princeton University team, which also included researchers from Rice University and Xerox's Palo Alto Research Center (PARC), managed to crack four of the six techniques in the contest. According to the Princeton team, however, they did not officially enter the contest and, consequently, did not agree to the contest rules. They simply ran a parallel experiment.

In April 2001, it became apparent that the SDMI was not pleased with the success of Felton's team and even less pleased with its plans to present its findings at a workshop on digital security. The team members received correspondence from lawyers representing the SDMI indicating that public disclosure of the findings could contravene the DMCA because it fell outside of the parameters set up by the SDMI for the hacker contest. All of this became public knowledge very quickly. The legal 'threat' was posted online and a Princeton computer science Web page was set up to follow the progress of the issue. The updates are brief and illustrate some of the progress that took place over the course of the year – 26 April, 2001: 'We have decided not to proceed with our planned presentation at the Pittsburgh conference.' May 3, 2001: 'The RIAA and the SDMI now say that they never intended to sue us, and that they never even threatened us in the first place. This letter sure looked like a threat to us. Verance has not rescinded their threat to sue if we publish.' Verance is one of the companies that developed watermark technology that the Princeton team broke. June 6, 2001: 'Today we filed a lawsuit asking a federal court to rule that the publication of our paper would be legal.' And, at the time of writing this section of the book, 15 August, 2001: 'Today we published our paper at the Usenix Security Conference. This was done with the permission of RIAA, SDMI, and Verance. Our lawsuit continues, because they continue to insist on veto power over our ongoing work and future publications.'

The recurring references to Verance Corp are significant because its technology was already in commercial use and the view from its legal advisors was that the disclosure of information regarding this technology would not only jeopardize the technology itself, but the content it was intended to protect. There is also an interesting aside to this story, and one that brings the realm of intellectual property and the usefulness of competitive intelligence together. This use of competitive intelligence techniques was noted in an article by Steven Bonisteel of Newsbytes (2001). Bonisteel wrote that:

> *Challenge participants were not told which vendors created the six data-protection technologies. But the Princeton team noted in their paper that a search of the public US patents database helped confirm their progress on one of the tests. The team said it found a patent for a complex data-hiding*

scheme that seemed to describe what they were seeing in one of the digital audio samples. That patent was filed by Aris Technologies Inc, which became Verance when it merged with Solana Technology Development Corp. While the patent document didn't reveal a lot about the watermark, the team said it helped them zero in on the pattern with which a digital fingerprint was embedded in the audio data.

The view of the technology companies is fairly apparent. They have put a great deal of time and effort into research and development and now they need to go back to the drawing board. In the case of at least one company, there are commercial implications relating to the sale of a product that has been shown to be 'hackable' and perhaps not living up to specific claims made to customers. The digital security industry as a whole, or at least that portion of it represented by the SDMI, is trying to prevent widespread knowledge of means by which these digital watermarking technologies can be bypassed, and suppression seems to be its tool of choice. This industry, as well as the entertainment industry, perceives a genuine threat to copyright as a result of these issues.

If the issues relating to intellectual property rights were not sufficiently complex and controversial, there is another side of this story. And that side of the story extends beyond intellectual property law and encompasses, in some views, First Amendment rights. Professor Felten and his team have asked the courts to indicate that any discussion and/or publication of their work and research is a First Amendment right. Consequently, they are legally entitled to communicate their findings even if it exposes weaknesses in techniques used to secure copyright protected digital media. The DMCA, as we have learnt, makes it a crime to provide technology and information that can be used to access material that is protected by copyright. Fisher believes using the specific section of the DMCA that is in question to prevent the Princeton team from publishing their document would plainly curtail traditional First Amendment freedoms.

In his article, Bonisteel quotes opinion from the Princeton team's Web site. They refer to the criminalization of research masquerading as copyright protection. These views are worth repeating:

The main problem with the DMCA is that it hinders this analysis, restricting it in order to provide an extra layer of legal protection for existing copyright systems. But this causes the scientific process to stagnate. Imagine a federal

*law making it illegal for anyone (including Consumer
Reports) to purposefully cause an automobile collision.
While this may be a well-intentioned attempt to stop road-
rage, it also bans automobile crash testing, ultimately
leading to unsafe vehicles and the inability to learn how to
make vehicles safe in general. The situation with the DMCA
is analogous.*

In addition to the greater issue of legal constraints against research
and development, the Felten case was complicated by the contest
agreement. The agreement stated that participants were prohibited
from attacking content protected by the SDMI outside of the contest.
According to Felten, however, his team did not sign the agreement,
which was Web based. Consequently, the contest rules were not
applicable to his team. By late October 2001, the US Department of
Justice and the powerful recording industry were looking to dismiss
the copyright law dispute but for entirely different reasons. The
Justice Department's request claimed that the DMCA does not
preclude scientists from research efforts and publication in the realm
of digital media protection. The recording industry, on the other
hand, sought dismissal on the basis of withdrawing their legal
threats against the scientific papers that Felten and his team had
already written. Backed by the Electronic Frontier Foundation (EFF),
a leading civil liberties organization that works to protect rights in
the digital world, the dispute has been pushed forward in order to
gain some clarity regarding the law and the stance that will be taken
by the government. The EFF would not settle for a statement by the
Justice Department because it is not legally binding. It has not been
formalized by any court ruling or endorsed by the recording
industry. Interpretations of the DMCA by the pro-industry camp
also suggest that future research could be reviewed and censored on
a case-by-case basis. In response to this uncertainty, EFF Legal
Director, Cindy Cohn, stated, 'Since the government and industry
cannot agree on what the DMCA means, it is not surprising that
scientists and researchers are confused and decide not to publish
research for fear of prosecution under the DMCA. Regardless of
specific government or industry threats in the past, scientists should
not have to experience the ongoing chilling effects of this vague
digital copyright law.'

At the time of writing this book, the Felten saga continues. Clearly,
the Internet has added a complex dimension to traditional intellectual
property law-making and enforcement processes. The DMCA, if

nothing else, is symbolic of the overwhelming challenges facing lawmakers when they tackle the digital world. Coupled with the powerful influences of the various sectors of the entertainment industry and the 'anything goes' attitude that comprises a huge portion of the cyberworld's unwritten constitution, the issue of Internet rules will only grow in magnitude in the next few years. Arguably, it will become the main focus of intellectual property law in the wired world.

PROTECTING PROPERTY ON THE NET

So, how does intellectual property protection keep up with the Internet? Can it move at cyberspeed? According to Mark Cuban, it does not need to. 'Software has done okay without draconian protection methods', says Cuban. 'When they find someone who violates their licence, the SPA (Software Protection Association) goes after them, which is exactly what should happen.' The SPA is now part of the SIIA.

While other Internet entrepreneurs may have vastly different experiences, Cuban did not find intellectual property protection vital to the success of Broadcast.com. He was in a competitive business and he was prepared to do what was necessary to succeed, understanding that if he did something well, his efforts would likely be copied. The nature of Broadcast.com was such that it was more of a 'great idea at the right time' using existing products and technology to create a service. It did not create new technology or the type of brilliant invention that requires patent protection, for example. It was simply a matter of getting the system up and running and competing like everyone else. Cuban adds, 'Patenting the fact that we turned on servers with our left hands like some of these companies were trying only serves to saturate the government with nonsense.' This jab is directed at companies like Amazon.com and others that took advantage of the technological inexperience of patent examiners to obtain 'business method patents' for simplistic methods of using computer and Internet technology. In doing so, these firms effectively tied the hands of competing firms and other businesses that had been using, or certainly would have been using, such common-sense techniques. For example, Amazon.com was able to prevent Barnes and Noble, its main competitor, from implementing a book-buying system based on Amazon's patented 'one click technology'. This illustrates another challenge that the current intellectual property regime faces in its attempts to encompass the digital realm.

If piracy on the Internet is such a big problem, what can be done to prevent it without introducing more laws? The answers may eventually be found in new technology. Digital rights management (DRM) is a growing business projected to reach sales of US $300 billion by 2004. DRM technology is designed to support companies releasing copyrighted digital technology for profit while at the same time minimizing the likelihood of piracy. The simplistic explanation of DRM sounds like this: a copyrighted product is purchased and downloaded. The file is scrambled but comes with a key that is unique to the user and the computer on which the file is downloaded. It cannot be sold to another user or transferred to another computer without being discovered. The key often determines how long the user may retain the file for viewing or in the case of an audio file, how many times the user can listen to the recording. Growth in this industry will certainly lead to innovation and improvements. Keeping one step ahead of the hackers is a full-time job.

Digital watermarking, the technology that Felten and his team tackled, continues to be used to enforce copyright law on the Internet. This method embeds data, such as a numeric code, into the image, signal or file to be protected. In theory, it cannot be removed when a file is decrypted and acts as 'cyber fingerprint' – a telltale sign that the property has been stolen. Companies specializing in this technology often develop the watermarking capability as well as the tracking software used to uncover the unauthorized user. As we have discovered, work to develop such technologies must be encouraged and refined and one of the best ways to do so is by making the technology available for testing. It is in the best interest of these digital security firms to have their products and services rigorously tested and fine-tuned in order to best serve their potential clients. Drawing on the resources available – those who might otherwise expose flaws under conditions outside of the company's control – would appear to be a beneficial solution to all parties involved.

For all the entertainment, education and commercial benefit it can provide, we often forget the potential dangers of the Internet. In her September 2000 statement at the Symposium of the Americas regarding intellectual property protection, US Attorney General Janet Reno remarked that, 'I've seen the challenges posed by the darker side of the Information Age: how computers can be used as a tool for far more serious crimes, how someone half a world away can bring to a halt the vast computer operations of a government, a business, or a school, or can steal from a bank, making a gun an obsolete weapon.' In that same speech, Reno emphasized the growing involvement of organized crime in the manufacture and distribution of counterfeit and pirated goods and how this not only has a negative impact on consumers and businesses but how it can also can fund other illegal activities and promote corruption of government officials.

Reno supports efforts made by the European Commission to increase enforcement efforts, rather than looking to implement a greater number of laws. While she alludes to the need for greater cooperation among international law enforcement agencies she does not pretend that this will be easy. Domestically, it is a challenge and as she points out, 'responsibility for enforcing intellectual property laws is often fragmented, with a mixture of civil, administrative, and criminal penalties enforced by as many as 8 or 10 government departments.' Extend this into the international arena and you have some idea how challenging enforcement can be. The protection issue is greater than laws and enforcement however. A third important element is education.

The SIIA/KPMG study discussed earlier in this chapter could not adequately capture what may be a critical factor in the fight against piracy. I would call it the 'ignorance factor', and although it is inexcusable, particularly among business professionals, academics and students, it cannot be overlooked. Education on intellectual property laws is vital in order to decrease the damage caused by Internet piracy and related cybercrimes. It is discouraging to admit that highly trained and educated adults in our modern world also need a lesson in ethical behaviour but it is a sad truth. Of course, there will be mistakes. For example, I cannot wholly guarantee that everything that is not cited in this book is my original thought, idea or phrase. That would be impossible. Anyone could make a case that I have used their material. It is a question of intent and such questions are much easier to respond to from a point of understanding. We can make laws that are suitable to the Internet and we can gather and coordinate the necessary resources to effectively enforce the laws. But let us also educate those who wish to inhabit cyberspace about property rights, just as we educate our children about trespassing on the private property in our neighbourhoods, or stealing toys that belong to other children, or cheating in exams. Once we get the 'law-abiding' citizens on side, maybe the task of catching the criminals will not seem so daunting.

INTELLECTUAL PROPERTY RESOURCES ON THE WEB

We have examined a few of the serious issues that the Internet poses when it comes to intellectual property protection. Yet, it is important to remember how valuable the Internet is with regard to intellectual property information. There is only so much ground you can cover in one book on intellectual property. The good news is that there is always more information. If nothing else, the subject of intellectual property is dynamic and there is no indication that it will disappear, slow down, or lose its significance in the global economy. If you wish to keep abreast of developments in this area, I recommend you get online. The Internet is a double-edged sword when it comes to intellectual property information, as it is with any topic. Where do I start? How do I know this is accurate and verifiable? How can I narrow down my search to target what I am looking for? My co-author and I answered these questions in our previous book (Cook and Cook, 2000). Information gathering is an art. It takes practice and discipline to avoid wasting time and gathering a great deal of useless data. However, the Internet is by far the greatest inorganic information tool in history. Listed below are some sites that might prove useful in furthering your understanding of intellectual property in our world – the laws, the issues, the challenges and the potential solutions. They are in no particular order and mention of them in this book should not be confused with an endorsement. This list is far from comprehensive and undoubtedly some very good resources will have been overlooked.

While some of these sites are affiliated with specific organizations or businesses (law firms, for example), they all share a common trait: they provide a great deal of information and are good points of departure for further inquiry. I have intentionally avoided most academic sites for no reason other than sheer volume. But I urge you to conduct Internet searches on the Web sites of universities and other educational institutions for their valuable contributions to the field of intellectual property.

www.intelproplaw.com: the 'World-Wide Intellectual Property Links' at this site cover a wide array of related sites, including some national government offices, specific links to patents, copyrights, trade secrets and plant breeders' rights. There are links to international institutions and treaties, law associations and even careers in intellectual property law.

www.law.com: a law mega site with a comprehensive section on intellectual property. This site includes both free information and services for paying members. There is a section of timely and informative articles from other information sources, written by experts and covering current intellectual property cases, decisions and issues.

www.nsulaw.nova.edu/library/ushouse/105.htm: the Shepard Broad Law Center of the Nova Southeastern University provides this extensive collection of links covering both the United States and international Web sites.

www.apic.jiii.or.jp/: the Asia-Pacific Industrial Property Center (APIC) is a Japanese-based, government-supported organization that assists developing countries in the Asia-Pacific region with intellectual property education and training.

www.gseis.ucla.edu/iclp/hp.html: the Web site of the UCLA Online Institute for Cyberspace Law and Policy. The name says it all, as this site is dedicated to the ever-growing field of law that deals specifically with the Internet. We have seen that many of the legal issues in cyberspace are directly related to intellectual property and this site delves deeply into copyright cases, hacking charges and digital media protection challenges.

www.findlaw.com: a good general law Web site with a fair bit of intellectual property information. The main site is heavily focused on the United States; however, it does have a link to international resources divided by country.

www.corporateintelligence.com: the Web site of the IP Group of Information Holdings Inc, a company that offers paid services relating to intellectual property. While it targets corporations and law firms with these services, it also has an excellent selection of articles on diverse topics relating to intellectual property – accessible to anyone who visits the site.

www.ifla.org: the Web site of the International Federation of Library Associations and Institutions (IFLA). It includes a section on copyright and other forms of intellectual property complete with links to related articles from diverse sources. Currently these articles are found under the bibliography section.

www.arl.cni.org: the Association of Research Libraries (ARL) Web site also includes a copyright and intellectual property section. Similar to IFLA above, there a numerous links to articles on topics ranging from licensing issues, contracts between writers and e-book publishers and lawful uses of copyrighted works.

www.nea.org: this site is maintained by the National Education Association (United States) and provides users with a section of intellectual property resources from diverse sources. As is the case with the other sites focused on education and designed primarily for educators, much of the intellectual property information pertains to copyright issues.

www.ipmenu.com: this site is affiliated with Australian and New Zealand Patent and Trademark Attorneys Phillips, Ormonde and Fitzpatrick. They bill it as 'a global guide to intellectual property resources on the Internet' and they offer a credible attempt to back up this claim. The site also includes a section for the latest intellectual property news from around the world. There is no shortage of global intellectual property information on this well-organized site.

www.globaltechnoscan.com: primarily a science and technology site devoted to new technology, business opportunities and issues such as technology transfer, research funding and venture capital financing. Nevertheless, it offers a section dedicated to intellectual property. There is a special emphasis on patents considering the nature of the site content. Consequently, it provides valuable and specific information for anyone seeking intellectual property information from a scientific angle.

www.brint.com: provides a wealth of information on numerous business topics – business technology, e-business, knowledge management and intellectual property, of course. Numerous articles and reports are available for purchase, although there is free information as well.

www.patentcafe.com: it was hard not to list this Web site considering it has such a catchy name. Fortunately, it contains a considerable amount of valuable information within its network of intellectual property Web sites. In addition to sections to help you find intellectual property attorneys and other relevant products and services, the site includes an intellectual property Web-site directory, an e-mail newsletter and a 'Kid Inventors' section devoted to resources for young innovators.

www.delphion.com: this site is affiliated with IBM and contains subscription services for intellectual property research and analysis. This service may have value to those who are using patent analysis as a strategic tool to enhance their own decision-making capabilities.

http://usinfo.state.gov/usa/infousa/tech/ip.htm: the only government site included on this short list is from the country with the greatest influence on the intellectual property regime. InfoUSA's site contains a considerable amount of national and international information; however, most of it is policy related and generated from government sources or international institutions with intellectual property protection mandates.

www.computerlaw.com: the name of this Web site illustrates its focus; however, it has a selection of links in a number of areas, including trademark law, patent law and general intellectual property issues.

www.tradename.com: another source of diverse information compiled into one site. The intellectual property resources page includes a number of international patent offices and other national intellectual property agencies from around the world. The site also focuses on domain names and services for domain registrations.

www.marksonline.com: although it has a heavy focus on trademark-related issues, this Web site also includes some general links to further intellectual property information. If trademarks are your primary interest, you may find this site interesting. As with tradename.com, this site finds the relationship between trademarks and domain names sufficiently close to include domain search features and domain name information and news on its site as well.

www.lawsites.com: billed as 'a comprehensive quality controlled legal resource for lawyers' this site is cryptically refers to a 'Mr. Wilson' on its intellectual property resources page. I will not spoil the mystery of Mr. Wilson (I have no idea who he is) but the site is worth visiting for more reasons than that. The main focus appears to be US-based resources but there are a number of links to valuable international intellectual property sites as well.

www.megalaw.com: another great name for a Web site. And, what would a mega law site be without a mega intellectual property section? This one has it, complete with an international government intellectual property section with the Web addresses of (at last count) 34 different national offices. The other topics are equally thorough.

DEVELOPING INTELLECTUAL PROPERTY IN DEVELOPING NATIONS

What is the matter with the poor is poverty; what is the matter with the rich is uselessness.

George Bernard Shaw

When first read and considered, Shaw's comment appears to be a cruel and insensitive criticism of those living in poverty. In reality, the writer is acknowledging that poverty is a state that need not exist if the rich were not useless. It is entirely within the grasp of the people on this planet to eradicate poverty. It is not unreasonable to believe that the abundance of resources at our disposal can be used to everyone's benefit. I can almost hear the critics muttering 'communist' or 'socialist' under their breath!

This chapter is dedicated to the intellectual property issues affecting developing nations. It will examine some of the 'abundant resources' and the ways in which they are being mismanaged by the rich and poor alike. By presenting evidence from different perspectives, light may be shed on alternative solutions to help each developing nation reach a suitable standard of living. Clearly, that may bear no resemblance to the consumer-driven, spiritually bankrupt yet incredibly wealthy societies that dominate the Western world. It may be a way of life that ensures the needs of the population are met and the rights of individuals – including the rights to express themselves, the rights to profit from their innovations and the rights to sustain their heritage and culture – are protected.

In the technologically and industrially advanced nations of the United States, Europe and certain Asian countries, the business world is fuelled by innovation and knowledge. The capacity for creativity is immeasurable. Many of these nations are also centres for wonderful artistic and literary achievements. The economic wealth attached to these technological, scientific, artistic and industrial creations is also staggering. These nations recognize that, in order to fully benefit (at least financially) from all this creation, they must seek greater protection for their innovations, as well as broader intellectual property rights in all the countries and regions in which they conduct business. Strong international safeguards for intellectual property and increased access to lucrative foreign markets are a winning business combination for the leading industrialized nations because it allows them to exploit their economic superiority longer. Unfortunately, this strategy cripples developing nations.

The Western world is quick to forget or dismiss the wealth of innovation, creativity and knowledge that resides in other regions of the world. This may be due, in part, to the fact that commercialization of innovation is not always a priority in other societies. The concept may not even be clearly understood. In other instances, serious social and cultural problems may be more pressing. Even those countries that are making valiant efforts to close the economic gap by embracing technology and establishing stable governments with prudent fiscal policies remain at a distinct competitive disadvantage. Intellectual property rights and related protection issues are simply two of the countless difficulties these nations face in their struggle.

The challenges of establishing and enforcing intellectual property rights are not limited to the developing world, but they are magnified in the poorest regions of our planet. Even within nations that are signatories to the various WIPO or WTO agreements, the intellectual property rules may be on their books but there are no mechanisms in place to back them. It is admirable that a government makes the commitment to the international community to become a signatory to an international agreement. It is encouraging to see governments that develop national laws to protect the intellectual property of both domestic and foreign firms. But if there is neither the will, the intention, nor the resources to enforce the rules, the laws become meaningless. These are especially serious problems in the developing economies for a number of reasons. We will attempt to explore some of them in this chapter.

According to Jeffrey Sachs, a professor of international trade at Harvard University and the director of the Centre for International Development, 15 per cent of the earth's population provides nearly all of the world's technology innovations. A further 50 per cent of humanity is able to adopt these technologies in production and consumption. Sachs (2000) states that the remainder – approximately one third of the world's population – is 'technologically disconnected, neither innovating at home nor adopting foreign technologies'. This is particularly relevant to a discussion on intellectual property because technology is a driving force behind many of today's inventions. It is a driving force in the dissemination of knowledge, ideas and other forms of intellectual capital. Technology has also become a valuable tool with which to monitor and protect intellectual property and learn more about laws and rights associated with intellectual property.

It is an unfortunate reality that many developing nations lack the means to foster economic growth. Such growth can be accomplished in many ways but it requires resources outside the reach of these countries. Governments are challenged to create programmes to support entrepreneurs or create innovative knowledge-based and information sharing environments, regardless of how intelligent and motivated their people are. Imagine the complexity of such tasks when the legal infrastructure and political will is weak or non-existent. With virtually no investment in critical areas, such as education, research and development and information dissemination, effective economic outputs are negligible. As a result, there are few success stories such as profitable new businesses with useful products or services. According to Sachs (2000), 'Innovation shows increasing returns to scale, meaning that regions with advanced technologies are best placed to innovate further.' This is hardly surprising, but he also refers to the 'critical mass of ideas and technology' that is first needed to sustain innovation. This is missing in many developing nations and it is hardly reasonable, as some critics suggest, that these nations shape up, develop a modern and technologically advanced economy and compete like the developed world. Such arguments only serve to support the current inequity in the global economy and ignore the staggering technological, economic and social changes that have taken place in the last half-century alone. The conditions that spurred the technology driven economic growth in countries like the United States, Japan, and Germany simply do not exist any longer.

These technologically advanced nations seem to forget that over the last 300 years, they borrowed, copied and stole ideas, inventions, technology and even the writings of foreigners in their drive for industrial advancement. The widespread implementation of laws and enforcement mechanisms in these world powers is a relatively recent phenomenon coinciding with their successful industrialization. It is always going to be a game of 'catch-up' for developing nations without greater intervention from the wealthier countries. We are familiar with the common practice of corporations investing in developing nations in order to benefit from lower labour costs or other money-saving reasons. In return, these corporations offer a certain amount of employment to the local population. Frequently, these are low-pay, low-skill jobs that may offer the employee greater security and income than subsistence farming, for example. These jobs do little in the way of enhancing the individual's talents or capacity to innovate. In the best-case scenario, the corporation provides a modest amount of training and opportunities for a few management positions or jobs requiring specialized skills.

The return for governments that seek this type of foreign investment is minimal. The overall skill level of the workforce is virtually unchanged and any additional income that is injected into the economy is often spent on products and services provided by foreign multinationals. Additionally, it is common practice for these firms to implement secondary or outdated technology in foreign operations. This strategy allows them to limit exposure to their leading-edge technology and safeguard their competitive advantage in the event that they lose ownership or control over their foreign facilities. Consequently, technology transfer – a source of industrial sustenance for many developing nations – does occur; however, it is always the second, third or fourth best technology. Even if these nations manage to capitalize on such transfers, they will inevitably remain in the shadow of the current industrial leaders. Somehow, a new recipe for success is needed to replace the choices that both the industrialized world and many developing nations are now making.

HONOURING INTERNATIONAL OBLIGATIONS

As we learnt in earlier chapters, nations that contract into international agreements face specific obligations. For example, signatories to the TRIPS Agreement are responsible for taking appropriate steps to ensure they meet the minimum standards for intellectual property protection. What the Agreement does not do, however, is provide these nations with a budget, experienced people and training to implement their plan of action. Clearly, that is beyond the scope of an organization like the WTO, as it currently exists. As a result, adherence to the requirements of the TRIPS Agreement or other international conventions can be a slow, costly, and seemingly unrewarding process. This is especially true for developing nations that have thriving underground economies that flourish due to a complete lack of regard for the intellectual property rights of foreign and domestic firms. The termination of such criminal activities can present serious short-term economic repercussions for certain nations. Even if corruption has not reached epidemic proportions within the government and the ranks of decision-makers, there is little outward incentive to pursue a legally responsible approach to economic growth. Such an approach is a long-term strategy in terms of benefit, while the pain of clamping down on piracy and other forms of intellectual property theft is felt immediately in the economy. How do impoverished nations fill the void? Is it entirely up to them or should they expect assistance from wealthier and more experienced foreign governments? Is there a role for the WTO in this regard? The questions seem endless and the answers are scarce.

The current intellectual property regime clearly has a negative impact on many of the developing nations of the world. Patents, in particular, come under heavy attack. The anti-patent argument is wonderfully captured in 'The right to good ideas' (*The Economist*, 21 June, 2001):

> *So patents are obviously bad for poor countries – or so the activists argue. They are largely the preserve of western multinational companies, allowing them to establish monopolies, drive out local competition, divert research and development away from the need of poor countries and force up the price of everything from seeds to software. In the process, patents prevent the poor people from getting life-saving*

drugs, interfere with age-old farming practices and allow foreign 'pirates' to raid local resources, such as medicinal plants, without getting permission or paying compensation.

That is not a bad presentation of half of the story. The author points out the other problem in the very next paragraph of the article. Local musicians in Mexico are struggling to sign contracts with the large international recording labels because over 60 per cent of the musical recordings sold as CDs or cassette tapes in Mexico are pirated. The music industry is not going to invest in a market in which the recording stars' main audience is already getting the music it wants from an illegal source. Nor are they going to be interested in any opportunities in Mexico until the situation is rectified. Simply put, lack of intellectual property protection makes for bad business. There are enough lucrative markets with more protection than that found in Mexico. Picking the 'lowest hanging fruit', in this case markets with adequate safeguards, makes for good business.

It would appear that intellectual property is here to stay and with over 170 nations represented in the WIPO and over 140 nations following the rules of the WTO, the sooner that governments establish rules to help their own entrepreneurs and inventors, the sooner they will benefit from the international laws. Granted, there are severe problems with the way intellectual property rights are defined and enforced. We have covered many of these throughout the book. This chapter will examine some of the problems facing developing nations when it comes to honouring intellectual property rights and the 'damned if you do, damned if you don't' dilemma that many governments face when they look at their economic and legal woes. These issues extend beyond the realm of intellectual property and must be explored in this manner in order to understand the more specific issues.

THE PROBLEM WITH PIRACY

Copyright piracy is arguably the easiest intellectual crime to commit. Books, movies, music and software are popular targets for unauthorized copying and distribution. Software piracy, for example, has become a global epidemic. Asia in particular is home to some of the worst offenders. If we look at the software industry, China, Vietnam and Indonesia stand out as the three most problematic countries for software piracy. It is estimated that 95 per cent of the software used in

China is counterfeit product. An article on the subject entitled 'Phonies Galore' (*The Economist*, 10 November, 2001) noted that US software giant Microsoft launched Windows XP in China on 9 November, 2001. The cost of the product was 1,498 yuan or approximately US $180. Yet computer users in China had been purchasing copies of Windows XP for weeks at a greatly reduced price of 20 yuan. This was not a pre-launch, goodwill sale by Microsoft. Rather, it was business as usual in a nation that will be a WTO member state by the time you read this book. That means that China will have enacted intellectual property laws that meet or exceed the minimum standard required by the WTO's TRIPS Agreement. Even with these laws on the books, intellectual property theft in the form of software piracy remains a growing concern due to the lack of enforcement. Typically, this is a resource issue but many are questioning the will of countries like China to take an aggressive stance with pirates and counterfeiters. As the above-mentioned article humorously noted, 'In China, an anti-piracy propaganda film recently created some optimism, until it was discovered that most people were watching pirated copies of it.' Whether this is true or not, widespread corruption and ambivalence towards the concept of property rights is not helping the situation in China and other offending nations. The *Economist* article also indicated that Asia was the only part of the world where piracy rates rose in 2000, to an estimated average of 51 per cent.

In the last month of 2001, law enforcement agencies in the Asia-Pacific region seized an estimated 45,000 copies of counterfeit software from dealers in China, Hong-Kong, Taiwan, Thailand, India, Singapore and the Philippines. Not surprisingly, Microsoft was hardest hit as pirated versions of its new Windows XP operating system, as well as the related Office XP package and its Windows NT server software, were among the more popular items. This statistic is from a single month and accounts for over US $4 billion in losses to the software industry in this region of the world alone. Collateral damage to the economies of these nations is even greater because they have developed notorious reputations as places were legitimate business cannot flourish. Both the monetary losses and the breadth of the criminal activity boggle the mind. This seizure occurred in a region in Asia. Is it even possible to calculate the extent of the problem if you factor in North, South and Central America, Europe, Africa, the Middle East, the rest of continental Asia and Australia and New Zealand? Granted, Asia is a piracy hot spot and the enforcement of intellectual property rights has not been a universal priority for its nations. But it is not a priority for much of the world, including parts of Eastern Europe and Latin America, for instance. Many economies in these regions are in a 'danger zone'. They could take positive steps forward in terms of stable economic and social growth policies, including an effective legal system. Conversely, they could tumble back into lawlessness and oppressive regimes, and squander an opportunity for integration into the global economy. Taking the tumble creates a breeding ground for intellectual property abuses.

WHERE THERE'S A WILL...

It becomes increasingly apparent that the nonchalant approach to intellectual property protection and enforcement in many developing nations is robbing them of what they most need: economic growth and technological 'know how' to assist with an almost limitless supply of social, financial, medical, political and cultural crises. Companies that wish to tap into new markets will weight all the factors before entering any. Technology intensive industries, companies with valuable brand names and other businesses with considerable intellectual assets will be looking for safety and security as well as sales. The incentive to invest in foreign markets that cannot guarantee a lawful business environment is minimal. This robs the local population in these countries from opportunities – some would say opportunities to be exploited while others would say opportunities to grow and experience new ways of doing things, perhaps earn a better living or take advantage of new products and services to enhance their well-being.

Regardless, by creating an environment where the opportunity cannot exist, the people are robbed of the choice to say 'yes, this is a good thing for us' or 'no, this impinges too much on our way of life, which we celebrate in its current form'. And, if the local population has already adopted some of the changes as positive things, they may wish to grow new businesses on their own. Such entrepreneurial efforts are fantastic and should be rewarded. Whether it is a health business, a computer business, musicians selling a recently recorded CD or growers in a specific geographic region selling herbs with therapeutic properties, these business people require a stable business environment in which to operate. Lawlessness does not simply prevent foreign investment in developing nations. It also stifles local economic growth and development efforts.

Recent lawlessness in Zimbabwe over another kind of property (farms in this case) provides an excellent analogy for some of these intellectual property issues. Robert Mugabe and his thugs have thrown law and human rights to the wind by expropriating privately owned farms throughout the country and handing them over to 'squatters'. These people have no legitimate right to the land and, in many cases, have no skills to operate a farm. They simply support Mugabe's corrupt regime and oppose the wealth of some of the farmers have attained. As a result of these farm invasions, crops were neither planted nor harvested. No income has been generated, therefore it cannot be injected into the economy. Foreign businesses will not go near the country and innocent people have died. More innocent people will die as the country spirals downward at the hands of an incompetent and dangerous tyrant.

While few deaths have been attributed to intellectual property crimes, many of the problems that Mugabe has created over real estate in Zimbabwe can be seen in nations with intellectual property problems: political actions that discourage foreign investment; stagnant economic growth or economic decline as a result of policy decisions; and domestic instability. The following two examples highlight specific problems that developing countries face with regard to developing intellectual property on their home turf, and for their own benefit.

INDIA

India is considered a developing country despite its size and stature in the global political arena. According to the World Economic Forum, India is:

- the world's largest democracy;
- one of the fastest growing economies as of 2001, despite the global economic downturn and serious border conflicts with Pakistan;
- an emerging knowledge power, with software exports projected to reach US $50 billion by 2008. Indian information technology companies also count one fifth of Fortune 1000 companies among their clients;
- a potential global leader in biotechnology;
- the third largest car market in the world;
- home to a strong and diversified private sector accounting for 75 per cent of the nation's industrial gross domestic product.

In 1947 India became a sovereign and independent nation following two centuries of British authority. The nation remained a closed economy until the early 1970s. While the country grew in many ways, both direct and indirect foreign investment were discouraged by the government. Most of India's industrial and economic reforms have occurred in the last decade. The Foreign Exchange Regulation Act of 1973 stated that no foreign business shall 'permit any trade mark, which it is entitled to use, to be used by any person or company for any direct or indirect consideration without the approval of the Reserve Bank of India (RBI)'.

The country also maintained weak patent laws so that local business would be able to exploit technology without the costs associated with patent protection. Not surprisingly, foreign firms were not enamored of this strategy. In the area of copyright, India actually signed two international agreements – the Berne Convention and the Universal Copyright Convention (UCC). The early adoption of these laws made sense because India was a major producer and exporter of films (arguably the largest film industry in the world) and musical recordings. As time passed the country's software development and book publishing industries grew and supported a focus on copyright protection. Yet, despite the strong copyright laws on the books, enforcement remained a serious problem.

More recently, India became a signatory to the Paris Convention and the Patent Co-operation Treaty (PCT) in December 1998. That same year, the government notified 130 WTO signatory countries and 150 Paris Convention countries for the purposes of claiming priority under the Indian Trademarks Act (Trade & Merchandise Marks Act, 1958). The country was making bold moves to align itself with the international regime, including compliance with the WTO's TRIPS Agreement. It also began recognizing different patent offices, such as the United States and the European Patent Offices, as authorized international search and examining authorities.

India has long been known as a great source of software development talent. In fact, Indian engineers and scientists are largely responsible for the success of many technology firms in the United States and other countries around the world. Until recently, the only Indian companies that were making their presences known in the technology industry were outsourcing firms like Infosys, which has skilled programmers providing information technology services to numerous international corporations. While the monetary benefits of doing this work for other companies were attractive, India was developing very little intellectual property of its own in the area of technology. This is now starting to change and Indian businesses are experiencing the positive results of the shift. Excellent researchers, scientists, and computer experts have returned home from all over the world to work in Indian start-up firms in areas as diverse as telecommunications, life sciences and various software companies. Such changes have even attracted venture capital from a number of foreign sources, including Indians who struck it rich in Silicon Valley and other technology hotbeds around the world.

Biotechnology firms in India face a different problem. While they may be making inroads with their products in other countries, Indian patent law does not fully protect pharmaceuticals. Weak patent protection in the past is now coming back to haunt the nation. As a result, these entrepreneurs are not particularly comfortable about the prospects of intellectual property protection at home. They lose out, the Indian consumers who are interested in biotechnology products and services lose out, and the economic gains that can be accrued from a thriving biotechnology industry will have to wait until India is better able to address the needs of these businesses. Realistically, those economic gains will be lost to other countries and other companies. Businesses, as well as investors, will go where the money is and where their interests are adequately protected. Even the Indian courts have realized this and have clearly stated such opinions in rulings on other intellectual property issues such as copyright. If piracy continues unimpeded, it will adversely affect the trade, commerce and industrial production of the country. In turn, this will adversely affect the economy and the revenue of the state.

CHINA

China shares many similarities with India in terms of its recent push to develop and commercialize intellectual property. However, its late start in this regard was more the result of fundamental ideology and inward focus than novice marketing practices and poor intellectual property strategies. China also has a notorious reputation for allowing the intellectual property of non-Chinese individuals and businesses to be pirated. Its poor reputation not only drew the criticism of other governments, it hampered investments in China that might have assisted in the development of a strong base from which to develop its own intellectual property. China has experienced a number of dramatic changes in the last few years, many of which have contributed to a more open commercial environment. With that new environment, the Chinese government has become somewhat more stringent regarding the protection of intellectual property. More important perhaps is the desire of Chinese businesses and entrepreneurs to be taken seriously in the international business world. In order to compete globally, to attract clients, customers and investment from outside their borders, they know that the enforcement of fair rules is necessary. Clearly, it will benefit both foreign companies and Chinese firms.

Like Indian employees, many Chinese citizens have found success and wealth working for foreign firms. Many have returned to China to grow businesses based on the experiences they have accumulated in the United States, Europe and in other parts of Asia. A fair and equitable intellectual property regime would give them a better chance at succeeding. A regime that is enforced will be better still. Ever so slowly, China moves to the open market and the world gets a better view of this potential global economic giant. Both the leadership and the general public are openly embracing certain forms of technology to improve the domestic economy and establish specialized expertise. This approach will spur further growth. For example, the University of California concluded that China accounts for half of the developing world's expenditures on plant biotechnology research and development.

In other areas, assistance from the Western world and a relaxation of intellectual property rights is helping China improve its current state of affairs. Kexing, China's largest biotechnology company, is a prime example. According to a report in *The Economist* (28 June, 2001), Kexing sells 60 per cent of the drugs used in China to treat hepatitis B, a disease affecting over 20 million Chinese. To date, these drugs have been made by Kexing even though they are the intellectual property of foreign firms. An agreement between the United States and China allowed for this breach of patent protection. Any patents registered in the United States before 1986, and certain US patents between 1989 and 1993, are not protected in China. There is a humanitarian reason for this and it has created a commercially advantageous situation for Kexing as well. The *Economist* article points out that, of the 20 million Chinese citizens affected by full-blown hepatitis, only 100,000 can afford treatment. Enforcement of international patents would reduce that number to close to zero. Kexing, however, can manufacture a drug that costs 80 per cent less to purchase. As a result, it has a large market share, growing profits, and enough cash to re-invest into research and development. This strategy has allowed the company to pursue its own patents. By the end of the decade, Kexing aspires to be one of the top 10 biotechnology companies in the world. By playing by the rules, the article points out, Kexing benefits and helps push China closer to international standards for intellectual property.

THE TECHNOLOGY SOLUTION

Technology is not a panacea for developing nations, particularly when it comes in the form of exploitive or destructive changes to a society. Many opponents of globalization seem to believe that this is the case with all technology. That is simply untrue. Societies and cultures evolve as a result of both internal and external influences. The 'revolution' that industrialized Britain spanned a couple of centuries. Still, many critics found the magnitude and the pace of change in the country horrific. Likewise, the technological revolutions that are changing developing nations and causing such upheaval are frightening, at least in part, because they are happening so quickly. Rather than spanning a couple of centuries, they are spanning a couple of decades or a couple of generations. The stress of such rapid change cannot be underestimated. Both the people in these countries and the well-meaning outsiders who deplore these assaults on the traditional way of life in these nations are struggling with this real time revolution. But poverty, sickness, despair and hunger do not constitute a traditional way of life.

Technology, when it is applied thoughtfully to human problems, can vastly improve the lives people lead. And it does not have to be at the sake of traditional values, norms and traditions. People can make up their own minds in this regard. Guest (2001) captures the essence of this thought in the following article:

> Young Thai men used to spend years in Buddhist monasteries, cultivating their spirituality. These days they cannot spare so much time. Typically, they spend only a few weeks studying the sutras before they rush back to the city. No one forced them to change their priorities. If they choose, they can spend their whole lives in a monastery. But for the most part, they choose not to. No one is forced to take part in our modern, technology-adoring society. Anyone who would rather go and live on nuts and berries in the forest is free to do so. But most people like what modern technology has to offer, and fret only that they cannot get enough of it.

Technology provides the nations of the developing world with fabulous tools to raise their standards of living in all respects. As the people in these nations free their minds and energies from the challenging tasks of merely staying alive – whether the challenges arise from hunger and malnutrition, viruses and bacteria, militant dictatorships and war, or other desperate situations – they will be able to explore the opportunities to create great things and further contribute to the collective wealth of the world through their arts, scientific discoveries, local products and services. Equally important, they will be able to benefit from their creativity and efforts, through recognition and financial remuneration. A fair an equitable national and international intellectual property protection system promotes such benefits. One can only imagine the latent genius that exists in these developing nations. Considering that developing nations make up the bulk of the world's population, sheer numbers alone make a compelling argument for the potential wealth of intellectual assets in this part of the world.

HOPE AND HELP FROM DEVELOPED NATIONS

Before the accusations fly that this chapter is entirely biased against the Western powers and their efforts to assist developing nations, I must acknowledge the great amount of good that does flow from the wealthier nations on this planet to those who face less fortunate circumstances. For every horror story of corporate exploitation and labour abuse by multi-nationals in developing countries, there are successes that have given people hope and a higher standard of living. There have been business alliances that are truly equitable partnerships in which all parties involved prosper in every meaning of the word. On the government level, there has been considerable financial aid pumped into the developing world. Unfortunately, too much of it is grossly mismanaged, misdirected or stolen by corrupt officials. It would appear that the message is getting out that Western solutions to the problems of developing nations are not necessarily effective solutions, so there is hope that the voices of those in need play a larger part in fixing future problems. Many governments and non-governmental financial organizations have also rescheduled debt payments, refinanced or absorbed the debt of developing nations.

In the area of intellectual property rights, there have been some exceptional efforts made to establish alliances and partnerships in order to further the development of a fair and workable intellectual property system in developing countries. The Franklin Pierce Initiative was launched in December 2000 with the assistance of The Electronic Community Project, a non-profit organization that provides onsite and Web-based training and content to civil society organizations. The Franklin Pierce Law School is one of the premier intellectual property law schools in the United States and this initiative aims to foster civil society in developing nations while establishing a legal foundation or infrastructure to assist with sustainable economic growth. Obviously, the use of the word 'civil' in this context does not suggest that developing nations are uncivilized. It is used in the legal context and is more closely connected with what the Western world would view as stable and reliable legislative, judicial and governmental institutions for the people. The launch of the Franklin Pierce Initiative coincided with the signing of agreements with three African universities and focuses on strengthening the understanding of, and access to, intellectual property rights, which in turn will cultivate an environment that is more attractive to private investment. Additionally, the establishment of the legal infrastructure is intended to spur the growth in civil advocacy in the traditional trouble areas of developing countries, such as healthcare, environmental protection, gender equality and access to capital.

The mission of the Initiative is particularly encouraging because it gives equal weight to the concerns of the people it is designed to help rather than impose a Western solution resulting from Western analyses. The mission, according to The Electronic Community Project, is:

> To create a network of partner Universities and institutions with the dual goals of creating and sustaining a legal infrastructure for the protection of (1) private and collective intellectual property rights; and (2) public interest advocacy that provides protection for the public interest within the context of developing the economic and legal framework for private investment.
>
> The Franklin Pierce Initiative will seek to identify and collaborate with Universities, Law Schools and other appropriate institutions to foster development of these legal frameworks in a manner that respects indigenous

*values as well as general legal principles and the human
rights of all people.*

The last part of this mission is particularly interesting because it may provide even greater visibility for one of the most contentious issues between developing nations and the more influential proponents of intellectual property rights as they currently exist. The legal and commercial expectations of the industrialized world are often insensitive when examined against the predicament of the rest of the world. Consequently, the Franklin Pierce Initiative is hoping to 'advance the dialogue that is necessary to help develop a framework that protects the interests of indigenous peoples and advances economic opportunity'. The objectives include the development of an International Institute for the Protection of Indigenous Intellectual Property Rights and higher visibility for these important global issues through conferences that focus on the intellectual property challenges facing developing nations.

At the political level, there are national governments that recognize developing nations are disadvantaged by existing international intellectual property agreements. In the UK, for example, the Department for International Development has established a commission on intellectual property rights. The commission has a specific mandate to examine how international rules need to evolve in order to fully account for the needs of poor countries and poor people. This commission is also looking at the intellectual property issue in terms of sustainable human development. Like-minded efforts and continued pressure directly from the developing countries will bring more attention to the issues. It is not simply a matter of fitting these nations into the current system but ensuring that the current system is altered so that it does not disable developing nations more than they already are.

Despite all the controversy and apparent inequality, the creators and inventors in these developing countries are not dormant. The world is blessed with wonderful works of art, thought-provoking theories, and useful products and services from every part of this planet. It is very difficult to completely suppress innovation and genius, even if you are entirely focused on how you will survive over the next week. But we can only imagine at this point in our development what wondrous creations the rest of the world might experience if these people were presented with the opportunities and resources that the Western world takes for granted. Technology, warts and all, is helping to narrow this gap. So are the efforts of many individuals, organizations and even some governments. Human spirit, combined with a broad-based desire to close the gap between rich and poor, will help even more.

LOSING YOUR MIND

The challenge to each human is creation. Will you create with reverence, or with neglect?

Gary Zukav

Congratulations on reaching this point in the book. We have covered a great deal of territory and a multitude of opinions on the subject of intellectual property and no single position has been taken, other than to verify that it exists and it is not perfect. Consequently, the system still supports a large number of people called intellectual property lawyers. Businesspeople are well advised to remember this simple truth: intellectual property protection is not perfect. It will never be perfect because it is an arbitrary and artificial creation. And, at this point in our development as humans, we choose to operate in a realm in which intellectual property exists and its protection is important. With this in mind, it is interesting to consider where our preoccupation with safeguarding inventions, ideas and innovation may lead us.

The benefits of intellectual property rights are often presented in a very compelling manner. WIPO literature claims that these rights 'reward creativity and human endeavor, which fuel the progress of humankind'. The Organization claims that nearly two-thirds of all modern medicines may not have been developed had adequate patent protection not existed. And the revenues obtained from these patented (protected) medicines would not have been available to fund future research. Depending on how you feel about the proliferation of synthetic drugs, the increased dependency of much of the Western world on these artificial creations, and the suppression of more natural remedies, this may not seem to be the best example of humankind's progress. Considering that the greatest use for many of these medicines, at present, may be in developing countries that cannot afford them, patent protection seems to have rewarded pharmaceutical manufacturers and few others.

WIPO also claims that the entertainment provided worldwide by the multi-billion dollar film, recording, publishing and software industries would not exist without copyright protection. Perhaps, but the greatest change may simply be that entertainment would not be a multi-billion dollar business, and people would be entertained by those who sing, act, dance and create games for the love of it, even if they do not become obscenely wealthy in the process. It is also suggested by the Organization that consumers would have no means to confidently buy products or services without reliable, international trademark protection and enforcement to discourage counterfeiting and piracy. However, counterfeiting and piracy are merely symptoms of a global culture driven by commercial excess and marketing propaganda. Trademarks, at best, protect companies that do their utmost to convince as many people as possible that life is not worth living without their product or service. And while these companies deserve to have their intellectual property protected, this protection arguably has little or nothing to do with consumer confidence in the products they buy. There is no shortage of useless, worthless trademarked consumer goods and services on the planet.

When we consider intellectual property protection for what it is – an attempt to protect the intellectual assets of an individual or group so that that individual or group may commercially exploit the assets – we can examine the successes and failures of the current systems. When we expect it to be anything more, we encounter all kinds of interesting challenges to the very notion of intellectual property. And, that is not a bad thing to have happen. The proliferation of Internet users around the world, combined with the proliferation of Internet uses, is just such a challenge. We have seen domain names rival trademarks in importance and financial value. Companies have paid millions for catchy dotcom names that they believe will draw online consumers to their Web sites. Unlike trademarks, domain names are not intellectual property – yet. Although the dawn of the new century included the downfall of many Internet businesses, cyberspace will continue to challenge our current notions regarding intellectual property and enforcement methodologies.

We have also discovered that freedom of speech issues and copyright infringements are on a collision course in the United States and other parts of the world as 'legitimate' hackers expose inferior technology designed to protect intellectual property. For their efforts, they are threatened with lawsuits and prosecution for infringing upon intellectual property. Technology continues to be both an asset and a liability in the intellectual property sphere. The challenges that we have seen to date will pale in comparison to those of the future.

With a little foresight, it is possible to pre-empt some of the problems that will surface. It is never too late to declare that, in some areas of intellectual property protection, we may have jumped the gun or overlooked a really critical issue. I believe that there are specific criteria that are recognized as integral to the success of a global intellectual property regime. However, recognition is not synonymous with implementation. They are the elements that make intellectual property rights and the protection efforts truly powerful, rather than exploitive. These criteria include:

- Understanding, acceptance and espousal of the definitions of intellectual property. Understanding is required to ensure that everyone with a vested interest in the intellectual property system is reading from the same page. And understanding is required for stakeholders to make informed choices regarding the acceptance or rejection of these definitions. History is chock full of examples of people being exploited because they lacked the understanding needed to make the best decisions for themselves and those they represented. Whether it is the result of communication barriers, cultural insensitivities or outright hostility and disdain towards others, proceeding without a clear understanding among all parties early in the process will disable the process at a later date. Greater focus on the equitable treatment of all participants is critical for acceptance. Acceptance becomes the first step to ensuring a firm commitment to the definitions of intellectual property rights.
- Development of a secure and stable environment in which entrepreneurship and innovation can flourish. This does not necessarily mean an abundance of venture capital and business incubators in every town. While those elements may be useful, they are not the primary concerns for most countries. Rather, an infrastructure comprising a fair government and a credible legal system implementing policies and legislation that serve the needs of both people and businesses would be a great start. Coupled

with sound economic planning and a focus on education and health, positive change will be inevitable. Not only will domestic business grow, foreign investment will increase because of the greater confidence in intellectual property protection. History illustrates, however, that the challenges in accomplishing this seemingly basic task are monumental. This book has stressed the role of wealthier societies and influential powers in assisting those less fortunate with not only basic human rights, but with the opportunity to thrive. If we raise our standards and our expectations for the developing world and for those nations suffering under tyrannical policies or social and economic mismanagement, they may also raise their own.

- Respect for, and protection and cultivation of local/indigenous intellectual assets. We have examined the deplorable manner in which traditional knowledge, cultures and local plant species have been expropriated by outside interests for the sake of profit. The words of concern voiced by international intellectual property authorities in this regard have not been adequately backed by action. As a result, a modern-day plundering of some cultures' property is taking place and these people are not in a position to fully understand the implications. This must stop regardless of how the law is worded. It is morally and ethically deplorable.

- Equal access to tools designed to make the international intellectual property system more efficient and effective for all participants. Organizations like WIPO have created some wonderful technology-based tools for the benefit of all member states, yet they are not adequately accessible to all member states. Clearly, it is not the role of WIPO or anyone else to hardwire nations so that they can take advantage of WIPONET, for example. In all fairness, WIPO hosted over 11,000 men and women from developing countries to over 170 courses and seminars and courses as part of the Organization's cooperation and development programme. These limitations cannot be overlooked, however, if one of the goals of international institutions is to create an even playing field for all of their members. Additional attention to establishing and implementing the basics for all parties to international intellectual property agreements is paramount. Again, nations that have had economic advantages in the past might be able to spare some resources in this regard. WIPO is largely self-financed with member states contributing a mere 15 per cent of the budget. Some additional contributions from the wealthiest members could go a long way to addressing these limitations.

These contributions could be used to establish and fulfil specific projects to help developing nations take advantage of modern tools and techniques associated with intellectual property rights and protection.

This wish list would establish a healthy foundation for a fair and equitable intellectual property system. It certainly is not comprehensive and it does not take into account many external factors, such as the desire of governments to help each other and to help their own people. It does not take into account the unfounded and unspoken fear that exists in the Western world that there is not enough to go around and, if the poor people on the other side of the planet raise their standard of living, it will be at our expense.

Whether we like it or not, people and businesses on this planet are becoming increasingly interdependent. Those who view this as a negative side effect of globalization will continue to protest and focus on the horror stories. Those who recognize the opportunities only for themselves will continue to exploit others. And finally, those who acknowledge this interdependence as an extension of a natural human condition will be more sensitive to finding ways to improve the outlook to everyone's advantage. After some of the more pressing issues of health, welfare, racism and sexual discrimination are addressed, I have no doubt we could find time to improve upon the current approach to intellectual property protection. We might find that some of those rights we kill for are not quite so important in the long run.

NOTHING IS REALLY NEW

Many thinkers, writers, philosophers and mystics have expressed views that suggest that there are no original ideas or thoughts anymore. What we might call original ideas are simply variations on ancient themes, placed in present context or surrounded with the trappings of contemporary society and perspective. It has been suggested by many spiritual thinkers that our role as humans on this planet is simply to experience and remember; in other words, 're-member' to become one again with the all-knowing, all experiencing Oneness or God or whatever name is invoked to represent this idea. On that basis, it would be difficult to claim that a recently released book of poetry, a musical recording or a great slogan for a product is novel and worthy of protection from unauthorized use by others.

Perhaps that is why so many artists claim to be inspired by a higher power. They are simply remembering something that was already in existence. Interestingly, most of them still want credit and remuneration for what they have taken from this particular higher power. How does that explain those patented semiconductor components or that secret formula for Coca-Cola you ask. It does not, unless you undergo a giant, cosmological shift of your view of the world and your role in it. For better or for worse, we will not be travelling down this path in this book.

Clearly, the intellectual property system conflicts with some New Age beliefs and concepts. I would be worried if that surprised anyone but it does raise an intriguing question. With the number of patents, trademarks, copyrights, and other forms of intellectual property increasing annually, will we reach a point when nothing is really 'new' but simply a variation on an existing theme? Have we reached that point already in some areas? On those rare occasions that I listen to a pop music station on the radio, an hour may pass and I will feel like I have heard the same song for the duration. Movies typically fall into a few popular genres, such as romantic comedy, action thriller or horror. Within these genres, we explore the same plot and characters using different actors and settings. Many contemporary themes can be found in works of earlier literary figures, such as Shakespeare. And Shakespeare drew on Greek tragedy for inspiration, and the Greeks drew on a more ancient source and so on and so on.

Perhaps it is not something so blunt and short-sighted as the quote attributed to Julius Frontius some 2000 years ago and found at the beginning of this chapter – a statement echoed by a United States Patent Office official at the end of the 19th century. That poor fellow suffers a double indignity: he was outrageously short-sighted and unoriginal in his proclamation! Since the beginning of the 20th century, the world has experienced more technological advances than any other period in known history and most of these advances have become someone's property. Did this explosion of innovation occur because intellectual property protection became a more serious global concern? Whatever the reason may be, we created this environment by enacting new laws, enforcing them more stringently and providing the confidence to creators of all types that they could make a living introducing unique and valuable ideas into society. Maybe it was just one of those seemingly inexplicable quantum leaps that humanity takes every so often. This one just happened to focus on technological innovation. Regardless, human beings will continue to figure things out, improve upon existing ways of doing things, and probably look for ways to profit commercially from the effort. Is that so wrong? Like most basic questions, the answer is both no and yes.

We have already explored many of the benefits and disadvantages of the current intellectual property regime. This book contains many stories and opinions that capture both its value and its foolishness. We begin to understand that the overwhelming message from the top – the WIPO, the WTO, the wealthy nations, industries and corporations of the world – is that we need intellectual property protection. It is paramount to our livelihood, our very existence. According to WIPO, 'the progress and well being of humanity rests on its capacity for new creations in the areas of technology and culture'. This statement alone may be a truth for you; however, it does not support the creation of an intellectual property protection industry. WIPO adds a second compelling reason. By providing solid legal protection for new creations, there is motivation to expend additional resources leading to further innovation. In reality, the main motivation to expend further resources and continue 'innovating' is money. You need it to start innovating and you need it to keep innovating. It does not matter if it is your money or someone else's. Legal protection does not ensure that you will have the money to continue innovating unless you have that 'one in a million' invention, best-selling novel, hit musical recording or 'to die for' design. It would be interesting to determine the amount of money expended on trademark applications, patents, industrial designs and other forms of intellectual property that yielded no return for the creator. Further, it would be frightening to know how many people staked their savings or a second mortgage on efforts to protect a creation that no one else wanted. The ratio of poor inventors to rich inventor is extremely high.

Finally, WIPO tells us that 'the promotion and protection of intellectual property spurs economic growth, creates new jobs and industries, and enhances the quality and enjoyment of life'. Undoubtedly, it has spurred economic growth and new jobs are often a residual effect of economic growth. However, the bulk of the economic growth occurs in the areas of the world that have reached a rather advanced level of economic prosperity to begin with. Generally, nations that pushed for increased protection of intellectual assets were: 1) in decent economic shape; 2) developing a more open view to international trade; and 3) experiencing both growth and diversity of domestic business at the beginning of the 20th century. And generally, these are the same nations in the driver's seat today. You can rest assured that they will continue to protect their own interests even when serious attempts are made to address inequities in the system. With regard to WIPO's assertion that intellectual property protection 'enhances the quality and enjoyment of life', the statement is entirely subjective. There will be as many answers as there are people suffering on this planet.

INTELLECTUAL PROPERTY AND THE WRONG KIND OF GROWTH

Consider the story recounted in an article entitled 'The Secret of Abundance' (*Aquarian Times*, Autumn 2001). It comprises an interview with journalist, filmmaker and environmental entrepreneur Kenny Ausubel. He is the founder of the Bioneers Cultural Heritage Institute, a non-profit organization that seeks out natural solutions for the ever-increasing environmental balances that we create on our planet. The term Bioneer is defined as a 'biological pioneer' and refers to someone who believes in the interconnectedness of all living things and the incorporation of this belief as the basis for fixing environmental problems. In the article, Ausubel discusses how another man, Gabriel Howearth, was hired to help revive traditional native agriculture. He had collected seeds from across the Americas and had created a garden in San Juan Pueblo, New Mexico. The garden had hundreds of different varieties of tomatoes, for example, in all colours and shapes. Considering that most people are accustomed to seeing three or four varieties in grocery stores, this was a remarkable collection. Yet, all of these extraordinary tomatoes were natural creations, evolving as humans have evolved. Howearth began approaching people in the pueblo and asking them if they had any old or interesting seeds that they had not been planting. The local people responded enthusiastically to his request and he often found new and interesting specimens on his doorstep. One day, a farmer arrived during a film shoot, holding scarlet red corn seeds that he had found in a little clay pot in the adobe wall of his home. While the farmer did not know of their origin, two elders in the village recognized the seeds as the sacred red corn of San Juan Pueblo. No one had grown it during the previous 40 years by their estimation.

A number of 'food plants', such as corn, are not found in the natural world. As Ausubel states in the interview, 'There's one funky little runt of a plant in Mexico called "Tey-oh-Shintey," which is the mother of all corn. Somebody discovered they could do something with the plant and then 10,000 years later, Native Americans had created 1,000 varieties of corn.' Ausubel adds that there are 5,000 varieties of potatoes, grown in virtually every ecosystem in the world. While it sounds distinctly reminiscent of the stories we read today of genetic modification gone awry, it is exactly the opposite. This is the natural diversity of our planet – developed and tended to over thousands of years. It is this natural diversity that is threatened by intellectual property and, more directly, big business. As Ausubel states, 'The main reason is because of patents that corporations have on plants now, which they started getting in the 1930s. They claimed these plants as their "invention". Because you can't patent traditional plants, they weren't interested in them. So thousands upon thousands of varieties of food were lost day by day essentially because of corporate greed.'

Fortunately, the San Juan sacred red corn was not lost; however, for every plant that is spared, there are hundreds that perish because of unnatural intervention for the sake of potential corporate profit. This is just one of the ugly and often overlooked aspects of the intellectual property regime we have created. It is spurred by the same forces that make many people reach for soft drinks instead of water, fast food instead of nutritious fruits and vegetables, and toxic pharmaceuticals instead of medicinal plants and herbs. It is the disturbing element that gives globalization its negative reputation.

Before I get painted with the same brush as the WTO protesters and other anti-globalization radicals, I actually do believe in the incredible benefits that can be realized from international trade and the sharing of culture, products and services. I also believe firmly in the right of anyone to offer a product or service for sale, and to make a great deal of money in doing so. As long as the product is not harmful, dangerous, unsafe or exploitive and the transaction is fair to both parties, I would love to see everyone profit. And it is equally important that the creator of the product be able to benefit financially from the sale of his or her creation, if that is what the creator chooses. If only it were so simple. Unfortunately, we often assume that the way we are conducting our affairs now is the way we must conduct them. The only barrier to changing the way we conduct our business and relate to others is the barrier we chose to sustain.

Trade policies and economic strategies are no different than any other form of relationship between human beings. They can become stale, outdated, overwhelmingly negative and damaging to all parties. Conversely, they can also flourish, enrich and nourish the parties involved. These policies can take a mature and sensitive approach to overcoming challenges and supporting outcomes to benefit both parties involved. If there are more than two parties involved, even better. There will be greater opportunity for creative and innovative solutions if every voice is given a fair opportunity to be heard and the merits of all arguments are respectfully considered. It is becoming increasingly obvious in both the realm of international trade and the realm of intellectual property protection that there is a distinct hierarchy among the voices, and those at the top are getting far more opportunity to articulate their arguments and illustrate the merits of their solutions.

Having lived with the presence of intellectual property for many generations now, we often forget that it is a relatively new phenomenon. We are well advised to remember that the first patent law surfaced in the early 1500s and primitive forms of copyright appeared in the early 1700s. While 500 years seems like a long time, simple maths reveals that it is a relatively brief period in which we have attached such importance to these laws. As unlikely as it seems, the world progressed quite well without the concept of intellectual property and all of its rules. We still draw on the arguments of Plato, Socrates, Aristotle and other Greek philosophers in our attempts to understand our existence in this world. We can only marvel at the great pyramid structures in Egypt and throughout Latin America and imagine how these ancient cultures managed to create such architectural wonders. And the beauty of William Shakespeare's sonnets has touched generation after generation. Not only has the world progressed without intellectual property protection, it continues to do so in many ways. We must not forget that the concept has a distinctly 'Western world' flavour to it and remains virtually meaningless to a significant portion of the population even today.

Has there been a fundamental shift in humanity that prevents creativity from occurring unless there is financial reward? Obviously not, but it certainly appears that way in our modern society. Time changes most things, but creativity is a constant. If the people we define today as great creators and artists believe they cannot produce their magic without an incredibly complex safety net, we must question their motives for creating in the first place. Perhaps we should simply refer to them as businesspeople and remove the artificial gloss we willingly place on recording artists, celebrities and any industry that places profits ahead of progress. And until we accept that progress is not measured by quantity of patents that are issued, the size of a company or its revenues, or the speed with which biotechnology research can be commercialized, we will exacerbate the problems our societies are facing. Progress is measured by contributions to the welfare, peace and security of this planet. It is measured in increases in joy and happiness among living things. The creative genius of da Vinci, the inspiration of Handel's music, the wisdom of the Buddha and Confucius and the unknown genius who has found his or her way into so many cartoons and other spoofs as the inventor of the wheel did not suffer from lack of intellectual property protection. Granted, there are horror stories about starving artists in years gone by. Undoubtedly, brilliant individuals were exploited in any number of unpleasant ways, ultimately gaining little or no credit for their creations. If someone can tell me how this differs from today when we have more laws than any individual could possibly memorize, I would love to hear about it. We still have the exploitation. It just goes by a different name and has become institutionalized in many ways.

THE POWER OF IDEAS

Next to love, ideas may be the most powerful force on Earth. And if you have learnt nothing else from this book, you may now realize that ideas are especially powerful when they are unleashed on the world. We have focused on the incredible commercial power of ideas formed into artistic and literary works and industrial property. We have examined both the negative and positive aspects of this power because virtually all ideas are two-sided coins. Some are just more clearly one side than the other. Hitler's powerful ideas captured much of a nation (as well as many foreigners) and led to one of the most horrific events in recent history. As overwhelmingly negative as his ideas were when they were unleashed on the world, they prompted a great many people to say 'never again', and dedicate themselves to multiple causes to ensure that such atrocities were not repeated. Unfortunately, we have since failed in Africa and other parts of the world, where genocide has become a political strategy. Osama bin Laden's powerful ideas unleashed terror, as well as a concerted assault against terrorism on an unprecedented scale. It remains to be seen whether the world can follow through on this important project without it deteriorating into a 'special interests' agenda.

The next step for humanity in this regard is to rise to the occasion without being spurred by a single monumentally tragic event. Clearly, powerful ideas can be unleashed to improve the oppressive and sexist environment in which many women are forced to live. How many women need to be beaten, murdered or diminished as humans in one recorded incident before the world recognizes that this largely 'man-made' problem has already reached epidemic proportions. Powerful ideas could solve hunger and ensure that all babies enter a peaceful world in the best of health. Powerful ideas can also lead to techno-logical advances that, combined with more respect for our natural environment, will help us combat pollution, soil depletion, and global warming so that we may heal the planet on which we depend for survival. One day, in the not too distant future, I am confident that these causes will be more important than patents or profits and we will see just how powerful ideas, innovation and creativity really are.

References

Baker, D (2001) Ending intellectual property 'rights,' the first step toward a serious debate: reflections on the Pocantino Retreat on HDR 2001, CEPR, Washington, DC

Bonisteel, S (2001) Music-encryption crackers ponder SDMI warning over tech paper, infowar.com, 24 April 2001

Campbell, T (2000) What's the big deal with prior art, anyway? corporateintelligence.com, 5 December 2000

Cook, C and Cook, M (2000) *Competitive Intelligence: Create an intelligent organization and compete to win*, Kogan Page, London

Fisher, W (1999) *The Growth of Intellectual Property: A history of ownership of ideas in the United States*, Vandenhoeck & Ruprecht,

Goldstone, D (2001) Deciding whether to prosecute an intellectual property case, *United States Attorney's USA Bulletin*, **49** (2)

Gronroos, M and Stahle, P (2001) *Dynamic Intellectual Capital*, WSOY, Helsinki

Guest, R (2001) A survey of technology and development, *The Economist*, 10 November 2001

Halligan, R M (2001) The importance of trade secret audits and protection programs in the Information Age, corporateintelligence.com, 14 February 2001

Kleinbert, P (1991) The intersection of information, economics and universality in the 1990s, *Journal of Information Science*, **17**, pp 137–43

Mortensen, J (1999) *Measuring and Reporting Intellectual Capital: Experience, issues and prospects*, Royal Netherlands Academy of Arts and Sciences

Rogers, S A (2001) *Pain Free in 6 Weeks*, Sand Key Company Inc

Sachs, J (2000) *The Economist*, 24 June 2000

Sharman, D (2001) Intellectual property: an historical perspective on the commodification of information, University of Alberta, Edmonton, Canada

South Bulletin 19 (2001) Lessons from the history of intellectual property rights, Human Development Report, United Nations Development Programme, Geneva

Swartz, R G, (1992) Wordsworth, copyright and the commodities of genius, *Modern Philology* **89**, pp 482–509

Van Dyke, R and Pedersen, S R (2002) How big are patents?, *Legal Times*, re-printed by law.com, 8 January 2002

INDEX

1984 148

Adidas 113
Adobe 153
African Regional Industrial Property Office 41
Agreement on Trade-Related Aspects of Intellectual
    Property (TRIPS) 39, 46, 51, 54, 57, 58, 59, 82,
    84–89, 100, 103, 113, 114, 117, 130, 174, 179
AIDS 114
Allen, Paul 98
Amazon.com 41, 162
Ambrose, Stephen 125, 126
anti-circumvention 72
apomixes 139
Apotex 114, 115
Aquarian Times 194
Archimedes 11, 12
Aris Technologies Inc 160
Aristotle 196
Asia-Pacific Industrial Property Center (APIC) 166
Association of Research Libraries (ARL) 167
Aubryn International 102
Australian aborigines 16
Ausubel, Kenny 194

Backbone Magazine 156
Baker, Dean 43, 143, 144
Barbie 101, 102
Barliant, Claire 49
Barnes and Noble 162
Bayer AG 114, 115
Beecher Stowe, Harriet 19, 20
Berne Convention 20, 53, 63, 64, 86, 87, 88, 179
Bill of Rights 144
bin Laden, Osama 197
Bioneers Cultural Heritage Institute 194
BMW 118
Bonisteel, Steven 159, 160
Boston Consulting Group 139
brint.com 167
Broadcast.com 155, 156, 162
Brunsman, Shellie 124
Brussels Convention Relating to the Distribution
    of Programme-Carrying Signals Transmitted
    by Satellite 70
Budapest Treaty on the International
    Recognitionof the Deposit of Microorganisms
    for the Purposes of Patent Procedures 75
Buddha 21, 197
Business Software Alliance 24

Campbell, KK 156, 157
Campbell, Tim 41
Canadian Alliance Against Software Theft
    (CAAST) 24
Carbone, Barbara 152
Center for Economic and Policy Research 43, 143
Center for International Development 172
Centre for the Application for Molecular Biology to
    International Agriculture (CAMBIA) 138, 139
cetyl myristoleate (CM) 44
Childers, Thomas 126

Chiron 142
Cipro 114, 115
Coca-Cola (Coke) 4, 23, 58, 96, 192
Cohn, Cindy 161
Commodore 64 146
common heritage of mankind 20
computerlaw.com 168
Confucius 21, 197
Consumer Reports 161
Cook, Curtis 51
Cook, Michelle 102, 110, 122, 165
Copernicus 13
Copyright Act (Canada) 155
Copyright, Designs and Patents Act of 1988 (UK)
    51
Corinthians 49
Corporateintelligence.com 166
Cro-magnons 10
Crusades 17
Cuban, Mark 48, 155, 156, 157, 158, 162
cybersquatter 49

Dallas Mavericks 155
Datang Telecom Technology Ltd 122
daVinci, Leonardo 11, 12, 21, 196
DEFCON 153
Dell 25
delphion.com 168
Democritus 11, 12
Department for International Development (UK)
    185
Dickens, Charles 19, 26
Diel, Harry W 44
Digital Millennium Copyright Act 7, 129, 154–61
digital rights management 163
doctrine of equivalents 140
Dow Jones 49
due diligence 109, 110

eBay 158
eBusiness Journal 155
Economist 174, 176, 181
Economist.com 137, 138, 139
*Educator's Guide to Intellectual Property, Copyright
    and Plagiarism* 124
Edvinsson, Leif 34
Electronic Community Project 184
Electronic Frontier Foundation 161
Emarketer 150
Enlightenment Period 52
European Commission 164
European Patent Convention 90
European Patent Office 6, 14, 41, 62, 90, 179
European Patent Organisation 90

Farmer's Right 131
Federal Bureau of Investigation 99
Felten, Edward 158, 159, 160, 161, 163
Festo 140, 141, 142
findlaw.com 165
Fisher, William 13, 14, 15, 19, 36, 37, 113, 114, 118,
    119, 121, 122, 129, 158, 160

Ford   142
Foreign Exchange Regulation Act (India)   179
Forrester Research   150
frankenfoods   139
Franklin Pierce Initiative   184
Frontius, Julius   192

Galilei, Galileo   11, 13, 21
Gates, Bill   98
General Agreement on Tarriffs and Trade (GATT)   85
General Motors Corporation   122
Geneva Convention for the Protection of Producers of Phonograms Against Unauthorized Duplication of their Phonograms   67
Gilmore, Lynn   124
Global Trade Solutions   29
globaltechnoscan.com   167
Globe and Mail   126
Goldstone, David   98, 99, 100, 101
Groonroos, Mauri   20, 21, 30, 31, 34, 102, 104, 105, 119, 120, 131
Gucci   119, 127
Guest, R   182
Gutenberg, Johan   14, 15, 17

Hague Agreement Concerning the International Deposit of Industrial Designs   77, 83, 136
Halligan, R Mark   104, 105
Hamlet   8
Handel, George Frideric   197
Harris, Daniel   50
Harvard University   13, 43, 158, 172
HDTV   157, 158
Health Canada   114, 115
Hitler, Adolph   39, 197
Holder, Eric   99
Hollywood   155, 156
Holocaust   39
Howearth, Gabriel   194
Howkins, John   3
Hubbard, Elbert   27
Human Development Report 2001   43, 143

IBM   23, 28, 29, 142, 168
Indian Trademarks Act   179
Industrial Revolution   18, 26
Industry Canada   155
Information Holdings Inc   166
Infosys   179
InfoUSA   168
Inquisition   11
Intellectual Property Constituency (IPC)   133
intelproplaw.com   165
International Convention for the Protection of New Varieties of Plants   59
International Exhibition of Inventions   63
International Federation of Library Associations and Institutions (IFLA)   166
International Monetary Fund   117
International Olympic Committee (IOC)   68
International Patent Classification   79
International Union for the Protection of New Varieties of Plants (UPOV)   59
Internet Corporation for Assigned Names and Numbers (ICANN)   133
Internet treaties   53
IP.com   41

ipmenu.com   167
ISO   47
ITU World Telecommunication Indicators Database   150

Jack Daniels   102
Jefferson, Richard   137, 138, 139
Jesus   21
Jupiter Research   150

Kexing   181
Kleinbert, Paul   17, 18
Knowledge Capital Scoreboard   23
KPMG Consulting   23, 31, 32, 33, 152, 153, 162, 164

Lappeenranta University of Technology   20
law.com   101, 166
lawsites.com   168
Lerch, Donna   124
Lev, Baruch   23
Linux   97, 137, 139, 154
Lisbon Agreement   54, 77
Locarno Agreement Establishing an International Classification for Industrial Designs   81
Lucas Film Ltd   102
Lucas, George   102
Lucent Technology   122

Madrid Agreement Concerning the International Registration of Marks   48, 83
Madrid Agreement for the Repression of False or Deceptive Indications of Source of Goods   68, 76
Madrid Protocol   48, 83
marksonline.com   168
Mattel Inc   101
McCarthy, Janeen   124
mcgalaw.com   169
Medieval Europe   17
Microsoft   23, 89, 97, 98, 109, 137, 176
Minrad   102
Mohammed   21
Monsanto   131, 139
Mortensen, Jorgen   34

NAFTA   94
Nairobi Treaty on the Protection of the Olympic Symbol   68
Napster   149, 151
National Basketball Association   48, 155
National Education Association (US)   167
neanderthals   10
New International Economic Order (NIEO)   20
New York University   23
newsbytes   159
Nice Agreement Concerning the International Classification of Goods and Services for the Purpose of the Registration of Marks   80
Nike   4, 109
Nova Southeaster University   166

OECD   20
Office of the United States Trade Representative   100, 120, 121
oncomouse   43
online arbitration   7
Online Service Provider (OSP)   135

INDEX

Organization for Economic Cooperation and
  Development   150
Orwell, George   128, 148

Palo Alto Research Center   158
Paris Convention   20, 54, 63, 64, 86–89, 179
Patent Cooperation Treaty   24, 41, 69, 70, 74, 82,
  83, 136, 179
Patent Law Treaty   69, 70
patentcafe.com   167
Pathstar   122
Pedersen, SR   142
Perens, Bruce   153
Phillips, Ormonde and Fitzpatrick   167
Plato   196
Prema Toy Company   50
Princeton University   158, 159
prior art   40, 41, 141
Protestant Reformation   15
Protocol Relating to the Madrid Agreement
  Concerning the International Registration of
  Marks   76

Recording Industry Association of America   156,
  157, 159
Reebok   109
Reno, Janet   163, 164
Reserve Bank of India (RBI)   179
Rice University   155
Rogers, MD, Sherry A   44
Rolex   119, 127
Roman Catholic Church   11, 21
Rome Convention for the Protection of
  Performers, Producers of Phonograms and
  Broadcasting Organizations   67
royalties   52

Sachs, Jeffrey   172
Saint Augustine   126
Secure Digital Music Initiative (SDMI)   158–61
Seneca   38
Shakespeare, William   8, 12, 192, 196
Sharman, Darcy   52
Shaw, George Bernard   170
Shepard Broad Law Center   166
Shoketsu Kinzoku Kogyo Kabushiki Co   140
Silicon Valley   180
Skandia   34
Sklyarov, Dmitry   153
Socrates   196
Software and Information Industry Association
  (SIIA)   23, 152, 153, 162, 164
Solara Technology Development Corp   160
South Bulletin   18
Star Wars   102
Statute of Monopolies   14, 90
Strasbourg Agreement Concerning the
  International Patent Classification   79
Sveiby, Karl-Erik   34
Swartz   52
Symposium of the Americas   163

tacit knowledge   5
Taco Cabana   121, 122
TeleGeography Inc   150
The Creative Economy   3
The Wild Blue   125

Thomas Aquinas   126
Trademark Dilution Act (US)   50
Trademark Law Treaty (TLT)   69
tradename.com   168
Traditional Chinese Medicine (TCM)   132
transgenomics   139
Treaty on Intellectual Property in Respect of
  Integtrated Circuits (IPIC)   59, 89
Two Pesos   121, 122

UCLA Online Institute for Cyberspace Law and
  Policy   154, 166
Uncle Tom's Cabin   19
Uniform Dispute Resolution Policy (UDRP)   133
United International Bureau for the Protection of
  Intellectual Property (BIRPI)   63, 64
United Nations Development Programme   43
United Nations   63, 82, 128
United States Constitution   19, 144
United States Customs Service   99
United States Department of Justice   89, 98, 99,
  101, 161
United States Espionage Act   123
United States Patent and Trademark Office   141
United States Supreme Court   140, 142
Unites States Court of Appeals for the Federal
  Circuit   140, 141, 142, 143
Universal Copyright Convention   179
University of California   181
University of Illinois   124
Uruguay Round   84
Usenix Security Conference   159

VanDyke, R   142
Verance   159, 160
Vienna Agreement Establishing an International
  Classification of Figurative Elements of
  Marks   81
Volkswagen   122
von Bingen, Hildegard   12

Wall Street Journal   50
Warner-Jenkinson   142
Welsh and Katz   104
Wilson, Woodrow   22
Wings of Morning   126
WIPO Copyright Treaty   71, 72, 134
WIPO Performances and Phonograms Treaty   72,
  73, 134
WIPONET   134, 190
Wordsworth, William   52
World Bank   117
World Economic Forum   178
World Intellectual Property Organization   5, 6,
  24, 39, 40, 41, 42, 48–53, 60, 62, 63, 64, 69, 70,
  74, 79, 82, 83, 86, 87, 94, 117, 128, 129, 130,
  133–37, 154, 171, 175, 187, 188, 190, 193
World Trade Organization (WTO)   6, 39, 54, 58,
  62, 82, 84–87, 100, 103, 113, 118, 119, 128–30,
  148, 171, 174–76, 179, 193, 195
Wright Martin Aviation Company   116

Xerox   15, 158

Yahoo!   156

ZDNet   154